"I have witnessed the mental, physical, and financial d
afford nursing homes and who suffer every kind of di
some cases fifteen to twenty years. Caregivers are also
watch their loved ones vanish before their eyes while t
   "This book should be a godsend and will bring relie
tives of their homes. It so dramatically demonstrates tl
thinking, and hope—with unexpected humor. At one nursing home I said to an elderly
lady, 'Do you know who I am?' She replied, 'No, but if you go to the front desk, they will
tell you.'"

> **Art Linkletter**, television entertainer, producer, author,
> chairman of the board/president emeritus
> of the John Douglas French Alzheimer's Foundation,
> chairman of the board of the Center on Aging at UCLA

"As a psychiatrist, I've been called upon to help hundreds of clients who had Alzheimer's, feared
it, or were grieving its effects on a loved one. I am thrilled that *Twilight Travels with Mother*
deals with all these issues, plus offers many helpful hints on how to make Alzheimer's,
or senility in general, less likely or at least delayed in our own brains. I will use this book
to help clients who deal with these issues—and don't we all eventually?"

> **Paul Meier**, M.D., founder of Meier Clinics, author of *Unbreakable Bonds*,
> *Happiness Is a Choice*, and more than seventy other books

"In *Twilight Travels with Mother*, caregiver Mary Ann Mayo explains that it is not what
we do about an Alzheimer's diagnosis but rather what we do *with* it. As one who walked
the A-journey with a mother, and wonders if it is in my future, I found this book a gift.
Mary Ann's insights calmed my fears and could be a life preserver to someone you know.
You will need two copies of this book: one to keep and one to give to a friend who has just
heard the diagnosis."

> **Harold Ivan Smith**, D.Min., certified thanatologist,
> founder and president of friendgrief ministries,
> author of five books including *When Your People Are Grieving*

"Exceptionally well written, both moving and educational, and in a style so captivating that
once I started reading it I couldn't put it down! *Twilight Travels with Mother* is a fantastic
resource that all of us could benefit from, whether we fear getting Alzheimer's ourselves, have
a loved one who has already started showing the signs, or must live with an advanced case
of dementia. Mary Ann's approach takes away the dread and stigma of this now prevalent
disorder, giving us hope."

> **Archibald D. Hart**, Ph.D., senior professor of psychology and dean emeritus,
> Graduate School of Psychology, Fuller Theological Seminary

"Who would have guessed that a nonfiction book about Alzheimer's disease could be a
page-turner! Mary Ann Mayo has accomplished the nearly impossible. *Twilight Travels
with Mother* is engaging, funny, poignant, and rich in cutting-edge medical information
and reasons for hope. She answers precisely, truthfully those tough questions about aging
that we were too afraid to ask."

> **Lela Gilbert**, author and coauthor of more than fifty books,
> including *Heaven Is Not My Home* and *Portraits of Freedom*

Also by Mary Ann Mayo

Good for You! Smart Choices for Hormone Health
Praying through Life's Problems: Dealing with Life's Changes
The Menopause Manager
Woman by God's Design
Skin Deep: The Powerful Link between Your Body Image
and Your Self-Esteem
Body and Soul: A Married Person's Guide to Discovering
and Understanding Our Unique Sexual Personalities
A Christian Guide to Sexual Counseling: Recovering the Mystery
of Reality of "One Flesh"
Caution: Sexual Choices May Be Hazardous to Your Health:
Everything You Need to Know
Parent's Guide to Sex Education
God's Good Gift: Teaching Your Kids about Sex
In the Beginning: Teaching Your Children about Sex
Mom's a Bird, Dad's a Bee

twilight travels
with Mother

How I Found Strength, Hope,
and a Sense of Humor Living with Alzheimer's

Mary Ann Mayo

Fleming H. Revell
A Division of Baker Book House Co
Grand Rapids, Michigan 49516

© 2003 by Mary Ann Mayo

Published by Fleming H. Revell
a division of Baker Book House Company
P.O. Box 6287, Grand Rapids, MI 49516-6287

Printed in the United States of America

Library of Congress Cataloging-in-Publication Data
Mayo, Mary Ann.
    Twilight travels with mother : how I found strength, hope, and a sense of humor living with Alzheimer's / Mary Ann Mayo.
        p.   cm.
    Includes bibliographical references.
    ISBN 0-8007-5943-5 (pbk.)
        1. Alzheimer's disease—Religious aspects—Christianity. 2. Alzheimer's disease—Patients—Religious life. 3. Manahan, Mary Jo—Health. 4. Mayo, Mary Ann. I. Title.
    BV4910.6.A55 2003
    361.196′831—dc22   2003012833

Mary Ann Mayo, M.A., has written this book as an educational resource, not a tool to be used for diagnosis and treatment. The information presented is in no way a substitute for consultation with an individual's physician. Although the author has carefully researched all sources to ensure the accuracy and completeness of the information, the publisher and author shall have neither liability nor responsibility to any person or entity with respect to any loss, damage, or injury caused or alleged to be caused directly or indirectly by the information presented. Treatment of medical conditions and wellness should always be supervised by a physician or licensed health care professional.

Photo montage on the facing page: Frances Mayo (left), Mary Ann Manahan (center), Mary Jo Manahan (right)

To

Mary Jo Manahan
Frances Mayo
the loves of the past

and to

Cade and Cole Mayo
the hope of the future

Contents

Acknowledgments

One never writes a book alone. The material and inspiration are as much outside as inside. I am grateful to friends, family, and my pastors who encouraged me to keep writing. I was not convinced I was up to the task of producing a hopeful book about Alzheimer's—I worried that I might not have enough hope. But this book has forced me to look at the total picture, to be realistic, and to tell the story from my heart. The result has been that I have far more hope and much less fear than when I sat in my living room awaiting the dreaded visit from the "memory" nurse.

My husband's unwavering support and willingness to pick up the slack—and the dishes and the laundry and the grocery shopping and the cooking—have enabled me to finish this material in a timely fashion. He is my soul mate and my helpmate. If you find the book useful, bless him.

The loving encouragement of my editor, Jeanette Thomason, with whom I have a long history, imparted much more than she will ever know. Thanks to Mary L. Suggs and the "gang" at Revell.

Introduction

My mother began to manifest signs of Alzheimer's disease when she was about sixty. Her journey was a long one—more than twenty years. The pace was leisurely—meandering and lingering along the way. Interspersed throughout and generally with no warning, a corner would be turned leading to a new precipice; some were steep, others gradual. Occasionally the decline proved a mere detour; other times it necessitated a complete remapping and reorganization of her journey. Unremittingly the voyage continued, with each course correction resulting in greater hesitancy, additional anxiety, and less joy.

Mother did not make her journey alone. Those of us who loved her tried to stay on the road with her. Though for us the trek was tiring, for her the experience was firsthand and merciless. Contrary to what many believe about people with Alzheimer's, Mother was well aware that something was wrong. At times she would pound her head in frustration, perhaps with a vague hope that something might dislodge and reposition itself so that she could think better. Such awareness was present throughout much of her extended illness.

Twilight Travels with Mother deals with a daughter's often-humorous course through her mother's Alzheimer's journey. But it also faces head-on the fear that many sons or daughters experience when their parent has Alzheimer's disease—the fear that they are likely to be afflicted next. The questions are many: *Is "losing one's mind" inevitable? Is there anything that can be done to lessen the effects? What options are available to push back the clock? Is a diagnosis possible? How can dignity be ensured? How do we make sure our adult children have choices about our care? How do we know they understand what we value? Will they be doomed to bankruptcy as they struggle to provide the care we need and/or desire? Where is hope found?*

For those of us who want to face the prospect of Alzheimer's with the same confidence and success we have had when facing other challenges in our life, these questions are huge, but they are rarely addressed in books on the disease. We want to know what can be done early on to ease our mind while we still have one. Most books on Alzheimer's address the issues and needs of caretaking or the disease process itself. *Twilight Travels with Mother* focuses both on the truth that there is life after a diagnosis of Alzheimer's disease and the significant body of knowledge that is unfolding about its causes, diagnosis, and prevention. It is relevant to those currently caring for someone with Alzheimer's and anyone who wants to do all he or she can to ensure that aging does not automatically mean infirmity and despair.

Twilight Travels with Mother is not a book without hope. When I tell my mother's story, my feelings are not only those of sadness and despair. There were happy times and there were many poignantly funny ones. Mother's life to the end had value and never lost its humanity. I share her story as a rich source of material about what living with Alzheimer's has to teach us.

Mother was an ordinary woman whose journey through her disease speaks to us all about living and dying. My goal is to provide here a personal but balanced and disciplined look at a disease that is destined to touch, directly or indirectly, the majority of people in the United States sooner rather than later.

One

Make Me a Child Again

Backward, turn backward, O Time, in your flight. Make me a child again just for tonight!

Elizabeth Akers Allen

The Fear

I have never been bothered by birthdays. Such idiosyncrasy is due mostly to my mother, who had a healthy and honest openness about becoming older. It has been nurtured by the fact that I tend not to look my age. I've relished the exclamations declaring I couldn't possibly be as old as my birth certificate declared. "You look so young," friends (the real ones) exclaimed. "No, you couldn't possibly be . . . !" rolling their eyes in amazement. In truth, I've gotten so much mileage from looking younger than my age, I've actually considered lying about being even older—cashing in on a potential exponential ego boost.

When sixty began to press in on me, however, my feelings changed. There was something about "the big six-o" that was different. A disquieting unease descended on me that lasted several months. I suspect looking fifty but feeling more like ninety had something to do with it. Increasingly I found myself groaning as I got out of bed, simultaneously speculating about just what part of me might fall, fail, or flail. I began praising Eve for sinning and being responsible for the need for clothing. My prayers also paid tribute to contact lenses, red hair dye, Lycra underwear, dental hygienists, and, especially, to the lady who invented Barbie, because she also developed replacement breasts for those of us who have given ours up for a bad cause.

No denying it, I have begun to feel my age, even if I don't look it. That admission, coupled with worry over my family history of Alzheimer's disease, convinced me I had to bite the bullet—it was time for a long-term care insurance policy. Accordingly, my husband and I analyzed plans and filled out applications. His application sped through the system. We imagined the acceptance committee members gleefully ordering new boats, fur coats, and vacations to exotic lands as they calculated their premiums and the lifespan of a fifty-nine-year-old, one year post-myocardial infarction. No additional information, no mental tests—he was in.

Mine, on the other hand, was suspect. I was tentatively accepted, pending the outcome of a mental screening test. Visions of warehouses for the frail and forgetful forged their way into my dreams. There would be no afternoon teas, Friday sing-alongs, and activity director for me. Food would be shoved through the door to be eaten under twenty-four-hour lighting. Just the thought of an assessment of my memory shut down my brain's production of neurotransmitters and spiked my adrenocortical levels. In other words, I panicked.

I badgered anyone who had ever taken an insurance company's mental acuity test. "What did they ask?" I demanded. "How long did it take? How many things did you have to remember?" I reviewed seminar notes on tests for Alzheimer's. I kept my husband up nights helping me learn how to count backwards from one hundred by seven—subtract ten, add three, subtract ten, add three. I rehearsed associations, "When they ask you to remember *sport* see yourself in-line skating." I fretted, popped ginkgo, and awaited the call.

And then it came. The tester made an appointment to interview me—I couldn't believe it—*over the phone*. I was "beside myself," as Mother might have said. *I might even get a room to myself,* I pondered, already calculating what Martha Stewart could do to a 10' x 12' space. As expected, I breezed through the interview. I remembered every word she asked me to recall, aided of course by the notepad I had conveniently left by the phone. Just to be convincing, I reversed the order of some words. I was dazzling. The examiner was impressed. It was too easy.

I began to worry. Didn't she know what I was doing? Was the real test to see if I was together enough to cheat? What if she asked me if I had written the words down? Would I lie? Visions of no tea parties brought me to my senses. Yes, I would. The stakes were too high.

Apparently they were too high for the insurance company as well, because two weeks later a second interview was scheduled, this time in person. I tried to convince them it was a mistake; I had passed with flying colors. I enlisted the help of our financial planner; surely she could do something. My ruse was about to be uncovered, or, even worse, I would be rejected on the grounds of the rapid deterioration that had occurred in just two weeks. My fate was to be sealed, and it was ugly.

It is reasonable to ask why a person who a month before had spoken before nearly four hundred women and taped videos for two national organizations would be so paranoid about passing an insurance company's standard for mental sharpness. The answer, however, has nothing to do with reason. My response was unreasonable. It was irrational and illogical. I was afraid to face any evidence that might confirm the loss of my mind. Or, more accurately, I was afraid of the consequences of such a disclosure. After all, I had witnessed the payback when brain cells keep company with amyloid plaques. My fears weren't theoretical; they were real.

In my mind, positive proof of Alzheimer's meant I would soon be opening the dementia version of Pandora's box. Once that occurred, there would be no end to the paranoia, contrariness, and downright havoc I would be doomed to unleash. Wide open, Pandora's dementia box would embolden but not enlighten me. Who knows, I might take to prancing around my retirement facility in a blouse and nothing else. I would plan great escapes. And, if I forgot where the bathroom was, I would decide the trash can by my bed was a close enough facsimile. I would no doubt believe my son and daughter had malevolent motives toward me and write endless notes saying so. I might even develop a new vocabulary—one more suitable to sailors and bar owners. I would stamp my foot and develop my personal version of an "evil eye." I would use it when I couldn't have my way, like when I wanted to go home, even if that meant a trip back in time as well as geography. Worse yet, what if the contents of the dementia box included an eraser that would wipe out more than forty years of shared love and history with the man I married "for better or worse." While any of these fears could easily justify nervousness over facing a test, the bottom line is the same. My greatest fear is that I am doomed to repeat my mother's behavior and experience. Simply stated, it is that I am destined to become my mother.

I do and I don't want proof I'm losing it. My memory, since my early forties, works in quirky ways. Whether or not I am developing Alzheimer's, the disease casts its shadow on my life. I know I am not alone. It is a fear shared by anyone who has seen firsthand the ravages of Alzheimer's. And so, while I try both to educate myself and put into practice habits that will stave off what may be inevitable, I prepare for the worst. My hope is that long-term care insurance will provide some protection for me and my loved ones, ensure some dignity, and increase choices. It may also enable me to leave something behind for my children and grandchildren besides debt.

When the doorbell rang, I realized that Pandora and her dementia box had arrived. The insurance representative seemed nice enough.

I invited her in and got us both some green tea. With heart pounding, I tried my best to answer her questions. For all the medical problems I have had, I am in pretty good shape. My husband and I eat well and for the last ten years or so have been advocates of nutritional supplements. My bones are strong from good practices like drinking lots of milk as a teenager and a lifetime of physical activity of one sort or another. For my sixtieth birthday I bought myself a set of in-line skates. The eleven-year-olds at the skate park and I have developed a mutual respect, although they have been little help, despite great effort, in teaching me how to stop. They insist on doing a one-eighty in the air while I have mastered only a "crash and burn" technique.

An hour and a half of questions about my physical well-being were checked off with little difficulty. And, yes, the inevitable occurred. I was asked to remember ten words—I recalled eight and could recollect all ten for the next three weeks, real-life proof of how stress affects one's memory. I had to count backwards only from twenty by three. Still, you might be interested to know that I almost flunked. The last assessment, my blood pressure, was sky high. I was stunned. I am the low blood pressure queen. For the first time in my life, I was floating up there in the danger zone. What was it my mother used to say? "Sometimes you can't win for losing."

The Reality

The health site on the MSN web site defines Alzheimer's disease as "a degenerative disease of the brain from which there is no recovery. Slowly and inexorably, the disease attacks nerve cells in all parts of the cortex of the brain, as well as some surrounding structures, thereby impairing a person's abilities to govern emotions, recognize errors and patterns, coordinate movement, and remember. At the last, an afflicted person loses all memory and mental functioning."[1]

"Degenerative, no recovery, impairing, loses all . . ." anyone who has not discovered the fountain of youth has reason to worry.

Alzheimer's disease (AD) would not be anyone's choice for retirement. While technically accurate, this definition is about as blunt and discouraging as it gets. It is not the complete picture, however. It overlooks the fact that for most people AD is slowly debilitating, and a lot of living, loving, and humanity lie between the diagnosis of a "degenerative disease" and "loses all memory and mental functioning." Alzheimer's may not be a picnic, but neither is it the immediate end of a productive, meaningful, and joyful life.

If there is anything to look forward to, it is that anyone who suffers from AD in the next fifty years will not be alone. By 2050 one in forty-five Americans will be diagnosed. In case you worry that there is something in the water, most of this increase is due to an aging population. While 5.9 percent of the population was over seventy-five in 2000, by 2050, 11.4 percent will be. While the risk of AD at sixty-five is 5–10 percent, that risk is said to almost double every five years until age eighty-five. For you engineers, that means if you live to eighty-five, you will have an approximate 50 percent chance of also living with AD. It also means that if the onset can be delayed by just five years, the worldwide prevalence would be halved.[2]

Approximately four million people in the United States are currently diagnosed with AD. Based on the 2000 census, predictions range from eleven million to sixteen million by 2050.[3] It is estimated that nineteen million are currently affected in one capacity or another as caregivers of people with AD. A one-hundred-billion-dollar price tag is included, mostly out of the pocket of common folk. AD and lung cancer are currently tied in third place for the leading causes of death in the United States. By 2050 Alzheimer's will be second, overtaking cancer and nipping at the heels of heart disease for the number one spot. Among developed countries it is believed 13.5 million afflicted people in 2000 will grow to 36.7 million in 2050. Developing nations that had 8.6 million sufferers in 2000 will have 36.7 million in 2050.[4]

The main determinant of death, of course, is age. On average a person who is eighty will live about seven more years; an eighty-five-year-old will live about five more years. As noted, pushing back the onset of AD as far as possible can make a significant difference in the amount of care ultimately needed. There is room for debate as to how long one lives with Alzheimer's. My mother began to show the first signs of disease around her sixtieth birthday and died when she was eighty-four years old. Generally the younger one is when affected, the longer one lives. This makes sense for a variety of reasons, not the least being that younger people are healthier to begin with. A recent Canadian study reported a median of 3.3 years of life after diagnosis with memory problems. In their sample, the average age of onset was 83.8 years.[5] Other studies propose times more in line with heart disease and cancer, 5–9.3 years. The obvious difficulty is pinpointing when problems begin. It is a safe bet that it is not when a doctor officially declares it so.

The problem lies in the fact that the changes older people complain of are frequently dismissed as normal aging. But the truth is, significant impairment and disability are not normal parts of growing old. Education on how to make such a distinction in diagnosis is imperative. An accurate finding is important because there are dementias that can be treated.[6] Problems with memory can have many causes; for example, polypharmacy (interaction of multiple prescription and/or nonprescription drugs), depression, alcohol abuse, or drug toxicity, just to name a few.

Early diagnosis of Alzheimer's, the most common dementia, is equally important. Knowing what a patient is truly dealing with helps prevent costly trips down the wrong medical path and gives people time to prepare and to begin treatments for symptoms such as depression, wandering, and incontinence. Contrary to conventional wisdom that there is nothing that can be done after a diagnosis of AD, medications do exist that delay the onset and progression and that are most effective if begun early.

My reaction to my potential diagnosis of AD, while a bit over the top, is not unusual. I am joined by apprehensive Baby Boomers who spend millions on memory enhancement aids, books, mnemonics courses, and nutritional supplements. For them, minor glitches, like losing one's keys, become proof positive the funny farm is just around the corner. Though healthy and functional, they, like me, have become the "worried well."

The statistics concerning the number of people who will be touched by Alzheimer's are indeed grim. Personal experience with the disease merely ups the ante. Still, perspective is called for. If 50 percent of us are destined to lose our minds in varying degrees by the time we are in our eighties, there are still 50 percent of us who won't be afflicted. A study of centenarians, the New England Centenarian Study, conducted by gerontologist Thomas T. Perls under the auspices of Beth Israel Deaconess Hospital and Harvard Medical School, focused on what enables people to age well. With a similar outlook, this book is an effort to look at AD from the perspective of aging well.

Dr. Perls's goal is an overall decrease of disease. He has been known to comment that his interest is not looking for the "fountain of youth" but the "fountain of aging well." His hope is that research on the healthy aged will give clues as to how we can live life as disease free as possible. Then a full and generally healthy life will be followed by a short state of ill health that leads to death.

People who live to be one hundred years old have, for the most part, lived this healthy life. The oldest among us tend to have a sense of humor and an ability to adapt to their circumstances. They "mourn and move on." Positive attitudes abound. At least 25 percent have good cognitive ability; 9 percent still live on their own; most remain active mentally and physically. One striking feature is the very strong social networks and/or families that have characterized their lives. If they don't have family (or have outlived them), they create new ones. If they move to a nursing home, they make a life for themselves there. We "worried well" should take heed.

The majority of centenarians have taken good care of themselves, giving up smoking, watching their weight, eating a balanced diet, and getting appropriate exercise. There are exceptions. Madame

Jeanne Calment of France quit smoking at age 117 and died at age 122. While we may not have the genes to live to 100 plus, most of us, by adopting wise lifestyle patterns, can improve the odds of staying healthy into our eighties. If we have relatives with Alzheimer's or other diseases that impair well-being, it should be a signal to us that we need to do things right—the sooner the better. Dying with a worn-out body is infinitely preferable to suffering a debilitating disease, putting up with medications that make us sick while fixing something else, or slowly losing our mind.

A Brief History of Alzheimer's Disease

In the past, older people who were no longer thinking clearly were said to have senile dementia. For the most part, such mental changes were considered a normal aging pattern. In 1906 German neurologist Alois Alzheimer diagnosed a patient who seemed to have all the symptoms of old-age senility despite being fifty-one years old. Examination of her brain at autopsy revealed clumps of neurofibrillary tangles and areas of plaque. Until the 1960s such changes were believed to be a rare form of presenile dementia found in younger people. New research confirmed, however, that the same tangles and plaques were prevalent in older people as well, concluding they were evidence of the most common type of dementia and deserving of the name of the first person who described them.

The exact cause of Alzheimer's is not known. What is known is that there are more than one and probably many contributing factors. Why one person succumbs and another doesn't isn't clear. AD generally strikes people over sixty-five years of age, but it is also a disease of younger people, with almost all Down's syndrome adults showing signs of the disease. In the end most victims die from pneumonia, urinary tract infection, or heart disease.

Researchers have noted, and it was certainly true for my mother, that in the middle and late stages of AD, when cognitive impairment is great, individuals retain a broad range of emotions.[7] I was never comforted when people told me not to worry about Mother. They reasoned that since she understood little of what was going on, she was a vegetable. While their motivation was to ease my sorrow, I knew it wasn't true. If they had taken the time to look, they would have known she was at least a whole salad. She experienced happiness, contentment, surprise, pride, sadness, distress, fear, depression, worry, and anger. Unfortunately negative emotions frequently outweighed the positive, but they were all there. Mother, who had spent her life making an art of passive-aggressive behavior, spent her twilight years letting us know what she felt about most things, real or imagined. She occasionally graced us with a tirade of swear words she must have been saving for a lifetime. Gentle and non-confrontational all her life, she became forceful and demanding.

On the other hand, Frances Mayo in the throes of AD became as docile as a lamb. My mother-in-law had worried about "catching" Alzheimer's from my mother, and her fears materialized. While contracting AD from a son's mother-in-law (or anyone else for that matter) has never shown up in a list of contributing factors, I doubt we could have convinced her otherwise. Her powerful personality and bright mind had led to her being the mayor of her town, founder of innumerable good causes, and a woman who rarely refrained from telling you where she stood. Yet, as a victim of Alzheimer's, she was quiet and agreeable. The point is, emotions expressed by a person with AD may mirror her lifelong personality or may be entirely different. Either way, emotions remain a part of the sufferer's humanity.

Where Do We Go from Here?

The last decade has shed considerable light on brain function. New imaging techniques have provided clues to the literal places and chemistry involved in our ability to think and reason. Researchers are in a race for breakthrough drugs for AD. Brain researcher Tim Tully reports in the article "Viagra for the Brain" that effective memory-enhancing drugs are just around the corner. "It's not an 'if'—it's a 'when,'" he insists.[8] And work is also proceeding that will benefit the seventy-six million middle-aged "worried well" who are beginning to experience normal changes of aging, including memory loss.

Scientists are now able to define gradations of memory loss and are investigating whether or not mild memory problems foreshadow worse things to come. There is an approximate 10 percent increase in conversion to AD from a relatively new diagnosis of mild cognitive impairment (MCI). This intermediary stage gives researchers an opportunity to study why MCI increases vulnerability to Alzheimer's for some but not others and may help researchers discern the efficacy of early interventions.[9] Ongoing studies, done in conjunction with the National Institute on Aging, are designed to pinpoint who really needs to worry—I can hardly wait!

Ironically, as exciting and hopeful as these breakthroughs will be, technology and cutting edge research can have a downside. The medicalization of old age—in reality making old age a disease—means that doctors increasingly focus on a diagnosis while doing little to actually make the person feel better. Pursuing diagnosis affords a means to avoid looking at the now, providing distance from the pain and suffering. Indeed, once a diagnosis is reached, which may have been arrived at through great expense and physical and mental anguish, the doctor may continue to ignore suffering and may institute a plan of undertreatment that actually worsens discomfort.

Is it too much to ask our doctors, who take an oath to do no harm, to look beyond diagnosis? It has been argued that preserving independence and relieving misery are in conflict with adding years to life, but there is no evidence that this is true.[10] The goals of medicine remain to help and to heal. Comfort and happiness are very important at every stage of life, and to this end our hospice system needs to expand to assist more than the dying.

Many of us may share certain medical and emotional needs of aging, but often the needs are unique to each individual. Relief of a person's suffering, then, necessitates time and empathy, and neither of these essentials is part of a managed-care system. But medicalization of old age allows the medical profession a means of externalizing the experience and ignoring or failing to acknowledge that bodies get old and wear out.

We may focus on our mental acuity, but in actuality it is not likely to be the only thing we will have to deal with as we age. Parts and pieces break and no longer function optimally; degenerative diseases on simmer for years begin to boil. And on top of everything else, we can't remember our son's phone number! A trip to our physician reveals his reluctance to treat, at least not without confirmation from peer-reviewed, double-blind studies. But few of those studies apply to a sixty-year-old, let alone an eighty-year-old.

The fact is we have more chance of dying from a combination of medical problems than from any one of them. Only a few of us will greet old age with optimal wellness and high function. I don't expect to be in that fortuitous group. I do, however, intend to maximize my chances to live at my personal best. How successful I am has much to do with the responsibility I take to educate myself, rationally examine what I value, and pragmatically act on what I suspect is needed to best meet the unique needs of my mental and physical health. I must be realistic, open, and honest about my requirements and desires with my family, my physicians, and myself. I may be afraid, but I can't be timid.

It is true that the happiest old people have been found to value well-being and social functioning more than physical or even psycho-cognitive functioning.[11] Wow! That's great! Yet for me the truth is well entrenched that life is over when I can no longer remember—as my reaction to proof that I might be losing it mentally reveals. Mother used to fret she wouldn't be able to remember something she was experiencing. I would ask her if she was having a good time. Her answer would inevitably be yes. Alzheimer's is a crash course in learning to live in the moment. Successful old age, apparently, has less to do with avoiding the ravages of aging than with the ability to adapt. It is not so much the condition of our body but that of our attitude that gives us a sense of having aged successfully.

At the moment, most of us seem to have more fear than questions. Courage is required to read and educate ourselves about a disease that has the power to prevent us from doing either. Nothing will be gained by putting our heads in the sand. Besides, that has never been the style of this generation. There is no reason we cannot face the ramifications of Alzheimer's with the same confidence and success we have faced other challenges of our lives.

We live in a time when a significant body of knowledge is unfolding about AD's causes, diagnosis, and prevention. How we ensure our dignity, quality of life, and humanity in death depends to a significant degree on how much responsibility we choose to take. Life is not over with a diagnosis of Alzheimer's. Those afflicted do not wake up the next day with final-stage dementia. What then are the truths for us "worried well"? Chances are we will have to confront some very real issues and problems, and few of us will avoid all suffering. In the end our ability to age well will lie less with whether or not we get Alzheimer's or any other disease and more with our adaptability and continued desire for connection to others. We were created for relationships.

Thoughts on the Twilight Journey

When I was caring for Mother, I found it difficult to read the few available books that addressed the subject of Alzheimer's. I am sure they would have been helpful, but the sense of having every waking hour consumed with the disease kept me from reading even one paragraph. When the subject was Alzheimer's, a book that might have been uplifting and hopeful seemed something of an oxymoron. That thought also prevented me from writing.

With each passing year, however, new discoveries and more enlightened approaches have cracked the door and hope has crept in like a cat that knows it is supposed to be outside. I have changed too. I no longer see only the decimation of a life that was once vital and creative. The horror and despair that Alzheimer's brought were moderated by many good times and lots of laughter. Mother did a lot of living between diagnosis and death. She even managed to work in a final love story. Should Alzheimer's be my fate, my hope will be for good times mixed in with the bad.

The truth is that the majority of Americans will be affected directly or indirectly by AD in the coming years. But whether it is our fate or that of someone we love, the instruments of care, from the technical to the social, have changed radically. The approach to this plague has evolved from the hysteria I felt in trying to guess the best care for Mother to an atmosphere of greater understanding, improved options, and increased means to interfere with the rate of progression.

I am planning ahead. Should I succumb to AD, my children will not have to struggle to know my preferences; years will not go by with their wondering if I have just gotten ornery, lost my marbles, or if something is verifiably wrong, because I will seek a diagnosis at the first suspicion of onset. I am already working at ways to help pay for temporary help or permanent care, should I need those services. In the meantime, hope, not despair, must direct my life. It is my responsibility to maintain my unique, optimal (not perfect) health. My goal is not to live forever but to live well.

Brain Boosters

- A majority of Baby Boomers will be affected by Alzheimer's disease in one way or another.
- Normal cognitive changes due to aging do not signal AD.
- Some people are more susceptible to Alzheimer's than others.
- Modern technology can discern who is at risk.
- Keeping our overall health the best it can be is protective against AD.
- There is nothing to be gained by ignorance or avoidance; AD must be demystified.

Two

Get Me to the Church
on Time

Hope does not lie in a way out, but in a way through.

Robert Frost

Life Goes On

Every life is a story. This is the story of Mary Jo Alderson; more specifically the story of the last third of her life and how life goes on with Alzheimer's. Mary Jo was my mother; many aspects of her life make hers a story worth telling. Yet her battle with Alzheimer's disease prompts this assembly most. It is said we remember best what makes an emotional impact. Of all our shared experiences, few matched the last.

Mother's ability to reason and remember declined over a twenty-year span. This did not put an end to her capacity to love, be kind, adore small children, take part in her grandchildren's lives, and laugh. It did prompt new behavior, like becoming depressed, giving blank checks out to complete strangers (so they would know her address), and becoming unrelentingly paranoid about the devious plans of her only daughter (me) to steal her farm—or her red sweater—which were of equal concern depending on the day. And, because of her decline, when she decided to marry for the third time, the emotion was not joy but worry, felt not by the bride but by me.

Mother's first husband was the proverbial Jekyll and Hyde, a nice guy as long as he didn't drink. With him she had a son, Joe. When Joe was three, she did a most daring thing for women in that era. She left her husband. True to the times, she told no one exactly why. As a result, her family and acquaintances were embarrassed, angry, and decidedly unsympathetic. In 1933 women, especially those with small children, did not leave their husbands.

A kind gas station attendant aided her escape. As he filled her gas tank before her flight, he noted her balding tires and, wishing to ensure her getaway, charged her nothing to replace them with four retreads. He knew, like everyone else in town, that she had endured the humiliation of having her husband bring women to sleep in their bed while she and Joe huddled on the couch in the living room. He beat her when drunk, loved and apologized to her when sober.

To support her son and herself, she worked as a cashier in a dress shop and took in boarders in the house she had rented. With the help of the Shriner's Crippled Children's Fund, she made weekly all-day train trips to Dallas where Joe received extensive treatment for a severe clubfoot.

Around the time of Joe's seventh birthday, Mother had her first look at my father. They got acquainted and were considering marriage when Mr. Jekyll and Hyde insisted that my mother remarry him. He warned her that if she married someone else, she would condemn herself to a life of adultery and damnation.

Neither Mother nor the rest of the family told me much about this aspect of her life (I didn't find out my brother was my half-brother until I was thirteen years old). She did share that, from her perspective, divine intervention saved her from remarrying an abusive spouse. Miraculously, according to her, shortly after she agreed to return to him, husband number one was found murdered and robbed on the side of the road.

After this my mother decided to marry my father. She was nearing thirty and told her new husband that her wifely duty included one more baby, so ten months later I was born. It was a big disappointment when the "Billy" they expected turned out to be a girl, one whose hands were "almost human" according to my father. In the spirit of misguided fairness, he also announced he would show me little attention to ensure my brother would not feel slighted. Such is the grist for therapy!

This very traditional marriage lasted thirty years until my father's death from a heart attack at fifty-five. Mother bought a place on Lake Texoma and briefly filled her days with meeting friends for lunch, taking daily walks in the peaceful surroundings, and feeding the squirrels that lived among the one hundred trees on her property. Prophetically she was called Squirrelly Girly. Her time of mourning was cut short when her mother fell and my mother felt obliged to spend most of her time with her. She didn't want to be there. My grandmother didn't want her to be there.

Mother's motivation for insisting on staying was prompted more by unresolved issues from her childhood (I'll prove I'm the good kid and love you more than my older sister you thought was so perfect) and her vulnerability following my father's recent death than by my grandmother's physical needs. But as time wore on, this "loyal" daughter grew increasingly stressed and angry with her siblings for not providing relief. Though not a physician, Mother accurately pinpointed that this episode in her life damaged her brain.

By the time husband number three was in the wings, Mother was seventy. My husband and I had finally managed to resettle her into a condominium in our hometown. While we tend to think there is nothing good that can come from losing one's memory, in Mother's case it led directly to her becoming a new bride and a seven-year marriage that, with the exception of the last year, brought two very special people a great deal of happiness.

You see, husband number three was a well-respected Canadian physician who with his wife had become friends with my parents when my father was transferred to Canada to construct the Distance Early Warning Line in Alaska and supervise the building of oil refineries in Alberta, Canada. Their daughter, Marjorie Anne, and I had become friends at school. Marjorie Anne, like most kids, adored my mother—so much so that she used to refer to her as her second "Mum." Little did we know that it was predictive of what would come.

When his wife died, Dr. Jimmy Stirrat began the arduous task of notifying those who would want to know. Mother was deeply moved and, after her own experience of interrupted grieving ten years before, was concerned and sympathetic. The emotional impact of the news made an imprint on her mind—her phone calls of sympathy did not, however. Because of her short-term memory deficit, Mother called Dr. Stirrat frequently to express her sympathy. Each time, in her mind, was the first time. Her sensitive concern and sympathy shared several times a day made an impact on the good doctor. At their wedding he told me how much her calls had meant to him.

Before long, Mother announced that Dr. Stirrat wanted her to meet him and his family for a weekend in San Francisco. Confirming date and location, I found myself with the dilemma of how a woman with a pretty severe memory deficit would travel alone. It took weeks of organizing. I arranged for a limousine driver and paid extra to ensure she was met as soon as she stepped off the plane. I color-coded her clothes and attached a list to her suitcase. On Monday she was to wear everything that had a blue label, on Tuesday, the yellow labels, and so on.

At this stage of AD, Mother did well as long as she was one of the crowd, participating in some group activity. My friends found her delightful; they had no way of knowing that the stories she told didn't always have a basis in fact or were interesting compilations of events she masterfully intertwined. Her experience on her San Francisco adventure was no exception. The activities, schedule, and reminiscing all resulted in everyone having a fine time.

On her return, daily phone calls continued. One day Mother mentioned Dr. Stirrat had talked of marriage. Alarm bells went off. They were temporarily quieted when she later denied any such conversation. By this time hallucinatory episodes were occurring, and I was having a difficult time distinguishing what was real and what was imagined. Mother always had just enough current fact woven into her revelations that I sometimes wondered just exactly who it was that was losing her mind.

More and more stories of marriage began creeping into the conversation. It would take place "after Dr. Stirrat's appropriate mourning period of one year." While that was a sweet sentiment, it was not the issue that concerned me! I had always been fond of Dr. Stirrat; indeed, I loved him. The last thing I wanted was for him to think he was marrying the girl of his dreams and discover it was a nightmare. I was concerned he was marrying a memory instead of a reality. I knew he believed Mother to be the cheery, kind woman he knew from the past. I wasn't sure that image could support the woman who repeatedly asked the same questions and didn't always recall what she had had for breakfast—or if she had even had it. He deserved to know the truth.

I briefly thought of laying down the law, taking back the parental role and telling Mother she couldn't remarry. Assuming the parental role is an inevitable but dreaded step for many children whose parents have Alzheimer's disease. It is never taken on lightly or willingly. Grown-up kids with gray hair and grown-up kids of their own find comfort and order in the universe when parents are still parents, even when they have no need for them to be. I was unsure that this was our time to reverse roles.

Before saying anything, I presented my dilemma to a group that had considerably more experience as children and parents than I did. I took my concerns to some elderly men at my church. To them it was simple. Their recommendations were unanimous. I

had no right to command that Mother not remarry. I did have an
obligation to let Dr. Stirrat know exactly what he was getting into.
It was recommended that I ask him to fly down from Canada and
accompany Mother and me to UCLA, where a team of doctors
could examine her and objectively report on her condition. Dr.
Stirrat readily agreed.

Since this was early in the science of Alzheimer's, the doctors
seemed comfortable confirming and documenting the extent of
Mother's memory problems but decidedly less at ease with attribut-
ing them to AD. Perhaps they picked up on the reluctance of Dr.
Stirrat to accept such a diagnosis. Or, being academic researchers,
maybe they were reluctant to make a diagnosis without the definitive
proof of autopsy. Possibly they were concerned that such a diagnosis
might invalidate her medical insurance. At that time, insurance
companies often reneged on coverage after such a diagnosis. Dr.
Stirrat heard what he wanted and needed to hear. Mother had
simply suffered a "few small strokes," which affected her short-term
memory, but it wasn't Alzheimer's and we were never to suggest that
it was, he insisted. That was that. The marriage was on.

If getting Mother ready for a weekend in San Francisco had been
a challenge, preparing for the wedding and the extended trip to
visit relatives in Texas afterward became equivalent to preparation
for an invasion. But all that pales when compared to "getting her
to the church on time."

The marriage was to take place in Reno. Dr. Stirrat's frequent
trips to this gambling mecca had made him a welcome guest, so
welcome that for such a special event one hotel gave him the penthouse and a wedding cake, courtesy of the management. The plan
was for us to make the ten-hour drive to Reno, bringing everything
mother would need for the next few weeks.

My husband, Joe, declared he couldn't join us—too many babies
waiting to be born. Smart man. The children and I—Joey (15)
and Malika (11)—would have to make it on our own. The day
we were to leave, trouble began immediately. Mother was to pick
us up at 6 A.M. She finally answered her phone at 7 A.M., speaking

almost incoherently and in tears. She announced she wasn't ready and couldn't get ready. I assured her everything was packed; she just needed her last-minute items. She was not consoled. "Not to worry," we assured her. We would drive to her place.

By 7:30 A.M., two reluctant kids, a distraught and confused mother, and an impatient, stressed daughter headed for the appointed marriage altar 547 miles away. The first two hours were spent on two topics.

Mother: "We have to go back, I don't have my glasses."

Daughter: "Yes, you do, Mother. They are in the trunk. I put them in your overnight bag. We will get them later, since you have your contacts in now."

Mother, a few minutes later: "I forgot my glasses."

Daughter: "No, Mother, we have your glasses."

Mother: "I didn't bring my glasses. We have to go back."

Daughter: "Your glasses are in the trunk. Do you want me to stop and show you?"

Mother: "I don't have my shoes."

Daughter: "Yes, you do. They are in the suitcase in the trunk."

Mother, a few minutes later: "I forgot my shoes."

Daughter: "No, Mother, we have your shoes."

Mother: "I didn't bring my shoes. We have to go back."

Daughter: "YOUR SHOES ARE IN THE TRUNK. YOUR GLASSES ARE IN THE TRUNK. ALL IS WELL."

Silence. Five minutes would pass. Then it would begin again.

Mother: "We have to go back, I don't have my glasses."

Daughter: "Oh, yes, you do . . . and your shoes too."

As tedious as the conversation was, it was better than what was to come. Suddenly, thoughts of glasses and shoes were forgotten. Mother's face was as sweet as an angel as she asked, "Where are we going?"

"We are going to Reno so you can marry Jimmy."

The panicked howl from the adjacent seat nearly sent me off the road. "No," she bawled. "I'm not getting married. Jimmy has never asked me to marry him. I don't want to get married. I can't get married." The angel now looked like a trapped animal. I don't know how I looked but it couldn't have been good. The debate continued.

"You are getting married," I insisted.

She snapped back, "No, I'm not. Where did you get such a silly idea?"

"But, Gram," wafted a small voice from the backseat, "his family is waiting in a penthouse in Reno, with a wedding cake. We're all going to see you get married." Suddenly, even Joe and Malika were paying attention.

With all the strength of a woman who had walked out of an untenable marriage and raised a child on her own, she insisted, "No, you can take me, but I'm not getting married."

I believed her. I raised my voice, gripped the wheel, and with each rising decibel pushed harder on the accelerator. "Mother, it's all planned. *We are going to Reno where you are going to marry Jimmy.*"

Her reply filled the car, *"No, I'm not!"*

Blinking red lights and a siren broke into the palpable anguish that had infected the passengers of the wedding car. Stunned back into reality, I dutifully pulled over.

Officer: "Do you know how fast you were going?"

Daughter: "Well, when I realized I was going as fast as I was, I began to slow down."

Officer: "You did, but you passed three cars and an eighteen-wheeler before slowing."

Daughter, incredulously: "I did?" My mind fumbled for an explanation. Briefly I considered the truth. My mind formed the words, *You don't understand. I should be forgiven. I should be given a gold star not a ticket. You see, I'm taking my mother to her wedding and she forgot she was getting married.* Accepting that no one who hadn't been in the car could possibly understand, all that came out was, "Would you like a donut or would that be seen as a bribe?"

Hours later, stomach churning and body rigid, I pulled into the hotel unloading zone. I had no idea what would happen. My hands were clammy, my heart was racing. Marjorie Anne, her children, and Dr. Stirrat were at the door. They were all smiles. It was the moment of truth. Like the perfect Southern woman, Mother smiled meekly and slipped out of the open door into the arms of her groom. Hand in hand they entered simultaneously the lobby and their unique and satisfying marital relationship. Incredulous, and with the last functioning brain cell I had left, I helped sort luggage and get directions for parking my car. The kids remained catatonic in the backseat. No doubt the fear of someday delivering me to a groom I didn't remember was playing out in their heads.

For the next two days Mother was the requisite blushing bride. Her fears and hesitancy, if she remembered them, had given way to the compliant woman she had been most of her life, the one who didn't make scenes—especially in public. Marjorie Anne had arranged for hairdos and manicures, caviar and champagne. A limousine dropped the newlyweds off at the white wedding chapel, and the deed was done. I allowed myself to take a deep breath—the first one since arriving. I thought of Joe, hard at work delivering babies all weekend and throughout the night, answering a hundred phone calls, with no time to eat except what might be grabbed from a patient's leftover tray. I thought how lucky he was.

Jimmy was thrilled. Mother's wedding night present to him was a belly dance with bells on her toes, he reported. This, I might add, was in stark contrast to his first wife and more than I needed to know about my mother. We sent them off on their honeymoon. All was well.

Am I Losing It or Is This the Way It Is Supposed to Be?

If you've entered your "golden years," you're well aware that parts of you do not work like they used to. Perhaps you've taken to kicking a piece of trash under the couch rather than bending over to retrieve it. Because your eyes have changed, you realize that your last trip to the grocery store was in an outfit comprised of three unmatched shades of pink. Thirteen pairs of magnifying glasses are located by the phone, in the bathroom, on your desk, or around your neck but never where you want them at any given time. Suddenly, everyone seems to mumble. And food no longer tastes like your mother used to make it.

Sensory changes normally occur as we age; it follows then that brain function does too. Until 1998, when technological advances (PET and CAT scans and MRIs) proved otherwise, textbooks declared we lost neurons at the rate of 10,000 a day, 3.65 million in a year from middle age on. At that rate functioning at any level above an amoeba should have been cause for celebration. Today we know that we don't lose much of what we started with and are actually capable of generating new brain cells. This is great news. It does not, however, change the fact that the brain ages. For instance, brain cell metabolism slows down, just as it does in the rest of your body, but the major change of an aging brain seems out of step with the rest of the body—it shrinks.

Brain Function 101: A Trip to the Wild Side

The brain has three major parts: the brain stem, cerebellum, and cerebrum. From its perch on top of the spinal cord, the brain stem relays information it picks up from your five senses (taste, touch, sight, smell, and hearing) and controls the basics such as breathing and heartbeat. It is not where you organize a dinner party or worry about your friend who was just diagnosed with cancer. It's a relay station, hardware if you will. The cerebellum lies just behind the brain stem and helps your body move—the coordinator of your muscles. It retains memory of movement, which is why I was able to take up in-line skating at sixty. My cerebellum pulled the file on my skating life as an eleven-year-old. It could do this easily since this area of the brain experiences few age-related changes.

The cerebrum is the most complex of the three. It houses thoughts, emotions, and memories. If we stretched out its convolutions, it would cover two and a half square feet. God clearly knew what he was doing when he devised a way to give us lots of thinking room without having to figure out how to get our heads through a door.

While there is some overlap, the four lobes of the cerebrum have specific duties. The frontal lobe is where we do abstract problem solving, like how we can make our grown kids open a savings account. Shrinkage in this area can be significant—up to 30 percent by the time we are ninety—resulting in difficulties with complex thought, focus, and multitasking. In other words it can be risky for us to try to get the cereal and cat food in the right bowls while we watch the news and look up a telephone number.

The temporal lobes, obviously positioned by your temples, shrink up to 20 percent as you get older. They manage many activities, including memory, speech, and hearing. Impaired hearing as one ages is not necessarily due to brain function but is often related to weaker stimuli from nerves running from the ear to the brain, making processing less reliable. Calcification of the inner ear bones results in less vibration and thus the weaker signal. In the same way, our vision can become poorer with degeneration of signals from the eye to the occipital lobe located at the back of the cerebrum. Its job is interpreting and organizing what we see.

The combination of a slower metabolism, brain shrinkage, and reduction in the neurotransmitter dopamine in the frontal lobe area explains why we no longer get the same degree of pleasure once experienced from favorite things, activities, or people. These changes can result in a tendency to be more impulsive and to have less control of our emotions—the "grumpy old man" syndrome!

Resting on top of the brainstem is a ring of brain matter known as the "feeling" brain. Technically it is the limbic system. It includes

Normal Aging Fact 1:

Distractions keep you from laying down strong memory paths.

Normal Aging Fact 2:

You can't recall what you never learned.

Normal Aging Fact 3:

You must increasingly make active choices about what you want to learn.

Normal Aging Fact 4:

Once you decide you want to remember something, the more ways you reinforce your memory, the more likely you will be able to recall it.

Normal Aging Fact 5:

Wisdom attained from living and acquiring knowledge over a long period of time offsets slower brain processing time.

Normal Aging Fact 6:

For older people, retrieving information may be more complex, but what we have learned is still there.

Normal Aging Fact 7:

Failing to remember is likely to be evidence of irrelevance, not pathology.

the hippocampus. Shrinkage and chemical changes in this area are of great concern because it is here that memories are formed and retrieved. The hippocampus is like a keyboard on a computer, inputting and calling up information stored on the hard drive. In this case the hard drive is the neocortex, the large convoluted surface of the brain. The hippocampus's role in short-term memory means its malfunction is involved in those "senior moments" of temporary forgetfulness and in full-blown Alzheimer's.

It is the limbic system where mind and body meet. It is literally where thought meets emotion. It is why your attitude makes a difference. What you think becomes important because there is a physiological connection. Remember my experience with the long-term health insurance interview? The level of norepinephrine from my adrenal gland, released in response to my anxiety, resulted in a self-fulfilling prophecy. My fear of not remembering prevented me from recalling what I knew. While small doses of hormones can enhance memory, an overload explains why we freeze during test taking or forget our best friend's name when we are trying to introduce her to a new acquaintance.[1]

Memories, so vital and vivid to us, are nothing more than chemicals and electrical impulses in our brain. Every memory is stored several times in a variety of ways in a network of neurons. My first date with Joe is encrypted in the areas that registered how great he looked and the feel of his arm around me on the dance floor. The knot in my stomach and the pounding of my heart were emotional responses that meant the memory of that Saturday date would be registered in something like indelible ink, making that night, now more than forty years ago, seem like it was yesterday.

Laying down memories in a variety of tracts means that it is difficult to wipe out a memory completely. People who have the best recall normally lay down memories using auditory, visual, and kinesthetic memory patterns. Most of us lean heavily on what we hear. Whatever pathways we have used, the fact that we have a number of them means that, as individual connections become weak, we can access a memory in a variety of ways. Retrieval takes more time, but the memory remains accessible.

Signs of the Aging Brain, or Get Used to It Kid—It's All You Got!

Our working memory is very short term.

> **Normal Aging Fact 8:**
>
> Controlling our level of stress can significantly affect the rate at which our brain ages.

> **Normal Aging Fact 9:**
>
> We do not lose our capacity to think, just to think quickly.

> **Normal Aging Fact 10:**
>
> God grant me the senility to forget the people I never liked anyway, the good fortune to run into the ones I do . . . and the eyesight to know the difference.

People tend to panic when they can't remember what their spouse told them to pick up at the store or to whom they were just introduced. They ignore the reality that short-term memory is just that—short term. Unless what comes in is reinforced in some way, the brain doesn't record it. It should be some comfort to realize that you can't retrieve what isn't there. You didn't forget—you never "knew." Your teenager can study and retain information for a test while watching TV, talking on the phone, and painting her toenails. You no longer can. If recalling something is important, a memory pathway must be established. For something to stick, repetition must reinforce the path.

One of the significant changes of aging is the fact that you must give your full attention to laying down memory pathways. The more distractions, the less likely you will remember. It is not Alzheimer's if you must reinforce the memory of turning off the lights by saying out loud, "I turned off the kitchen light." It is not AD if, in order to remember a phone number, you must repeat it five times while simultaneously writing it. Such practices are intelligent adaptations to a brain that with age requires concentrated effort for something to stick. It is a reality of aging that it becomes difficult for us to take in or do several things at once and learn or remember. Technically this is known as channel capacity and it is one of the first brain functions to decline.

The inability to focus when there are distractions is often at the bottom of why we of a certain age find ourselves going to another room and forgetting why. Blame it on deteriorating channel capacity rather than AD. This is normal aging because you continue to know how to get to the other room and you are aware you are looking for something even if that something escapes you. An individual with dementia wanders into another room and hasn't a clue why he is there. Unable to stick to the task to figure it out, he becomes distracted and involved in some unrelated task.

Language skills, IQ, abstract thinking, and verbal expression have been proven to remain fairly steady throughout our life span except when affected by disease. It is good news that brain cells can and do replenish themselves, even if it is also true they may not make connections that are as strong or lasting as the original ones. The more mentally active a person has been and remains, the more connections are made in the brain. When information needs to be put in context, all those associations give an older person a leg up on a recent college graduate. Experience enables a person to reach good decisions with less information. A twenty-one-year-old may be able to program a VCR but lacks the wisdom acquired through living and experiencing life for a very long time.

The downside of having many connections in one's brain is the amount of material to filter through. It is likely your filing system may have become quite complex. Stated another way, your Rolodex is huge and, while all the names and numbers are there, looking up a specific one takes time. In the same way more time is required to filter and find information in the labyrinth of your mind.

Among individuals there is great variability in memory. Lapses of memory occur for all ages. "It's on the tip of my tongue" is universally experienced. However, older individuals tend to worry more and read the worst-case scenario into any memory glitch. Perspective can be gained through a realistic acknowledgment that an aging brain means no longer working with the fastest and most up-to-date computer.

Younger brains are able to register more detail and etch a stronger memory around new learning. What we remember depends on what else was going on in our life at the time. Information is encoded according to what is deemed important. We remember best the meaningful and relevant events, actions, or thoughts associated with something we already know. Things that we are expected to remember and that are unique to our experience are rarely forgotten.[2]

If we had to use one word to define most accurately the changes of the aging brain, it would have to be *slowing*. The fact that we need more time to learn and remember does not mean we can't learn or encode new memories. It does signify we must give ourselves more time to learn new things. We sabotage learning and recall by putting pressure on ourselves to perform quickly. Even though the aging brain continues to be capable of most of what it could do in the past, demanding that it perform like it did at twenty-one is as silly as demanding the same of our body.

Thoughts on the Twilight Journey

To me, the amazing thing about Mother's marriage to Dr. Stirrat is the magnitude of genuine joy it brought two dear people in the twilight of their lives. I was certain that this seventy-two-year-old pathologist would soon tire of the incessant, repetitive questions. I did, but she was my mother. He was choosing to take on what I was convinced he would come to see as a burden. He deserved to sit back, enjoy his grandchildren, and live out his life as the retired and esteemed professor of a major medical center that he was. How little I understood. Never once did he express frustration or raise his voice to her or to us. "It was a little thing," he insisted. Together they vacationed at his ancestral home in Scotland, toured China, and visited with family in Texas.

He found her charming and fun to be with. She was a tease and flirt with him. She talked him into his first pair of Levi jeans. He wore them with his sealskin bowtie that had become his trademark after his work at the Arctic Circle. She introduced him to a profundity in their relationship and a dimension of being that were new to him. In return Mother got companionship—someone who would play whenever she wanted. They ate cookies together and made cups of coffee for each other. He was unendingly patient.

She told him repeatedly how kind and special he was. In or out of his presence, she would say to me, "Isn't Jimmy kind? He is the nicest man." And I would agree. He protected her. Her stories and paranoia about her finances prompted us to "open the books" to him so he could restore her confidence that all was in order. He grasped the details and would gently reassure her when her anxiety became unmanageable.

When not traveling, they would sleep in, fix a light breakfast, and at noon go out to lunch. Dinner at home was fruit or cereal. Mother never again cooked a full meal and she loved that there was no expectation for her to do so. In the twilight of their life, they forged a union that fulfilled both previously unmet and new needs. And they did it despite Alzheimer's.

Being together was reason enough to begin a new day. It did not matter that Mother could not remember. "It was a little thing." Why do I keep forgetting this? Why do I keep thinking life has purpose and joy only when every detail is remembered? No doubt life is richest when it is emblazoned with recollection. But what ultimately counts is patience and kindness.

Brain Boosters

- Alzheimer's is not the end of a quality life.
- Aging slows down brain processing speed.
- The chief culprit in forgetfulness as we age is our not paying attention.
- The more associations we make with something we want to remember, the more likely we will be able to recall it.
- Wisdom acquired with age makes up for what we forget.

Three

Don't Worry—Be Happy

A heart at peace gives life to the body, but envy rots the bones [or brain as the case may be].

Proverbs 14:30

Shedding Light on the Darkness

My grandfather constructed wooden derricks as a Texas oil rig builder. He died of pneumonia before I was born, because, although penicillin had just become available, no doctors he knew had access to it. My grandmother, Mommaw, was a terrific cook, at least a terrific from-scratch biscuit maker, which she produced daily through most of her life. I still enjoy reminiscing about my annual week-long summer vacation at my grandmother's house, building tree houses with my cousin, drawing water from the well on the back porch, and discovering the particular delights of outhouses and slop buckets.

I never suspected that this proper church lady had eloped when her folks objected to her choice of a husband. Recognizing that

43

the little streak of rebellion she once possessed was full blown in her daughter Mary Jo may explain why she found my mother so trying.

Mommaw's life was one of feast and famine. When the oil fields came in, there were Pierce Arrow cars and tennis courts. As fate would have it, my grandfather's death occurred during one of the down times, leaving Mommaw to cope on a meager income.

She had four children: Esthma, also known as Cissy; Mary Jo, my mother; and Margurette, the baby girl. The youngest was a baby boy, JC, fondly called Budo. Like the story of the three little pigs and the kind of houses they built, these three sisters each chose a distinct lifestyle for keeping the wolf from the door.

Both my mother and Margurette would come to believe that Esthma was their mother's favorite. Equally important, she was popular at school and a good student, undoubtedly setting a standard that was hard to equal. Mother chafed under the comparison. She liked to play and have fun. She was a cheerleader and "very pretty," according to a ninety-two-year-old gentleman who still remembers their dates. It was no surprise she won first prize in the Charleston contest and liked to beat the boys on the tennis court. Time and again I heard stories about how she never broke more rules than Esthma; she just didn't hide her behavior. If she wanted to kiss a boy, she would do it in the open. Esthma, however, would "neck" in the car—God help her! But Esthma's penchant for being respectful of current norms and being a responsible "mother's helper" legitimately won over their mother. On the other hand their mother worried about what an uninhibited spirit like Mary Jo might do behind her back, so her social life was limited to tagging along behind Esthma. Throughout her life Mary Jo expressed envy and frustration that she was not appreciated as the "good" child.

Esthma liked to read and she was a career woman for most of her life. Her husband, Pete, had a small accounting business, and she worked as office manager and all-round assistant. She did not spend much time preparing healthful meals.

Pete was not always an easy man to live with. He smoked much of his life and his wiry build matched his edgy personality. Living with him couldn't have been easy. Her stress level throughout her life was high.

I would say that Esthma was the one whose house was built out of straw. Her vulnerability lay within her genes. In 1985, when she was seventy-seven years old, she suffered the first of four strokes. They left her unable to move on her own or verbally communicate. Still, she remained a sweet and loving person and was very aware of what was going on. She was able to read until the last year of her life at ninety and a half years old.

Mary Jo, my mother, left home when her mother insisted she go to a girl's college. She once told me that since her mother had refused to let her go to her coed-college choice, getting married after six months was the best way out. As you might guess, selecting a spouse as the lesser of two evils is not the beginning of a fairytale romance. Within three years, her husband was periodically beating her and bringing home women he picked up off the street. Since she never revealed to anyone why she left the marriage, her decision did little to endear her to her mother. And yet she felt fury when others didn't support her.

Other than the Bible, which proved a comfort to her, I don't remember Mother reading many books. She was a decent artist and an excellent writer, masterfully spinning tales of her travel adventures or of our life in a foreign country, even if it was Canada. She was also the best Sunday school teacher I ever had. Our home was frequently filled with the cardboard tube inserts from carpets in the process of being transformed into palm trees, authentic Holy Land costumes, and flour-and-salt-paste–covered milk cartons that became little houses, ultimately filling out the whole city of Jerusalem in Christ's day. Other than when she and my brother were living alone, she did not work outside the home.

Mary Jo's house was built of sticks, somewhat stronger than Esthma's straw version, and she was probably in her late fifties when her stick house began to collapse, sixty years old when I first suspected something was wrong. Following my father's death, she had settled into her own lakeside home and appeared to love it. As the years went by, however, near hysterical phone calls set off alarms that something was wrong. She was concerned about her finances and my brother's requests for financial help. She felt compelled to assist him but was terrified she would not be able to support herself—although she was in fairly sound financial shape.

More alarming were Esthma's reports that during a visit Mother had acted "crazy," retreating to a closet and beating her head against the wall. Mother's explanation to me was "Since they think I'm crazy, I just did something so they wouldn't have any doubt—it was just an act." The defiant little girl was still at it, providing the necessary wind to blow her own house down. She was clearly depressed. Her charged emotions and disorganized thinking left her furious that neither Esthma nor Marguerette would take more responsibility for Mommaw's care. Mother was insistent that their mother needed someone with her around the clock long after recovering from falling and breaking a hip. It was possible that she had fallen as a result of a stroke; her own mother had become incapacitated in the same way.

Mother left her home and spent weeks at a time taking care of her mother. Weeks rolled into a couple of years, and Mother's mood deteriorated. She hated the confines of Ector and its three hundred denizens; when home, she despaired when fending off my brother's requests for just "one more loan."

My grandmother's eventual move to a nursing home did not deter Mother's visits. While she can't be faulted for wanting to make sure her mother was well taken care of, it was not her only motivation. Into her seventies she still expressed her frustration at not being recognized as the most caring, loving, and dutiful daughter of the bunch. She was Cinderella and no one was admitting it. The depth of this unresolved issue came to light when I told mother about Esthma's stroke. Mother, one of the most compassionate and caring people I have ever known, looked me straight in the eye and responded, "Well, it serves her right for making everyone think she was such a Goody Two-shoes." It pains me to share that she could say something so unkind. I would like to pass it off as a further sign of a deteriorating mind—the disease speaking. But the truth is she brought a serious unresolved life issue into her Alzheimer's. My father's early death coinciding with Mommaw's fall kept Mother from ever learning to live on her own. Her conflicts and despair excluded choices that would have been less stressful and this undoubtedly contributed to the progression of her disease.

The final gust of wind that collapsed her stick house was the series of small strokes that left dead and damaged brain cells in their wake, but an autopsy revealed no cardiovascular disease anywhere else. While her love of sweets necessitated occasionally beginning dinner with dessert (to insure she would have room), her diet included adequate vegetables and fruits. Her cholesterol was not a problem. The four strokes that downed Esthma's house were four big bullets; buckshot brought down my mother's. Esthma clearly inherited the family's propensity for stroke. Unlike Mother's little versions, her massive variety occurred in spots that resulted in major damage—still her mind was not affected.

Margurette was young enough to be out of the Mary Jo/Esthma loop. She didn't get into much trouble and apparently escaped into a fantasy world of books for stimulation and companionship. Around age two or three, she almost lost her life to scarlet fever. Her hair fell out and, when she recovered, her voice was very gruff and low-pitched, remaining so today. Any damage done by such an early near-death experience appeared to be more psychological than physical. She has remained more of a private person than either of her two sisters.

She reports being delighted when Mary Jo left for college because she was at last able to have her own room and luxuriate in its privacy. She attended college for two years and married at twenty-five, late for a woman of her era. Like Esthma she worked all her life. In fact it wasn't until she had surgery for colon cancer at age eighty-six that she quit. Shortly after her surgery, she moved to an assisted-living facility. She was not thrilled.

Unlike her sisters she had no children. Her husband, Lloyd, was a heavy smoker and died at sixty of a heart attack after suffering from emphysema for a number of years. Margurette was not an advocate of regular exercise, but in her fifties she became best friends with a woman who owned a health food store. She became a believer in the benefits of supplements, taking twelve to fifteen pills a day for almost twenty years. In addition to a multivitamin, she took doses of vitamins E, A, D, and C. I remember her chewing vitamin C tablets like candy.

Whether or not Margurette's supplement habit kept her brain functioning and helped her avoid the strokes that befell her sisters is something that can't be proven. It certainly was a factor in the rapidity of healing following her colon cancer surgery and the doctor's observation about her overall good physical health. While my cousin found evidence that Margurette had not kept on top of her finances, she was able to get up and go to work long after most of us have collected our gold watch and settled down with the *TV Guide*. There is no question that she is now, at eighty-seven years old, showing wafting and waning signs of dementia. Still she is able to function in an assisted-living setting, where meals are prepared but the resident is basically responsible for her own care.

Margurette's life was not without travail but it was relatively stress free in comparison to her sisters' lives. She was an independent woman who maintained contact with people by working for more than fifty years at the same store and by visiting friends. Her lifelong habit of reading and the fact that her life was uncomplicated by children may have given her an edge. We can conclude that her house was built of bricks.

My husband and I visited Margurette shortly after she moved to the assisted-living facility, and it was as much a highlight for us as it was for her. Joe and I had decided we would get "old-folk practice" by checking ourselves into the facility for a week, actually into their guest room. Our old-folk practice meals proved the most challenging aspect of the visit. Wolfgang Puck was not the chef. People were nice, and the facilities were clean and adequate, but we all perked up when we signed out for our daily adventures. Margurette trooped around with us in the 110-degree heat, relishing every meal away and always on time for the next day's agenda. She was sharp and pleasant. But such a schedule was not her usual routine. As we expected, as the months have passed, her ability to focus and remember has slipped considerably.

Of the three, she continues on, not having escaped dementia but somehow succeeding in staving it off to the end. Her sisters have passed on, one with a great body but very little functional brain; the other with a functional brain but a body that just quit working. Margurette and Budo, the younger brother with no sign of AD, give me lots to think about. They also give me hope.

It is difficult to look back at the lives of these three sisters and determine why each suffered her unique fate. As children they were raised with the same good cooking in the same quiet town. But their emotional perspectives of their household and their mother were quite different. For Mary Jo this set up a lifelong struggle that gnawed its way to the surface as life's burdens increased and her mind slipped. While she appeared happy-go-lucky, she always had a sense of not measuring up—at least in the eyes of the one person we tend to think is the gauge of our lovability. If our own mother (parent) doesn't think we pass muster, who else will?

I remember Mother being very proud of my accomplishments and certainly supportive of them. No mother ever sewed on more sequins or carted a kid around to more activities. Still, as she got older, her joy over one of my new publications or articles was tinged with envy. In my own mind I have always felt I have taken Mother's particular strengths and pushed them forward. She was Mother Confessor to all the kids in the neighborhood and to any hurting friend; I became a professional therapist. She wrote her twenty-eight-page Christmas letters; I wrote books. It is clear Mother's wound caused by the feeling that she didn't measure up was like an underground tsunami that hit the beach when dendrites failed to keep up a defense.

The result was twofold. First, because of her increasingly distracting obsession with Mommaw's failure to acknowledge her as the favored child, she was unable to fully enjoy her grandchildren and her life in general as she aged. Second, the years of stress and depression resulting from her insistence that she had to take care of her mother while still grieving my father's death literally manufactured the toxic cocktail that began to destroy her brain. Even mother acknowledged her choices had resulted in "something happening to my brain." Are we guessing? Not at all. There is plenty of research to confirm that AD is more likely to manifest its symptoms if depression is longstanding and life feels beyond control. Maybe Mother's lifelong addiction to sweets was a means to obtain a sugar high and lift her spirits. Add a few small strokes to the mix and you have Alzheimer's.

There were other factors. As a child, Mother wasn't a good student or avid reader. Her years as a single mom were complicated and her life stressed by my brother's medical needs. Three marriages to heavy drinkers couldn't have been easy. She walked regularly for a few years during her fifties, but when she remarried in her seventies, after the first few years, she settled into a very passive lifestyle, passing the time watching television with little stimulation beyond the adventures presented on *National Geographic.* Dr. Stirrat's heavy smoking meant she secondarily inhaled the equivalent of a pack of cigarettes daily.

Unraveling the Mystery

As a therapist, sometimes treating married couples whose lives have been turned upside down by an illicit relationship, I am always struck by how no one ever sets out to have an affair. Instead, a series of "little yeses" lead a couple where they never planned to be. Most cases of Alzheimer's disease are like that. It is as if the body permits a series of "little yeses" slowly to erode what was meant to be. At this point we know that at least sixty "little yeses" can alter normal brain function. While early changes are so subtle they are missed, the cumulative effect of each individual's quantity of unique "yeses" eventually leads to conceding that something is wrong. Like the affair, the significance of such an admission is difficult, confusing, and frightening.

I have some subtle and not so subtle "yeses" that are primed to stamp out my neurons. Some I still have time to do something about. Others are already on their dastardly path, playing havoc with dendrites, toting that plaque—running amok with wild abandon. Mother was aware that "yeses" were piling up, but she had no name for them. She would complain that something was wrong with her brain and that knowledge in itself was driving her crazy. Like the majority of persons with AD, her decline was the slow road to mental, physical, and social deterioration. I hate having to admit that life was easier for me when her "yeses" raised their victory flag and she forgot for good that she was forgetting.

AD is a process. Decades pass while the brain chemistry interacts with environmental and physiological factors. This is what we know for sure. If you decide to get old, you have an ever increasing chance of being affected. If your family inheritance included AD along with Grandma's silver, you may be in trouble. If you refused to listen when your mother told you not to run around the swimming pool and you fell and knocked yourself out, you may live to regret it. Finally, your penchant for comic books instead of Latin 101 may come back to haunt you.

In other words, there are several possible contributors to Alzheimer's disease:

family history
head injuries[1]
limited education
an Alzheimer's gene[2]

Genetics Plays a Role but Rarely the Only Role

You can develop AD without a gene for it and you can have an AD gene and escape its ravages. It is obvious that genes and other risk factors work together to increase or decrease risk. There are a few families (and you would know if yours was one) whose genes set up the equivalent of a paved superhighway to AD. Their inheritance can include three mutated genes, any one of which almost invariably ensures they will end up with early-onset (before sixty years old) Alzheimer's. While this is rare, accounting for 3 to 5 percent of all cases, the late-onset form also has a genetic component and is much more common.

Persons with Down's syndrome are at high risk for developing AD—or at least their brains look like that of a person with Alzheimer's even though not all of them express the symptoms. The research is incomplete but one factor is the overproduction of the beta-amyloid precursor protein (APP) that manufactures beta-amyloid.

Another gene known as A2M and located on chromosome 12 appears to mediate the rate at which beta-amyloid is produced. Other discoveries are forthcoming. In the meantime, knowing you have the gene can be a worrisome burden if there is nothing you can do about it. Even if you have the gene, it does not guarantee that you will succumb. At the moment, genes are the tools of the researchers. Our job is to stave off damage by incorporating as many preventive methods as we can, gene or not.

It is well known that persons with head trauma can produce excess amounts of amyloid plaques. Being knocked unconscious increases the chance for AD threefold, particularly if the injury occurred early in life.

Higher education and occupational status may be protective. Statistically, there is greater risk with lower educational and occupational standing. But then there are Iris Murdoch, prolific British novelist and philosopher; Ronald Reagan, president of the United States; E. B. White, essayist and storyteller; Aaron Copland, composer. These cases are proof again that more than one factor is at work when, as Iris's husband John Bayley writes, "Dr. A" takes up residence.

It may just be that brilliant folk can hide symptoms longer, by appearing more intelligent, or perhaps more connections between brain cells have been established. It is hard to know. Education is linked to other lifestyle habits like diet, not smoking, quality of medical care, education, and stimulation early in life. A recent study that examined an older rural Black population with fewer than seven years of schooling found Alzheimer's was six and one-half times higher than the average. Perhaps education is like a vaccine. It offers some protection. A brilliant, complex thinker like Iris Murdoch is an individual case standing out from overall patterns. Clearly that happens. When the points converge and a person is diagnosed with Alzheimer's, all such odds become a moot point. Then the statistical probability becomes 100 percent.

There is no doubt that brain development can be influenced in the womb, in infancy, and in adulthood. A brain that has been exposed to stimulating experiences in multiple forms has a lot of "reserve." Envision a map that has your home at one point and your workplace, school, church, or mall located elsewhere. If you took the same route each day, you could probably drive it with your eyes closed. Should you wake up one day and discover the route had been blocked as a result of an earthquake, you would be at a loss as to what to do. If on the other hand you had made a habit of taking new and different routes periodically, even throwing in a few side trips, you would have some options—some reserve routes.

Educated people have alternative pathways to choose from. More paths or reserves mean that the amount of damage may not reflect the degree of AD. Symptoms may not be significant until so much damage is done it overrides the many routes and detours. Stronger brains have more alternatives, efficiency, and processing ability.

There is controversy about whether just being a woman increases the odds for AD.[3] Women live almost five and one-half years longer than men and age is a major risk factor. But women also lose estrogen as they age. Estrogen replacement may be controversial but there is no denying the important overall role that naturally occurring estrogen plays in a woman's health. Included in its more than four hundred actions is the enhancement of blood flow to the brain.

In my mother's case, small strokes contributed to memory problems, but the association is not as straightforward as one might expect. Still, while I may not be able to do much about my genes, I can do something about my risk for stroke. Large or small, strokes are mostly preventable and treatable. This will be discussed fully in chapter 4 but involves keeping blood pressure down, not smoking, and watching blood lipid levels, particularly LDL-C.[4]

Researchers who have studied the brains of Catholic nuns in the ongoing Nun study are skeptical that small strokes are a singular cause of Alzheimer's.[5] In all, they have discovered only one nun who had been diagnosed with vascular dementia who actually had enough damage solely due to stroke to cause the problems she had. In most cases stroke seems to be a contributing factor when plaques and tangles are present. Maintaining a stroke-free brain is worth the effort. If you have a stroke, make sure you minimize damage by taking one of the new clot-busting stroke medications within the first three hours.

A number of research studies have shown that individuals who are on cholesterol-lowering statins reduce their chance of AD compared to those whose cholesterol remains high. High cholesterol levels are undeniably related to risk of dementia. It is one of those "yeses" we can do something about. In fact anything that reduces blood flow, such as TIAs (transient ischemic attacks), hypertension, smoking, or hyperlipidemia, will affect cognitive function after age sixty and accelerate decline after seventy.

A few studies hint that race and ethnicity can protect or put one at greater risk. African Americans and Hispanics of Caribbean origin have in some studies been shown to be at greater risk than other racial groups.[6] Cherokee Indians in Oklahoma have very low AD rates. The only definite conclusion, however, is that culture has something to do with how genes and environment interact.[7]

Since some viruses and bacteria cause neurological problems, it is theorized that they may increase susceptibility to AD. Infection by a microorganism, as in untreated syphilis; a virus, as in AIDS; or by a prion, as in Creutzfeldt-Jakob disease or its variant, mad-cow disease, suggest infectious agents can negatively affect brain function. A bacterium, common in sinus infections, bronchitis, and other respiratory ailments, may trigger inflammation if it enters the brain. It is treatable with antibiotics. British researchers have linked the herpes virus, which causes cold sores and genital herpes, with an increased chance of AD. Inflammation from any cause is now recognized as contributing to AD.

Dementia occurs with Huntington's or Parkinson's disease. Some scientists believe autoimmune problems that increase as we age are a greater risk than bacteria and viruses. As with diabetes and arthritis, antibodies become confused and attack the cells of the person they are supposed to protect—perhaps even their brain cells. The question is which came first? Was the brain already susceptible because of developing AD, or did any of these factors increase the risk of AD?

As for me, I worry about cooking with aluminum pans. The fear of aluminum stems from the fact that excess aluminum is found in those pesky neurofibrillary tangles. While there is weak evidence of aluminum being a risk factor, I confess I simply can't ignore the possibility. I have searched out aluminum-free deodorant (impossible to find one that is effective) and antacids. I have made note of the many medicines that are high in aluminum. If you already have AD, it is realistic to avoid aluminum since the gastrointestinal tract of a person with AD can't excrete aluminum effectively.

Other substances that may affect the development of AD are lead, organic solvents, such as benzene and toluene,[8] glues, pesticides, and fertilizers. Zinc plus aluminum silicate, found in nondairy creamers and nonprescription antidiarrheal medications, accelerates amyloid plaque production. A small study suggests electromagnetic fields may interfere with concentrations of calcium within cells, which increases beta-amyloid production.

You Are What You Eat, We Think

People with memory problems, including Alzheimer's, are more likely to have low levels of folic acid and vitamin B12. A shortage of folic acid and high homocysteine levels are associated with brain shrinkage, the one place you don't want to lose weight. Excess homocysteine is a culprit in vascular disease. B12 and folic acid combine to break down homocysteine into a useful form. While the importance of vitamin E to brain health depends on the study you read, even the ones that claim no cognitive improvements cannot ignore that people taking vitamin E differ from people who are deficient in regard to the timeline involved in death, institutionalization, and ability to care for oneself.[9] Preliminary work suggests a high fat diet is no better for your brain than it is for your hips.[10]

Even mild hypoglycemia, low blood sugar, affects memory. Just like your car, the brain won't run on empty and is highly selective about what it uses for fuel. The brain is a fuel burning fool—kind of like a muscle car. It may account for 3 percent of your body weight but it uses 20 percent of its energy. You simply don't think well when you are hungry.

The Role of Stress

While I eat pretty well and take supplements that include a well-balanced B complex, the "yes" I worry about most (other than genetics) is the stress level I have lived with most of my life. It is true that it is not how much stress but how it has been handled that is important. I cannot say this helps me. Most of my life I have been passionately involved in whatever challenge I have accepted; I have always been too busy. Besides, having a perfectionist streak has placed me in the classic dilemma of the need to perform perfectly or consider myself a failure. In other words, I haven't been my own best friend. As I have aged, I have handled my stress better and am less apt to manufacture it—long-term care insurance applications excepted. My hope is that I have decreased my vulnerability, but the early days may have already done me in.

Big events or inevitable things like planning a wedding and then having your daughter elope to Thailand and the death of a loved one or a relationship are definite risk factors. But habitual anger and depression will do the trick as well. Veterans with post-traumatic stress syndrome have demonstrated major and selective atrophy of their hippocampus and their odds of an increased incidence of AD are currently being investigated. Studies of people who began life with lots of stress in their environment have shown their lifelong mental impairment, and they age faster than those who started life in a loving, calm setting. A connection between emotions and heart disease is well established. Why not emotions and brain disease? I'll come back to stress and the role the hormone cortisol plays in the next chapter.

Closely related to stress is depression. The Nun study documented that positive emotions often translated into a longer life, although negative emotions were not found to shorten life below the average. Depression is damaging because your body remains in a perpetual state of stress. When an elderly person has few resources and feels she has no control over her life, she will often experience depression.

Since depression affects memory, it is sometimes difficult to decipher which came first—losing one's mind is a good reason for feeling blue. There are many psychosocial causes of depression, but there are also biological causes. Some, like depletion of serotonin, are common with AD. Mother's coping mechanisms could not be maintained when the ravages of AD began. Her ability to enjoy her grandchildren and what was currently swirling around her was overshadowed by unresolved and hurtful incidents from the past. Long sealed away in the recesses of her mind, memories of hurtful events began to rise menacingly to the surface. They proved distracting and depressing, but therapy for a person suffering from AD is limited because of impaired reasoning and forgetfulness.

Other Risks

I saw firsthand how Mother's life journey, including her early life environment, affected her final journey. She is not alone; early life environment is linked to many adult chronic diseases. Heart disease, stroke, hypertension, diabetes, all have childhood links. Alzheimer's disease, as well, is associated with the environment in which you grew up and the number of siblings you had. Each additional child in the family increases the risk by 8 percent, and growing up in a rural area doesn't help either.[11]

When Mother lived at Lake Texoma, she walked fairly regularly. When she relocated to Redlands, California, I used to cajole her into going to aerobics classes with me. She would reluctantly agree to come and then just stand on her mat, occasionally making a move to reassure us she was alive. Lack of physical activity increases the chance of developing dementia, particularly among those who let their exercise slow down between ages twenty and fifty-nine. Couch potatoes beware, especially if you are smoking while you lollygag.

If you suffer a medical trauma, such as heart surgery or another severe illness, your risk of AD increases. Whether factors were already in place for loss of memory or whether they are caused by the medical crisis is unclear. What is clear is that a medical crisis is likely to escalate problems. Older people have a very difficult time restoring their health to their pre-crisis level and most never do. Sensory impairments, like becoming hard of hearing, contribute to cognitive problems in a number of ways. Just trying to follow what is going on can distract a person, keeping her from concentrating on what needs to be remembered. Misinterpretation of sounds can result in hallucinations, delusions, and paranoia.

There are some things you should not consider as risks for contracting Alzheimer's. It is not contagious. You cannot catch it from someone else. Behavioral changes resulting from life's traumas do not robotically set degenerative disease into operation. Psychiatric disease, other than depression, does not increase the possibility of AD. And, finally, AD is not God's wrath for bad behavior. No one deserves it; there is another kind of hell reserved for the naughty among us.

Aging with Grace

David Snowdon has written a wonderfully sweet and enlightening book, *Aging with Grace,* about his ongoing study of the nuns of the School Sisters of Notre Dame. The point of the study is not to test new drugs; it is to look at the differences between people and make a distinction between those who develop Alzheimer's and those who don't. Six hundred and seventy-eight sisters between the ages of 75 and 102 joined the study in 1988. As of May 2001 there were 344 who remained alive, ranging in age from 84 to 106. One hundred of those still do not have symptoms of Alzheimer's. Researchers have meticulously reviewed their personal and medical histories, subjected them to periodic tests of memory and physical function, and ultimately studied their brains after death.

The Nun study has reinforced the belief that education, complexity of thought, and a cheerful disposition have a connection with longevity and hanging on to memory function. The sisters were perfect study candidates because they shared so many of the same lifestyle factors. Researchers always struggle to eliminate as many differences between subjects as possible to increase the possibility that what they are measuring is truly the determining factor in why something does or does not happen.

Of greatest value was the serendipitous discovery of personal records dating from when the sisters took their vows as young women. Linguists who analyzed complexity of speech and vocabulary and "idea density" found that protective effects went beyond the level of education alone. Most of the nuns had been teachers and many had master's degrees. Idea density, the number of distinct ideas per ten written words, turned out to be a good predictor of what their fate would be. A mere one-page sample enabled psycholinguists to predict who would get AD sixty years later with 80 percent accuracy. Of the sisters with Alzheimer's, 90 percent had low idea density in their autobiographies, while low density was a factor in only 13 percent of the healthy sisters' writings.[12]

It is encouraging to those of us who fear the odds may be against us genetically that despite extensive physical brain damage, some nuns remained alert and functioning far beyond what one might expect. There were also cases where the effects of dementia did not match a marginally affected brain. Most often the level of dementia correlated with the extent of brain damage.

The results of autopsies were matched with linguistic scores, tests of memory, and assessments designed to measure the basic level of physical performance, like the ability to put on a sweater, get up from a chair, and walk six feet. The criteria for "rating" brains was done using the Braak scale developed in 1991 that defines stages of the disease by the location and number of tangles. A stage 0 brain had few or no tangles. Alzheimer's symptoms tend to manifest themselves at Braak stage V or VI, but there were cases where they emerged at Braak stage II.

Extremes were manifested by Sister Maria and Sister Margaret, for example. Sister Maria, despite severe dementia, had mild plaques and tangles, but she also suffered from longstanding depression and as is common with chronic depression had slight atrophy of the hippocampus. By contrast, Sister Margaret's atrophied brain had more tangles than 90 percent of the nuns studied, but it wasn't until she was eighty-seven years old that she began to have memory problems. She died at ninety. Overall, 22 percent of sisters in stages I or II, 43 percent in stages III and IV, and 70 percent in stages V and VI had dementia.

Sister Bernadette is another exception. She died at eighty-five years old with Braak stage VI, the most severe pathology for AD, but maintained normal scores, actually doing better on each test after age eighty-one. It is interesting to note that German researchers Heiko and Eva Braak and colleagues have discovered that 40 percent of people who die between the ages of ninety-six and one hundred are in Braak stage 0 or I. This conforms to what the Centenarian study, mentioned in chapter 1, said about the hardiness of those who live a very long time.

What all these findings mean is still not understood. Braak has shown that tangles can occur in the brains of very young people. Could it be that the brains of people who register linguistically as low density are affected at a very early age? What neuropathic changes early in life would compromise a person's linguistic ability? Or is it possible that poor linguistic ability escalates development of plaques and tangles?

The Nun study has confirmed previous work that demonstrated a cardiovascular and stroke connection to memory. These are "yeses" anyone can do something about. The role of head trauma in memory loss was also confirmed, so wear a helmet when you bike and don't forget to use your seat belt in your car.

Since problems can begin when the order of your day is potty training, reading to your children and grandchildren may be the most effective Alzheimer's risk reduction technique around. We are in debt to these wonderful women who were the subjects of the Nun study. "As sisters, we made the hard choice not to have children. Through the brain donation, we can help unravel the mysteries of Alzheimer's disease and give the gift of life in a new way to future generations," shared Sister Rita Schwalbe, explaining why the nuns were willing to participate in a study that has done and continues to do so much to unravel the mysteries of the mind.[13] Right on, Sister!

Thoughts on the Twilight Journey

Hindsight is a wonderful thing. If I had my life to live over again, I would choose a less stressful way to live. I would work on letting go of habits of perfectionism. I would not have worried so about developing a professional career while my children were young. I would have played more. A year or so ago I mourned the fact that I would not have a chance to do it over. Today for reasons I would share if I knew them, I no longer dwell on what might have been. I have this day. I can reduce my stress this day. I can laugh that my gourmet delight dessert served to my gourmet chef friend tasted like dirt. I can call my grandchildren and arrange trips to see them. I can visit museums on weekdays and go to matinees and never stand in line. I can play with my friends—on the spur of the moment.

In some ways I am happier and more content with life than I was when rushing through eras that were more productive. Perhaps aging has less to do with depletion than perspective. Some days there is so much to see, do, and read that I despair of getting it all in. Other days familiar surroundings beckon like the protection of a mother's lap. Life at sixty has an unexpected freshness and newness that I never anticipated. If I cannot remember, will this still be true? Could a muddled mind find its own joy? Maybe so, maybe so.

Brain Boosters

- Protecting your memory starts early.
- The best way to ensure your child's memory into old age is to read to him or her.
- Unresolved emotional and social issues can complicate cognitive difficulties.
- You are not a prisoner of your genes.
- Protect your head.
- Protect your heart.
- Never stop reading and learning new things.

Four

Staving Off the Beast

Look to your health; and if you have it praise God, and value it next to a good conscience; for health is the second blessing that we mortals are capable of, a blessing that money cannot buy.

Izaak Walton

Finding Hope

Mother's visit was unexpected. While she was always welcome to drop by, we generally tried to keep track of her comings and goings, but this time I hadn't expected her. I was at work in my small office when she drove up the driveway. Having sold her property at Lake Texoma, she was now living in a condo about two miles from our house. With carefully written instructions and a map we drew, she was able to find her way to our house and even occasionally pick up one or the other grandchild at school. This day she charged through my back door like a raging bull, her usual easygoing Texas manner replaced by agitation and obvious distress.

My welcome barely broke her concentration; she stormed past me, her manner brusque and determined. I trailed behind, already confused. She threw herself down on the couch and with equal force began her tirade, her face taking on the shade of a sun-ripened tomato, her coarse gray hair disheveled. She demanded, "Why didn't you tell me?"

I blinked; I hadn't a clue what she was talking about. With heart pounding, I asked, "Tell you what?"

"You know. You know," she accused. "You know and you didn't tell me—how dare you!" My mind began a crosscheck. What had I forgotten to tell her that was worthy of such agitation? She repeated herself, this time a little louder, like the problem was with my hearing, "You know and you didn't tell me."

"I know what? Mother," I repeated, "I don't know what you are talking about."

"Oh yes you do," she shot back. "You know about my brain and you didn't tell me. You know about my brain tumor. The doctor just told me and you already knew and didn't tell me." She placed her hands on her forehead, lightly pounding it, face twisted as if in torturous pain.

My mind began to race, reviewing all that had taken place and wondering if it were possible that I had stashed information like, "Your mother has a brain tumor," in some recess of my mind and forgotten about it. Had I missed something? Was she right? Mother was still lucid enough that I didn't automatically dismiss what she was saying. And then I remembered she had a checkup at the clinic the day before. Maybe the doctor had told her something was wrong. I tried to reassure her, "Mother, I know nothing about a brain tumor. I will call your doctor and see if he found something. I'm sure he would have called if there were anything serious."

"You knew and you didn't tell me," she insisted, getting up and storming out to her car.

I made a beeline to the phone. Could it be that the doctor told her something about a tumor at her appointment? Just what could he have said to her that might have been misinterpreted? According to his staff, the visit had been routine, and nothing out of the ordinary had been disclosed. Mother was so convincing that I insisted on talking to the doctor directly. He assured me there had been no discussion of any problem with her brain.

This incident marked the first time delusional behavior signaled that Mother's decline was more serious than depression and her readjustment to new surroundings. At this stage I had held out the hope that whatever was wrong could be fixed by making her an active part of our family and monitoring her health more closely. To that end we had made appointments with a number of physicians at the clinic where my husband worked. Getting a baseline health evaluation and establishing a relationship with new physicians seemed standard policy. We had also started to get her financial house in order. That process triggered another delusional incident that left me equally confused and wondering which of us would be the first to lose it completely.

Mother had been very clear as to how her property would be placed into a trust and was to be distributed. At issue was a farm in Texas on which an oil well or two had been a source of income. Her plan was to give our family the farm, which had been my father's, and for her to keep the mineral rights. The attorney had completed the paperwork, which needed only to be signed and recorded, when Mother called to tell me that she had changed her mind. Specifically, she intended to keep the farm in her name. I didn't argue. After all, it was her decision. While she didn't say why she felt the change was necessary, I could tell she was upset. She told me to set up a meeting with the lawyers. The day before our appointment, she was at the house, and, as she got ready to go, I reminded her I would pick her up at our scheduled time to change her will and trust. Her response was a surprise. "Why on earth do you think I want to take you out of my will and make sure you will not get my farm?" she asked.

"Because that is what you said you wanted," I replied.

"I never told you any such thing. You must be crazy to think such a thing," she insisted. I was beginning to think I was.

While both these incidents left me confused and upset, it was my supposed theft of her red sweater that almost did me in and that Mother apparently went to her grave believing. It all began when my very distraught kids reported that their very distraught grandmother had spent the evening going through every drawer and closet in our house determined to uncover the pilfered and apparently well-loved garment. No assurance could convince her of my innocence, and her search and accusation spanned years.

While it is not unusual for Alzheimer's to be accompanied by delusional and hallucinatory episodes, they are most often triggered by medication and/or occur late in the disease progress. Mother's experience of them so early is unusual and emphasized the great variation in how this disease expresses itself. The fact she was still considered high functioning for a person with AD, indeed she hadn't really been diagnosed as anything but depressed, made their occurrence very puzzling. She was lucid enough for me to question what I might have done or said to cause a misunderstanding.

Confusion over what was going on is typical of families whose loved one is experiencing the insidious changes of Alzheimer's. One always looks for an explanation other than the one that offers no hope. In the end, hope is found in slowing the progression of dementia. Good health practices enabled us to be optimistic about prolonging my mother's ability to enjoy and participate in life. While there is no way to prove it, in some ways it appears we succeeded. Her decline was slow. She would maintain a plateau for years then, usually abruptly, take a step down to a level of functioning that took her farther away from us.

Preventive Measures

It is no surprise that there are different attitudes about good health practices. Depending on the day, you have probably been a believer or a "let-the-chips-fall-where-they-may-give-me-the-rest-of-the-potato-chips" type. It's a surprise, at least to me, when physicians argue that keeping you healthy and enabling you to live longer is possibly a bad thing. They reason that greater longevity may bring with it greater disability. In other words, die young and skip the bad part.

It is obvious to us simple folk that persons with lower health risks tend to live longer and better than those with higher health risks. But some who have spent too much time hanging out in the rarified air of a university's ivory tower have insisted otherwise. Even a research study conducted by some of their colleagues, ones that apparently fell off the tower, couldn't convince them. That study concluded that people's lives are extended and the onset of disability is postponed (by as much as five years) and compressed to fewer years when their general health is improved. It proved that relationship between smoking, body mass index, and exercise patterns in midlife and late adulthood were predictors of subsequent disability. Duh! After years of argument between the two groups, it took a follow-up study by the same persistent group before their conclusions were accepted and the notion of staying as healthy as possible was begrudgingly established as a good thing.

Scientists have also learned that, after our peak at age thirty, we lose .5 percent of our physical capacity annually. A little calculation reveals that between ages thirty and sixty you can count on a 15 percent decline. If you are the type who thinks getting out of bed is your exercise for the day, plan on a steeper decline, especially if you also have spent most of your time looking for the closest parking space at the mall and sending your kid to do your banking while you nap in the car. In that case, research predicts your physical conditioning will be 60 percent of what it was at thirty.

Aging begins early and progresses gradually. Errors in cell division throughout the body cause genes to send out messages that, for example, order gray hair, less collagen and thus more wrinkles, and less efficient energy production. The Nun study shed light on the interaction of genetic and environmental factors. While we share the same set of genes with all of humanity, we are absolutely unique in the way our particular biochemistry causes mutations, triggers aging factors, and allows those factors to express themselves.

All this means that what you are exposed to and how you live your life make a difference. We know, for example, people who smoke age more quickly and are more susceptible to aging diseases like cancer and heart disease. The way you eat can result in obesity, which can also increase the likelihood of certain diseases, such as diabetes. Poor habits and nutritional choices, chronic infections, toxic exposure, poor aerobic capacity, trauma, and lack of attention to individual genetic needs make us susceptible to many classic diseases of aging, including dementia.[1] Many physicians give lip service to lifestyle because they don't always trust people will change, but more significantly they have been taught that a person is healthy until proven sick. But chronic diseases, particularly diseases associated with aging, can be insidious and develop slowly.

The tests that detect serious diseases are not designed to pick up your increasing propensity for an illness or the fact that an organ system is not functioning at optimal capacity. This is why you can feel lousy but all your tests say you should be out trekking through Nepal. In current medical practice you can't be sick until test results declare you are. Only then does the doctor go into action. Hence interventions that may stave off or minimize damage are delayed. This emphasis on disease diagnosis ignores individual susceptibilities and unique gene expression. It is why traditional physicians need to be more open to preventive/complementary medicine,

In case you need to know what aging feels like, consider the following biomarkers of aging: loss of strength, reduced flexibility, decreased cardiovascular endurance, increased body fat, reduced energy expenditure, lower kidney clearance, reduced cell-mediated immunity, increased hearing threshold, reduced vibratory sensation, compromised close vision and dark accommodation, reduced taste and smell acuity, altered hormone levels, increased autoantibodies.[2]

using the best of both worlds in an integrated manner. We need both—complementary medicine's focus on chronic disorders and traditional medicine's expertise dealing with acute ailments.

When we lose what is called organ reserve, we are vulnerable to biological aging. The good news is that as much as 75 percent of our health and life expectancy after age forty are modifiable on the basis of how we choose to live our lives.[3] This is a sobering fact when you consider that by 2020, 20 percent of the population in the United States will be sixty-five years old and older, with the greatest increase among those eighty-five years old and older.

Almost anything you do to improve your overall health will impact brain function. It is especially true that what is good for your heart is likely to be good for your brain. Like the rest of your body, your brain can be damaged and repaired. In fact we have much more brain capacity than we ever use. So what is in our control to repair and/or prevent damage? Here is what we know so far.

The Heart-Brain Connection

Undoubtedly sometime in your life you have played a hard game of tennis, run after a two-year-old grandchild, or tried to keep up with your great aunt Matilda who still runs marathons at eighty-five years old, and you have found yourself gasping for air. Your muscles simply refuse to work without oxygen. If you take some deep breaths and rest a minute, chances are you are once again on your way. Your brain doesn't like to work without oxygen either and when it is in short supply, as a result of a stroke or heart attack, it can be finicky about whether it will ever work as efficiently as it did before. With its penchant for being a prima donna, it is best not to put it to the test.

Twenty-five percent of all blood pumped by the heart is circulated through the brain. The oxygen that enters your lungs attaches to your red blood cells for a Disneylike ride through your heart and around your body. When it arrives where it is needed, it leaves your red blood cells and seeps into your tissues where it concentrates in

the mitochondria, each cell's power plant. There glucose is burned
to create the energy the cell needs to do its work. Anything that
interferes with the blood supply to the brain is dangerous. Without
oxygen your brain cells begin to die within minutes.

High blood pressure (hypertension), high cholesterol, diabetes,
and smoking put you at risk for a heart attack and also for a stroke
that can catastrophically prevent adequate oxygen from reaching
the brain. If you were scaling the heights on the blood pressure
chart when you were young, at midlife you have twice the chance
of difficulty with recall, abstract thinking, and judgment. Even
slightly elevated blood pressure over years is a concern. Whether
small strokes cause Alzheimer's or open the door for its development is a moot point. You don't want to have a stroke if you like
thinking clearly.

There are many interventions for reducing blood pressure. Some
people find easing up on the amount of salt they use is helpful while
others find it doesn't make any difference. Reducing consumption
of saturated fats and adding lots of vegetables and fruits works for
most everyone. A good mix of antioxidants, minerals, and fiber
explains why vegetables, especially cruciferous and green leafy types,
and citrus fruit and juice are so good for you.[4] The DASH study
out of Harvard and Yale, which got the majority of people off high
blood pressure medicine within a few weeks, added low fat dairy
products to ensure adequate calcium, and encouraged exercise.
Salmon and tuna are rich sources of omega-3 fatty acids, which
have been associated with lower rates of high blood pressure, heart
attacks, and depression. Persons who are at high risk may be asked
by their doctors to take blood thinners to reduce the occurrence
of clots obstructing arteries.

Stress and the Cortisol Connection

Robert M. Sapolsky, a Stanford researcher and author of a number of books including *Why Zebras Don't Get Ulcers,* tells of the
struggle salmon must go through to make it upstream to spawn.

Such a journey requires an immense expenditure of energy; couch potato salmon give up at the first gulp of fresh water. To complete their journey they must produce a tremendous amount of cortisol, the same chemical we produce when we need an energy boost or when we are stressed. When the salmon reach their goal and spawn, they do not stop producing cortisol. Their adrenals become enlarged, their hormone balance is off, and their immune system functions poorly. They develop kidney lesions, become susceptible to infection and parasites, and, as you might expect, die. Sapolsky points out, however, that if the adrenal glands where the cortisol is produced are removed, the fish return to health and live a year longer. We too continue to produce cortisol when we are under chronic stress. Like the salmon, damage results, particularly to our brain cells.

Cortisol is a memory-good-guy in small doses, but large and continual amounts result in hippocampal neurons functioning poorly and becoming vulnerable to damage. Ultimately it can cause cell death. Damage occurs in three ways. First, it robs the brain of its food. If you thought your child was picky, the brain easily has him or her beat. Don't even think about putting anything on its plate but glucose. Cortisol hinders its digestion, resulting in an energy shortage and inability of the hippocampus, the brain's primary memory center, to lay down memories. Second, not content to starve the cell, cortisol disrupts the function of the brain's messengers, the neurotransmitters. Unable to pass along clear messages, the mind is muddled and unfocused. Third, cortisol negatively affects cell metabolism, thus enabling excess calcium to enter the brain cells, ultimately killing cells from within.

Cortisol is not made in the brain. It makes a beeline there—and to your muscles—from the adrenal glands located above your kidneys when, for example, you are driving in Ireland and realize you are on the wrong side of the road and a tour bus is headed right for you. Because increased oxygen and glucose are at your disposal—due to the fight-or-flight response designed to give you what you need metabolically to get you out of trouble—you are able to react with the deftness of a NASCAR driver.

You may wish that your superhuman reaction time and ability to assess what to do to prevent impending disaster would last, but in about thirty minutes your cortisol level will be back to normal. Don't feel bad. Like a guest who has overstayed his welcome, when cortisol stays around too long, it becomes toxic. In a person already suffering from Alzheimer's or a stroke, it takes very little extra cortisol to cause further damage and interruption of memory storage and retrieval.

There is a connection between your thoughts and the hormones you manufacture and pump into your system. The complex agenda of your life causes thoughts that affect your entire endocrine (hormone) system. What is on your mind triggers biochemical responses that can excite, depress, and/or enable you to experience any other emotion. Any or all of these responses will likely affect your memory.

Mind over matter is not just New Age rambling; it has a biological basis—a mind-body connection does exist. Since no one can completely eliminate stressors, learning to cope with stress, particularly chronic stress, is crucial to minimizing damage. Techniques of stress management are beyond the scope of our present discussion but involve prioritizing your life and restructuring patterns of thinking and behavior that keep you apprehensive. A good support system is helpful. Physical exercise is particularly beneficial. Mostly, it involves being honest with yourself and deciding to make appropriate changes.

"I have to exercise early in the morning before my brain figures out what I am doing," insists a friend of mine. Even if you have to trick yourself into exercising, do it. There is no more valuable, more cost-effective, far-reaching benefit to your health than exercise. The payoff is far more than a hard body and being mistaken for your kid's older sibling. It is being able to recognize your kid for a lot longer.

Your brain benefits directly and indirectly from how active you are. Walking that extra block to the bank increases the blood supply to your brain and provides the fuel that enables you to activate the dendrites necessary to figure out how to use the ATM machine and remember your PIN number. But benefits don't stop there; increased blood flow prompts actual growth of new brain cell branches and burns off harmful stress hormones, protecting against damage caused by stress. A walk with your friends stimulates hormonal and neurological brain chemistry that enhances production of a number of neurotransmitters, including norepinephrine, which is associated with laying down new memories and moving them from short- to long-term storage. It also increases the level of a chemical component that acts somewhat like a plant fertilizer, protecting brain cells from injury and encouraging growth.

When you are tempted to use age as an excuse for not taking the stairs, remind yourself that compared to doing nothing, innumerable studies show that any physical activity will be of benefit in lowering your risk for any type of cognitive impairment and dementia.[5] Laboratory mice developed new brain cells when they were allowed to run their little legs off, ending up with twice as many brain cells as the mice that just hung out. These bodybuilding mice are responsible for the revolutionary discovery that new brain cells can be produced, which is known as neurogenesis.

A study that compared older healthy adults concluded that the group that walked forty-five minutes three times a week did better on tests of memory than a group that was asked to spend the same amount of time stretching. Still, don't overlook the value of the stress reduction ability of something like yoga. Even the mice agree. Throwing them into a swimming pool did not result in increased brain cells or increased ability to snap through their mazes despite Herculean efforts at the Australian crawl stroke, because their stress hormone, cortisol, negated the effects of the exercise. I suppose the lesson to be learned is whatever exercise you do, enjoy it. Being relaxed helps you notice and register more things, thus improving your ability to remember.

An added benefit is that exercise helps prevent depression, which is destructive to memory. Finally, it is well documented that for every mile you jog, you add one minute to your life.

Author and dementia expert Dr. Dharma Singh Khalsa says, "The mind is 'software,' the mystical and mysterious product of all that we are. The brain is 'hardware,' a bodily organ that requires nutrition, rest, use, and proper medical care."[6]

Food for Thought

A number of recent studies have confirmed how much better students perform when they have eaten breakfast. Adults are no different. Dieting and skipping breakfast affect thinking in the short term and, perhaps in ways that are not understood, increase vulnerability to long-term memory problems. This is especially so if your blood sugar levels tend to bounce around more than a kid on a pogo stick. Your diet is likely to be the primary *environmental* influence as to whether or not you develop AD. A well-balanced diet, which supplies most of your nutrients from whole foods, is important; still there are certain foods that the brain especially likes. They include the following:

- Fish oil: While the push to eliminate fat has caused some people to strive for a fat-free diet, this is not healthy. It is important that you distinguish between good-guy fats and bad-guy fats. Essential fatty acids (EFAs) are called essential because your body doesn't make them and you must get them from your diet. Both women and men have reduced heart attack and stroke risks when they eat fish. A large study out of Harvard determined that fish oil saves lives in people with no history of heart disease. All the research confirms eating fish is health insurance for the brain.
- Spinach: Popeye was no fool. The antioxidants (see below), beta-carotene, vitamin C, and folic acid found in spinach

keep blood vessels supple and help transport nerve impulses more efficiently.

- Strawberries and blueberries: Strawberries and blueberries, along with spinach, have officially been labeled brain food by Tufts School of Nutrition, because of the antioxidants they contain. Other foods that contain deep red and purple pigments, such as red cabbage, grapes, plums, and cherries also protect a neuron's ability to respond to chemical messengers and discourage the formation of blood clots.

- Garlic and soy: Garlic reduces cholesterol and has blood-thinning properties. Soy affects the way LDL (the bad cholesterol) oxidizes (loses electrons to free radicals), setting the stage for clogged arteries. Soy also has an antioxidant effect.

- Protein: Too much red meat increases homocysteine, which may contribute to heart disease. Still, your body needs protein. Our digestive system breaks down ingested proteins into amino acids and transports them through the bloodstream and into the brain. The amino acids are then linked together on orders from genes. While the brain uses only top-grade glucose for fuel, it could care less about the source of its amino acid building blocks. People who choose fish as their protein source, however, have lower rates of AD.

- Sugar: Your body can burn fat and protein along with glucose for energy, but your brain demands pure sugar. When its levels are too low, you are in a state of hypoglycemia. Headache, confusion, sweating, rapid heartbeat, and the inability to think well accompany it. A person who is easily hypoglycemic or who is (pre)diabetic or insulin resistant must keep on top of his or her blood sugar level. Eating small, frequent meals to avoid swings in blood sugar is a first line of defense. Stable blood sugar levels aid concentration and as an added benefit help keep weight down by eliminating the desire to binge. Most vegetables, whole grains, and nonprocessed foods supply glucose at a more even pace than do highly processed foods, potatoes, pasta, or rice.

- Green and black tea: Tea is an antioxidant and contains antioxidant boosters. It reduces the incidence of stroke through its abundance of flavonoids, which keep blood cells from clotting, and for some people boosts mental acuity by the caffeine it supplies. While tea actually contains more caffeine than coffee, its effect is mediated by a chemical found in tea leaves that is calming. Green tea is especially good for boosting immunity by improving the liver's detoxification capacity.

- Alcohol: Placing alcohol on a list for improving brain function might appear strange considering that its overconsumption can be deadly to brain cells and cause the depletion of thiamine (vitamin B1), which can result in extreme memory loss. It also temporarily lowers the vigilant guard of the blood-brain barrier that shields the brain from toxic substances (hence warnings about certain medications and drinking). On the other hand, moderate alcohol consumption appears to spare cognitive function. It is also beneficial to the cardiovascular system. However, keeping one's alcohol consumption to the moderate level (1 five-ounce glass of wine, 1 twelve-ounce beer, 1.5 ounces of hard liquor per day) becomes even more important as a person ages, since alcohol is then more poorly metabolized.

Saving Your Brain with Supplements

The controversy over nutritional supplementation lies not so much in whether vitamins, minerals, and herbals can be of benefit. Thousands of years of use in countries around the world speak to their efficacy. In some cases, however, new combinations, extraction of active ingredients, and use in combination with prescription drugs cause new problems. Sometimes it is the erratic manufacturing standards that are the source of concern. Purity, dosage, and unsubstantiated claims must be considered to ensure that benefits outweigh potential harm. The solution is to keep informed and to make sure that the company you buy from has sound business and manufacturing practices that equal more traditional pharmaceutical houses. In 2002 the American Medical Association, long a naysayer for vitamin supplementation, reevaluated its stance and in light of increasing scientific support recommended a daily multivitamin.

- A recent study indicated that kids who took a multivitamin every day increased their nonverbal IQ scores compared to kids who did not. A yearlong study at Memorial University of Newfoundland with older adults demonstrated that popping a vitamin improved short-term memory, concentration, abstract thinking, and problem solving. As we age, changes in our ability to absorb vitamins B12, D, and calcium may necessitate supplementation since we may not be able to get what we need through food. Don't make the mistake of thinking that eating your broccoli is no longer necessary if you take a multivitamin, however. Vitamins help us utilize our food—they *aren't* food. Tufts School of Nutrition has the final word: Alzheimer's risk is lowered among people who take their vitamins *and* eat their vegetables.

- Antioxidants help protect against free-radical damage. A free radical, as the name suggests, is a molecule that has lots of energy and simply loves to link up with other molecules to subvert their purpose and do the damage that makes us age while simultaneously contributing to a number of diseases. Antioxidants keep blood flowing to the brain and are important in heart health because of cholesterol-lowering and anti-inflammatory properties. Most antioxidants are found in ample supply in fresh fruits and vegetables and a multivitamin. Additional supplementation of vitamin E is sometimes suggested in cases of dementia.[7]

- By the time we are eighty years old, 40 percent of men and women cannot absorb vitamin B12; at sixty, it's 20 percent. If you aren't able to utilize vitamin B12 from foods, which can be determined by a simple blood test, you may need shots to maintain a healthy blood level. When vitamin B12 is low, pernicious anemia results, causing confusion and dementia. When you are anemic, you don't have enough red blood cells to transport oxygen and other essential supplies to your brain.

- Some nutritionists maintain that folate or folic acid is perhaps even more important for a healthy memory in older people than vitamin B12. Tufts University researchers have found that people with the highest blood levels of folic acid have little or no memory loss after middle age. The Nun study showed low serum folate was strongly associated with atrophy of the cerebral cortex.[8] B12 and folate are known to lower homocysteine. While taking a multivitamin can contribute to optimal levels, additional micronutrients are found along with folate and vitamin B12 in spinach, oranges, asparagus, fortified cereals, and beans.

- Thiamine (vitamin B1) deficiency can cause memory and mood problems, among other difficulties. An infection or, as mentioned above, alcohol abuse can cause its depletion.

- Like vitamins, minerals are essential components of enzymes and coenzymes and play their part in a healthy memory.

- Our production of phosphatidyl-serine, which helps keep cell membranes flexible and may have antioxidant properties, declines as we age. There is also evidence that it stimulates production of the neurotransmitter acetylcholine, the major neurotransmitter for memory. Studies show that it can improve concentration and the recall of names, faces, and phone numbers. Health food stores sell phosphatidyl-serine as a memory and energy booster. Most products on the market are derived from soy.

- Acetyl-L-Carnitine and N-Acetylcysteine, also available over the counter, function as antioxidants, brain energy enhancers, and antiinflammatory to improve cognition.

- Lecithin (phosphatidylcholine) is commonly found in foods, but studies suggest we may need supplementation to achieve the levels needed for protection against damage to our brain. It repairs neurons and is a building block for acetylcholine.

- By far the most accepted and useful herb for improving memory is Ginkgo biloba (leaf extract). The standardized dosage is 24% ginkgo flavonglycosides and 6% terpene lactones, 40–80 mg capsule taken up to 3 times a day. An important herb in Chinese medicine for thousands of years, it has recently shown promise with Alzheimer's. The many studies done with ginkgo have uncovered few side effects but may include headache, rash, or mild gastrointestinal upset. It is believed that ginkgo is probably more effective at delaying the onset of problems than in fixing them.[9] It is understood to work by increasing blood flow to the brain. It also has an antioxidant effect and is able to lower blood pressure. When doctors caution patients about the dangers of ginkgo, they are generally concerned about its anticoagulant effect. Studies suggest it is most effective in persons over fifty, probably because blood flow becomes more of an issue with aging. Personally, I give credit to a good quality ginkgo product for keeping me functioning at the level I have for several years. As with all herbs, the problem is ensuring good quality at a clinically effective dose.

- Huperzine A is an herb derived from Chinese club moss. It is sometimes used in combination with ginkgo and vitamin E. In China it is commonly recommended for memory problems and is believed to protect acetylcholine and work like a cholinesterase inhibitor. Its effectiveness has been demonstrated even in late-stage AD. Its long half-life and unique blood-brain barrier penetration has made it a target for continued research.

- Saint-John's-wort may help memory in several ways. It stimulates some neurotransmitters and alleviates depression in mild to moderate cases. It should not be taken with other antidepressants and can interfere with some prescription drugs. You must always check with your doctor before using it.

- If you were to complain of being tired and forgetful and you
wanted a general energy boost—and you happened to live in
Germany—your physician would likely give you a prescription for Asian ginseng (Panex ginseng). Choose a concentrated high quality extract standardized to 5–8% ginsenosides,
40–80mg.

The Effect of Drugs

There are many drugs for common illnesses that can cause problems
with memory. Memory loss often stems from the fact that the hippocampal region is very sensitive to reduction in its blood supply,
which can be caused by a variety of drugs. Most of the time this
side effect is reversible. If, however, cognitive problems exist or an
individual is already showing signs of AD, medications that are
currently being taken should be carefully reviewed. Drugs that are
known to affect memory should be avoided or a substitute found.
Halcyon, Valium, and sleep-inducing barbiturates all affect memory.
Antihypertensive medications such as beta-blockers, ACE inhibitors, and calcium channel blockers, prescribed for persons with
heart disease, through a series of chemical actions block the laying
down of memories. Steroidal hormones and drugs for Parkinson's
are a frequent concern.

The serendipitous discovery that medicines meant for one purpose
may have value for another has struck home twice in the case of
Alzheimer's. First there is the observation that people taking statins,
which are drugs given to lower cholesterol in general as well as
decreasing a specific LDL version—known as bad cholesterol—were
approximately 70 percent less likely to develop dementia.[10] Some
statins (lovastatin) appear to protect memory better than others. In
individuals with high cholesterol the connection is strong enough
to recommend its use, with reduction of dementia a bonus benefit.[11]
More research is necessary before it is known if statins should be
taken by persons at high risk for AD who have normal cholesterol
levels. While high cholesterol can be a risk for AD, whether or not

there is something about the statin itself that is responsible for the lowered risk isn't known. Like all drugs, statins have side effects, some serious.[12] Since they deplete the nutrient CoQ_{10}, supplementation is important.

In the same way, researchers have observed that nonsteroidal, anti-inflammatory drugs (NSAIDs, such as ibuprofen, Motrin, Advil, Nuprin, and Aleve) have an inverse relationship with AD. In plain language people with arthritis who had been using such drugs for years simply did not suffer the same risk of dementia as the general population. Those who developed AD but had used NSAIDs progressed more slowly and tended to show symptoms at a later age. The same effect has not been found with aspirin or celecoxib (Celebrex), despite their anti-inflammatory properties. Preliminary research indicates that the length of time the drug is taken is more critical than the dose. This is good to know because, like statins, side effects can be serious. At least sixteen thousand people die each year from sudden and severe gastrointestinal bleeding from anti-inflammatory use, many who had no warning that anything was amiss.

Staying Healthy

It may seem silly to suggest that a flu shot is protective of your cognitive function. But the truth is, the older we get the less resilient we become. Even a simple illness can lower immunity to other diseases that more directly affect brain function. Research confirms the value of maintaining a good diet to enhance immunity. As mentioned in chapter 3, there is evidence at autopsy that bacterial and viral infections (chlamydia, pneumoniae, and herpes) can damage the brain.

Flossing your teeth reduces the chance of heart disease by dislodging bacteria that may get into your bloodstream, causing inflammation of blood vessels. Healthy gums and teeth keep you eating well. Even having sex within the context of a monogamous relationship was recently shown to have health benefits. Do whatever it takes to avoid falling and hitting your head. Take a tai chi or yoga class to improve your balance.

Excess caffeine (five or more servings of caffeine a day) can raise your homocysteine level. High levels increase the chance of heart problems and have been noted among AD patients. Smoking increases homocysteine levels while robbing the smoker of oxygen and depleting all those good antioxidants.

Finally, get adequate rest. If sleep has become a serious problem, go to a sleep clinic for treatment or check for adrenal malfunction.

Work Your Brain

Confucius said, "The strongest memory is not as strong as the weakest ink." I confess I agree with Confucius. I have looked at a variety of memory-enhancing methods and have often been struck by how much easier it is to make a list and stuff it into your pocket. That said, it is true that most of us could do more to enhance and maintain our memory. What follows are some suggestions that, while deceptively ordinary and mostly commonsense, are known to maintain brainpower.

Research is full of studies confirming that participation in cognitively stimulating activities reduces AD or pushes it back as much as five years. Just reading the newspaper is helpful.[13] While we are familiar with the fact that our brain controls our behavior, it is also true our behavior can control the brain. For instance, besides rejuvenating existing neuronal connections, we can make new ones. Learning anything can change the structure of our brain and stimulate new cell growth.[14]

Challenging your brain to learn something new results in fresh mental pathways, strengthened connections, and increased nerve cells. Take a class, learn a new skill, and read. Go on a car trip where you have to plan an itinerary and read your map while simultaneously experiencing new things. Take a different route home. Try writing or brushing your teeth with the opposite hand. Cognitive function is improved when you use your hands while explaining something. Do crossword and jigsaw puzzles or paint; take up woodworking or ceramics, all of which help develop spatial relations and seeing how things fit together. Encourage coordination between your hands and head by playing video games with a grandchild or finally taking the time to learn to play a musical instrument. Make memorization enjoyable by learning all the birds that visit your yard. Get your gang together for chess, bridge, backgammon, or poker—anything that requires concentration.

That "gang" is crucial to keeping socially active. Older people who visit friends, join book clubs, and go to movies significantly reduce the risk for dementia. In general the higher our activity level, even leisure activity, the greater the possibility of reducing our dementia risk. The benefit of keeping plugged into life on many fronts is the sense of control it gives us. Staying upbeat and involved helps counter feelings of depression that can work biochemically to damage our brain and socially to narrow our world and diminish our function.

Seeing Is Remembering

Memory can be enhanced through a variety of techniques, many involving visualization. Lists can be recalled more easily when what is to be remembered is attached to something. One of the simplest techniques is derived from the ancient Greeks who "connected" words to various parts of the body. Recall was stimulated by visualizing the first item on top of the head, associating the second with the forehead, the third with the eyes followed by the nostrils, mouth, neck, chest, waist, hips, knees, and feet. For example, a ball, tennis racket, loaf of bread, and a can of coke could be remembered by thinking of a hat on the head with balls bouncing on the rim, tennis rackets fanning the forehead, a loaf of bread for eyeballs, and cans of coke rolling out of the nostrils like a vending machine and so on. The secret to using such devices is to use them consistently.[15]

One reason such memory exercises work is that they make us concentrate and decide to remember. Much of our problem with memory as we age is the fact that we don't pay attention and make active choices about what we want to recall, so the transference from temporary to permanent memory simply doesn't take place. The more ways we commit something to memory the better.

One of the most annoying and disturbing memory blips is to forget and block on the name of someone you know well—the senior moment experience. If it has happened to you, know that it is one of the first signs of an aging brain. Recalling names is a mental process that is especially sensitive to slower cognitive function. It is helpful when you meet someone to say his or her name and attach a visual cue that relates to it, maybe even visualizing it superimposed on the person's face.

The Importance of Religion

In the 1920s Sigmund Freud, father of psychotherapy, described religion as a neurosis. Twenty years later Albert Ellis called religiosity "irrational thinking and emotional disturbance." But generations have found comfort in looking to the spiritual during times of illness, and current research affirms that faith is good for the body as well as the soul. People of faith experience a number of health benefits including lowered blood pressure and less depression.[16] Religion promotes fellowship and connections between people that provide a sense of belonging, which in turn reduces illness.[17] Religious and spiritual experiences tend to promote positive emotions and are often accompanied by healthy lifestyles. Dr. Herbert Benson, the stress guru of Harvard's Mind/Body Institute, found that praying for ten to twenty minutes a day can decrease blood pressure, heart rate, breathing, and metabolic rates.

One of the first studies to show the effect of prayer involved a number of cardiology patients who didn't know they were prayed for but who had fewer complications and needed less medication than a matched group who were not prayed for. This historic study has been duplicated several times in large institutions. One of the findings from the Harvard School of Public Health was that regular attendance at church, temple, or mosque proved as effective as physical exercise at increasing longevity. (I hesitate to share that finding in case there are a few couch potatoes reading this.) Additional studies confirmed regular attenders had an extended lifespan by as much as seven years. Duke University's Center for the Study of Religion-Spirituality and Health found that people who attend services regularly are half as likely to have high levels of the blood protein interleukin-6 as those who don't. Elevated levels can be associated with AD as well as other diseases.

It is no accident that the words *healing* and *holy* are related. Prayer has no harmful side effects, costs nothing, and is proven to work.

Since the 1990s there has been a consensus that our brain, at least to a degree, is capable of growth and renewal. Minimally, it is accepted that new dendritic branches, the connections between nerve cells, are capable of re-growth. Mentally active people, as the Nun study revealed, have more dendrites. There is no dispute that there are things we can do to hold on to, prolong, and expand our cognitive powers. We must act on what we know while research continues to expand and specify what else remains to be done. Stay tuned.

Thoughts on the Twilight Journey

This is a chapter of hope. Those of us destined to get Alzheimer's will likely not be able to prevent it. But we are not helpless. There is a realistic possibility of pushing back the onset or at least minimizing its effect. It depends on how we decide to live our life. For me the payback goes beyond minimizing AD's ravages. Taking action enables me to feel less like a victim. I am not that big red dot in the center of a target just waiting to be obliterated by whatever has me in its crosshairs. I can do something. Whether or not it is enough, I must wait and see. But action gives me hope.

Action has other benefits as well. Taking care of myself enables me to enjoy today and the days I have in front of me, whether they are many or few. I can go and do. I can play with my grandchildren and take up new sports and activities. I surround myself with friends and people with great attitudes who are fun and stimulating to be with. I am not obsessed with an idea that life has to be lived any particular way or that I can never eat a bite of junk food again. Paradoxically, the discipline directed toward optimizing my physical and mental health has freed me.

I remember once telling someone I was "generally a healthy person." Afterward I thought about what I had said. It is not at all true. At fifteen I developed a severe back problem that has woven its way through most of my years. I was in bed all but three months when I was pregnant with my son. I had a bilateral mastectomy at thirty. I suffered for years with aches, pains, and debilitating fatigue. My thyroid gland broke years ago. I have had bouts of depression. But today, at sixty, I sit here feeling good, not in the shape I would like to be (sitting writing a book all day will do that) but ready to play and looking forward to the days ahead. The truth is—it's not over until it's over.

Brain Boosters

- What is good for your heart is good for your brain.
- Because of the body's mind-body connection, stress can damage your brain.
- Exercise is good for everything.
- Your most potent medicine is the food you put in your mouth.
- Vitamins and some herbs have been shown to improve brain function.
- If possible, do not let prescribed drugs undermine your memory.
- Play with your friends.
- Learn new things.
- Maximize your overall health.

Five

Distant Early Warning Signs

It's days like this when I'm sure I'm not going to make it to the end of my life . . .

From a greeting card

Clinging to Reality

My father died of a heart attack on my parents' thirtieth wedding anniversary. He was fifty-five years old; my mother was sixty, my current age. I had sent them a book of love poems as a present and after Mother passed away added it to my library. Just last year I picked it up and discovered the last remaining "notes" that Mother wrote in her desperate effort to make sense of a world that was slipping through her fingers like sand at the beach. At the bottom of the first page near the binding is written "The day my world stopped! 30th anniversary." Four arrows obviously added at a later time point to each word and above the "30th anniversary" portion "Wilburn & Mary Jo" is inserted, notable because she always called my father by his last name. On the front page is written the following:

87

I am sorry that Mom and Manahan went to Heaven *so soon*—but
will meet in heaven—
   This farm is Mary Jo's until I go to heaven—so all my notes say!—
True Mom said the farm was Mary Jo's until I went to Heaven! (so
true) YES TRUE
   And then came Joe-Lee! Yes—Mary Jo had a beautiful little girl.
We named her *Mary Ann* Manahan. *Mary Jo had Joe Lee then Mary
Ann True.* Mary Jo was married to Manahan. We all were people
who loved each other—correct!

Notes, thousands of notes popped up like weeds in an untended
garden, written as Mother proceeded through her twilight journey.
They were everywhere. I found them stuffed in her purse and in
every nook and cranny of her condo. The margins of Bibles and
other books were decorated with jottings, starting in one corner
and circuitously snaking their way up, over, in, and out, filling page
after page. Pads of stationery were never used for letters. Every page
contained her large script, its preciseness or lack thereof providing
a measure of her deteriorating condition. The notes were never
about mundane things—appointments or grocery lists. Most were
variations of the same theme—messages to remind herself that "the
farm" was hers. It had been inherited from my father's family, it was
a gift of love, it was all she had left, *and it was hers.* The underlying tone of every missive implied that, should it be taken away, all
would be lost and her world, once again, would stop.
   Along with underlining, often as much as three times, there
were two other elements that were almost always included, the
repetition of the word *true* throughout and references to my supposed betrayal. In one way or another, directly or indirectly, they
spoke to the despair and concern over the fact that I had deviously
wrangled away from her what she valued most. Possession of the
farm meant the difference between living on the street and having
a comfortable bed at night. I was greedy. How could I call myself a
Christian? It made no difference that Mother had never set foot on
"the farm" or that the sporadic income from some dying oil wells
would never amount to enough to keep her in her beloved cookies.

Her "beautiful little girl" had gone bad . . . was rotten to the core
. . . had crossed over to the dark side.

It was challenging to be at the bank with her when she handed
over a check containing all the usual note-details in addition to her
signature. The clerk would count out her money while giving me
a look that let me know "she knew." Her problems with me never
failed to endear strangers to Mother. And why wouldn't they, a
sweet gray-haired woman with a cheery smile and a Texas accent
who had to put up with an obviously calculating Type A who stole
from her. I felt lucky when I got out of the bank without the alarm
going off. Then there were the waitresses and hairdressers who
didn't have to depend on notes to know what was going on—they
just had to listen.

Periodically my husband and I would make a stab at collecting
and disposing of the accumulating piles of paper under the guise
of helping her straighten up. But the notes were far more prolific
than our efforts were effective. When we cleaned out her condo
to move her to an assisted-living facility, the sheer volume of
them was more impressive than upsetting. Still, for years, I would
accidentally come across another one, and my heart would stop
for a moment. The very last note, other than the poetry book, I
found while Mother and I were in a Social Security office. After
Dr. Stirrat's death we were making the necessary address changes.
Mother was having difficulty finding her card, so I took her wallet
and searched through the various pockets. In one I found a small
piece of paper folded into a tiny square. I unfolded it and there
written in miniature detail was *"The farm is* Mary Jo's. *True Mary
Ann* stole *it.* True. " I sat there stunned. My eyes filled with tears. I
looked at Mother, and she was the picture of innocence. She smiled
and her blue eyes twinkled.

What Is This Thing Called Crazy?

Paranoid and delusional behavior is not uncommon when a person
suffers from Alzheimer's. I used to try to make myself feel better by

putting myself in Mother's shoes. I would tell myself, if I were no longer able to keep any of my financial details straight, I would be paranoid too. Like Mother, I might decide to take my frustration out on someone else. But being a wise woman, she didn't choose just anyone; she chose the person who was closest—and safest. She knew I wouldn't take my marbles and run away. I felt like it, especially in the beginning, but I would not, could not, abandon her. I think it is the same principle that is at work with your teenagers. All your friends love them, but your kids don't have a civil word or manner for you. Still you would give your life for them.

Delusions involving people close to them may not always be an AD person's first symptom, but they can be very distressing, especially if the person is still somewhat high functioning and the accusations are directed at the person who is most involved with care. Changes in personality can also be disturbing. Mother's well-practiced passive-aggressive personality became confrontational and stubborn. She even began swearing. As the disease progressed, she would attack others when frustrated and tired.

Changes in memory are common to everyone and we compensate for them. But there is a difference in forgetting what you needed at the grocery store and leaving your food in the car—again. Needing to write yourself a list is not like being unable to concentrate, no longer being able to balance your checkbook, and becoming confused over which bills you just paid. It's not a matter of trying harder. As hard as a person with dementia tries, she can no longer learn or retain what she previously knew.

Even with these memory problems, the person with dementia may look and sound normal. Neither my friends nor Mother's doctor ever believed Mother had lost it to the extent she had. She could be delightful, and who knew her story about her relatives or what she did yesterday barely touched the truth? Impairment of recent memory is common in those with Alzheimer's, but other manifestations may be more prominent. It is almost universally true that hindsight is far better at picking up when problems began than awareness of any one symptom that may seem out of character but can be explained away. It isn't one thing that makes you a believer that something is seriously wrong; it is the cumulative effect.

The more educated a person is, the more she is able to cover her lapses. It often takes a crisis before the extent of the disease is revealed. My stepsister, Marjorie Anne, and I talked daily about what would be the best setting for Mother as Dr. Stirrat's health began to deteriorate and he was admitted to the hospital for what was to be the last time. I would need to fly to Canada, but first I had to determine if I could bring Mother back to her condo or would need to make arrangements for an assisted-living facility. At first, Marjorie Anne was convinced that with daily supervision Mother could live alone. After taking Mother home with her, each phone call involved a reevaluation and downgrade. Dr. Stirrat and Mother had hidden just how bad things had become. It is not unusual that the death of a spouse is the first occasion for relatives to come to terms with just how poorly the remaining partner is functioning.

In the beginning, forgetting can be very erratic. This increases the difficulty of knowing something is wrong, especially when combined with the desire not to see the truth. Like Mother, people may use notes to orient and remind themselves. Friends may notice repetition of the same story or question. Sexual drive can increase or decrease, a fact rarely mentioned by healthcare professionals. As fine motor coordination is diminished, handwriting is affected and perhaps also the ability to use silverware appropriately. Damage in the hippocampal area reduces the sense of smell and can secondarily affect enjoyment of food. Relatives may begin to suspect dementia, but when the short visit to the physician results in a proclamation that everything is fine, another two to three years will go by before an actual diagnosis.

The individual tries to cope in a variety of ways. Mother's stories that so regaled anyone whose ear she caught were examples of "misattribution." She would take the partial information she could remember and try to glue it together with other bits and pieces to make it complete. What looked like a misrepresentation of the truth was her effort to have her world make sense. We all tend to do the same thing, mixing memories that are vague and fleeting from a specific past experience with a more current memory. The chance of mixing up perceived and imagined parts and pieces increases when there is damage to the hippocampus.

Suggestibility causes this mixture of current information with personal recollection that results in a whole new "truth." And like all people, the person with a slipping memory still wants to be seen in the best light. Bias is a mechanism by which emotionally charged material (which is always remembered best) is summoned up in a way that makes a person feel good about herself. Mother's memories of her childhood and being second best probably involved all of these common memory mechanisms. We are guilty of using them as well, but in the mind of a person with dementia, the world may make no sense without them.

Planning meals, shopping, organizing a trip, following a complex movie plot or the storyline of a book, making calculations, even taking medication on time, are known as executive functions, requiring complex and abstract thinking. It is difficult for a person with AD to organize and track such tasks, because they require following a number of steps. It is a highly significant marker when a person who has been handling finances can no longer keep them straight or get bills paid on time. Getting lost or needing directions for a familiar route, forgetting names of familiar people, missing appointments, or not recalling recent events like a birthday party are red flags that should prompt action. Such changes are likely to be accompanied by poor judgment in hygiene—less bathing and insistence on wearing the same soiled clothing. These are evidence that the disease has significantly worsened.

As a victim's Alzheimer's develops, other symptoms may include confusion over where she is or what time it is. When recall of names and words, and maybe even sequence of words, becomes poorer, comprehension is severely affected. Understanding what one reads becomes impossible and following a conversation very difficult. Some people have spatial relation changes that make driving a car and even climbing stairs a hazard.

The goals of early intervention: prevention of acceleration of symptoms and maximizing functional level, preservation of patient dignity, amelioration of family stress, maximizing general health and safety, strategies for decreasing confusion and aggression, maintaining verbal and nonverbal interaction.

Whether or not a person is willing to accept help depends on the degree of awareness she has—which in itself can fluctuate. Forgetting she forgets is not denial and can result in a person's not realizing she needs help. While a person may not be able to hold a job, it is not correct to assume, as friends and family often do, that a person with dementia cannot do anything. In truth, many have the potential for years of high functioning.

There must be a balance between doing for someone and letting her do for herself. Support and encouragement versus a level of intervention that says you are inadequate is a delicate balance. Family and friends are sometimes in more denial than the patient, but they must be realistic about the situation, offering the level of help the person with dementia requires. In the early stages companions are needed rather than caregivers. I used to tell people Mother was happy as long as she had a "playmate." A caring and understanding companion may be the most significant factor in determining quality of life for a person with AD.

One of the best analogies of how AD reaches the point when life is disrupted is found in Daniel Kuhn's book *Alzheimer's Early Stages*.[1] In it he describes the development of AD as kin to an orchestra that works together in an intricate way to create beautiful music. When one musician misses a note or plays off-key, his glitch is likely to go unnoticed. But when his mistake affects his neighbor and his neighbor's neighbor, a discerning ear may pick it up. Should the missed notes and/or timing mistakes spread farther, the whole orchestra is apt to be affected and what was once melodic becomes cacophony.

Diagnosis

As you might guess, I am not a fan of those tests that appear in the latest issue of any number of magazines that profess to tell you, in the privacy of your own home—no brown bag needed—whether or not you have lost it. I don't take them. I confess I sneak a peak just long enough to conclude I would undoubtedly fail and thus, feeling utterly defeated, I go get something to eat. I find comfort in the fact that I can still draw a clock and put time on it and get up and walk nine feet and return to my chair in championship time. But there is no way I will take one of those tests, even if it is published in *Modern Maturity*.

I am not alone. Of the thousands of people each year who are beginning to have problems with memory, most silently ignore early signs until they can't be denied. It is easy for them to avoid what might be increasingly obvious to everyone else. It's unlikely anyone will bring it up. Spouses, friends, doctors, all comfort them with stories about their forgetfulness and the universality of the experience. But we don't do our loved ones or ourselves any favor by putting off a diagnosis.

Excuses for not finding out for sure if something is truly wrong are as numerous as the stars that shine over the vineyards in our dark Sonoma sky. But avoiding early diagnosis can have serious consequences. Most important, it denies us the opportunity to maintain control over our own destiny. It keeps us from beginning medications when they may work most effectively. Delaying AD's progression boosts our chance that, when new discoveries materialize, we can benefit. While we can still make an informed decision, we may choose to participate in a research study. A diagnosis motivates us to talk openly with people who are important to us and to plan with them the central theme of our care and what we believe is needed to maintain dignity. We can share our input on business and financial concerns. Finally, because it is hard to know how others can understand when we don't fully grasp what is happening to us, our gnawing sense of fear and isolation can be mollified by a support group of people with like-minded concerns. Avoidance of the truth can lead us into a crisis that precipitates actions and decisions we may later regret.

Without a doubt it is embarrassing to have to admit that you are not the same person you have always been. And after a diagnosis, it is easy to assume you are already far along in the journey. The part where you fall over the cliff, you tell yourself, must be just ahead. Rarely is this true. You will probably have many years of meaningful life ahead of you. More people die from causes other than their dementia than those who die as a result of its last stages.

Mary Jo is an example of one who had a full and meaningful life, even after her diagnosis. Her journey took more than twenty years. During that time, she traveled to China and Scotland, celebrated innumerable holidays and birthdays with her loved ones, got to know her grandchildren, and enjoyed thousands of desserts. After diagnosis she lived for years on her own, married for the third time, became a widow for the third time, and announced in her eighties with great pomp and circumstance that she had made the decision never to marry again—her husbands just kept dying, she declared.

Keeping perspective is vital to living life fully and well. Not knowing can be worse than knowing. But as one optimist noted, as you age, your secrets are safe with your friends because they can't remember either. Acknowledging a problem may be difficult, but it can be the springboard to a fulfilling life. Indeed, research studies have shown that most people react to a diagnosis of Alzheimer's by wanting to know more and calling into play the coping mechanisms they have always used.

It is wrong to assume that memory problems are always due to Alzheimer's disease. There are other possibilities that must be considered, as I itemize below. On the other hand, it is not unusual for AD to be misdiagnosed as something else or be overlooked or simply dismissed. Several research studies published as recently as 2001 indicate that primary care physicians often do not recognize dementia in their patients, especially in its early stages. In fairness, it is relatively easy on an HMO quickie exam to overlook or dismiss problems. Symptoms that are mentioned but not emphasized may result in the physician's deciding follow-up is not needed so that considerable time passes between onset and diagnosis. If physicians in your area do not have a reputation for diagnosing and treating AD or other dementias, it would be a good idea to contact the Alzheimer's Association and ask for a referral.

In the past a diagnosis of AD was made by excluding other causes for symptoms; today it involves inclusion of a number of markers. To meet the *Diagnostic and Statistical Manual of Mental Disorder*, fourth edition (DSM-IV) criteria, a step crucial for insurance reimbursement, evidence of decline from previous levels of function must be present. And it is not enough that you cannot recall what you gave your sister-in-law for her birthday; impairment in multiple cognitive domains must be shown, such as poor judgment or the inability to name objects (anomia), recognize them (agnosia), or carry out voluntary activities (apraxia).

In chapter 6 we will look at the various forms of dementia and how the symptoms of each can be distinguished. Here we are interested in how an accurate diagnosis can be made. What symptoms should motivate you and your physician to look further? Currently there is no one test that can determine if a person has AD. No laboratory test can reveal what might be causing symptoms and what the prognosis and treatment should be. Still, there is no reason a person cannot be reasonably diagnosed with an 80 to 90 percent degree of accuracy. It is true, autopsy remains the definitive answer, but now diagnostic accuracy is just as good for Alzheimer's as it is for most other diseases.

Alzheimer's accounts for only 65 percent of dementia cases; therefore, distinguishing it is crucial for defining appropriate treatment. Alcoholism; central nervous system infections like meningitis; syphilis; AIDS; metabolic diseases, which include hypothyroidism and hypoglycemia; nutritional disorders, such as deficiencies in vitamin E, magnesium, B12, folic acid, niacin, and thiamin; dehydration; vascular diseases, including multiple infarctions, strokes, and atherosclerosis; tumors; normal pressure hydrocephalus; delirium; and depression must be ruled out or treated. It is always wise to assume something physical is happening until proven otherwise. Besides eliminating other disease processes, a physician needs to be able to distinguish between the various forms of dementia that commonly fall under the umbrella of Alzheimer's and/or classify the stage as mild, moderate, or severe.

Certain triggers should prompt a physician to do an assessment. One trigger is a history that indicates cognitive problems have a significant impact on an individual and her ability to function as usual. Complaints of a gradual and progressive worsening of short-term memory, difficulties with orientation, language, judgment, and concentration alone or in combination—are clear calls for follow-up. In the past, a patient's own memory complaints were not considered to be correlated with a diagnosis of AD, but recent research has shed new light on a patient's ability to discern that something is wrong. Some people are very aware of changes in function—others may be oblivious. In most cases, observations of family, coworkers, or caregivers give the physician a balanced perception of memory problems, anxiety, changes in personality, as well as delusions, hallucination, paranoia, aggression, insomnia, and incontinence. Both the patient and others familiar with her should have an opportunity to speak to the physician alone.

A good history is developed through questions that elicit the rate of progression, revealing a gradual decline or plateaus followed by a stair-step drop in function. How the disease manifested itself, suddenly or gradually, is important. Patients with mild to moderate cases are able to report on memory with accuracy when questions are framed as, "compared to other people your age or compared to your function the last couple of years. . ." A psychological health appraisal should assess the use of alcohol and the likelihood of depression, apathy, agitation/aggression, and irritability, since they occur at higher rates in persons with AD than in unaffected peers. If AD is diagnosed, questions should be asked regarding medications, with an eye to eliminating or reducing drugs that negatively affect the central nervous system.

A physical exam and neurological screening include vision and hearing tests and a verbal and writing skill evaluation. Particular attention is paid to evidence of cardiovascular problems, diabetes, or Parkinson's disease. Results from laboratory tests can reveal disease processes and/or poor nutritional patterns, such as low B12 or folate. Finally, functional assessments and cognitive scales provide a baseline to compare progress or determine level of function. Neurological imaging is added to clear up diagnostic uncertainty, when additional screening is necessary for other medical or neurological disorders, or when a person has AD but might also have metabolic abnormalities, infection, or stroke.[2]

Depression must also be ruled out. Depression is the number one mental health issue for older people. It is estimated that 15 percent are affected, yet few complain about it specifically. Instead, as we age, we are more apt to grumble about aches and pains, problems with sleep, and disinterest in what we used to relish—including food and sex. Since depression often accompanies AD and can cause some of the same problems, distinguishing one from the other is important. A patient with AD is more apt to be disoriented than a patient who is simply depressed. A depressed person may have difficulty concentrating, but a person with AD also has short-term memory problems. Most telling is that someone who is depressed knows she isn't remembering well, whereas a person with AD may be oblivious to the forgetfulness. Two scales are helpful in diagnosing depression in older people, the Geriatric Depression Scale (GDS) and the Center for Epidemiological Studies Depression Scale (CES-D).

Why You Must Consider Medications

There you were shaking out your pills from that cute little Neiman Marcus pill case (or the ugly plastic one from the health food store) at your last family get-together when suddenly you realized your ritual had mesmerized your adult children. You look up just as they ask, "Just how many pills do you take?" You suddenly remember why you increasingly enjoy being with people your own age. A perk of getting older is that your friends no longer view you as a hypochondriac. Including vitamins, it is not unusual to find the number of pills you take to have some relation to your age. You may not realize that taking five prescriptions or nonprescription medications results in a 50 percent chance of a drug interaction.

But even if you don't take that many pills, the normal changes of aging make a difference in the way drugs are absorbed, transported, metabolized, and removed from your body. An adverse drug reaction may be immediate or take months to appear. An increase in body fat (whether you are overweight or not) means medication stored in fat has a less intense but prolonged effect. A decrease in overall body fluid means medicines accumulated in body fluids become more concentrated and their effect may be exaggerated. Absorption is influenced by a decrease in gastrointestinal tract motility. After years of work, the liver and kidneys begin to function with the same efficiency you do at the end of a very long and trying day. The result is less effectiveness in excreting drugs from the body, thus allowing them to accumulate. It may be that problems with recall, confusion, and inability to concentrate can be traced back to your medicine cabinet, and this must always be considered.[3]

Assessment by the Numbers

While I object to learning I have AD from a self-test in *Modern Maturity*, assessment scales of mental status devised and most often given by professionals provide valuable information that, in combination with other criteria, can yield a very specific appraisal of a person's capabilities. Such tests can be used to monitor progression, establish level of function, and even make predictions of functional status. It is very important to establish a baseline free of bias. There is really no excuse for a physician not to use any of the brief but formal testing instruments available for detecting cognitive deficits. While they may not measure perception or content of thought and mood, they provide information on recall and orientation, two of the most problematic areas of mental decline.

None of the following tests take more than fifteen minutes to give, some even less. They are available for physicians to use in their office as well as for assessment in care facilities. Despite their apparent simplicity, they are well researched and the results have been validated for accuracy. Most evaluate an individual's orientation (where she is, the date), recall (a test of memory), and ability to concentrate (math problems or following directions).

The *Short Portable Mental Status Questionnaire (SPMSQ)* quickly assesses how oriented a person is by asking her the date, day of the week, her phone number, address, date of birth, and age.

The *Mini-Mental State Examination (MMSE)* is probably the most widely used assessment tool. The only criticism of it is that people with more education tend to score higher despite actually having memory problems. The MMSE tests five areas: orientation, registering, attention and calculation, recall, and executive ability.

The *7-Minute Screen,* as the name suggests, is shorter than the MMSE but is considered highly accurate. It avoids many of the biases, such as higher education, that may affect the outcome of the MMSE. It is particularly good at differentiating between the elderly with normal cognition that has changed due to aging and people with Alzheimer's disease. In research tests it has been shown to correctly diagnose 90 percent of test takers with AD and with the same accuracy determine those who do not have dementia. Despite its accuracy, the 7-Minute Screen, or any other test of cognitive function, is not designed or intended to be used as the sole basis for a diagnosis. Additional medical, laboratory, and psychological tests must be considered as well. The screen has four parts: tests of orientation, memory, clock drawing (assessing visual-spatial skills), and verbal fluency.

An advantage of getting older is that you can eat dinner at four o'clock. A disadvantage is that you might forget to turn off the stove. It follows that another realm of assessment testing had to be developed to determine just how well you are taking care of yourself. Activities of daily living scales or ADLs measure the basic tasks needed for self-care and everyday jobs that support independent living. These scales are commonly used to determine when a person should no longer be trying to manage alone and perhaps be placed in a care facility. A person with AD tends to overestimate what she can do; family tends to underestimate. Although many families insist Mom (or Dad) is living independently at 116 years old, what is happening is that family or others are picking up the slack to enable her to remain at home.

Professionals are alert to this discrepancy and commonly make distinctions based on the diagnostic pearl, "Say do, can do, do do?" What is it that a person says she does, maintains she can do, and actually does? Tests provide an unbiased eye. An individual's ability to handle finances and shopping, for instance, are very telling.

Scales such as the *Instrumental Activities of Daily Living (IADL)* focus on the ability to follow a medication schedule, do one's laundry, use the telephone, and manage money. Even in early stages of dementia, such tests have proven valuable for assessing how much disease is affecting daily life and in determining the patient's ability to care for herself.

Activities of Daily Living-International Scale (ADL-IS) has proven especially useful for those with an early diagnosis. Its questions include those that measure a person's ability to find a desired TV or radio channel, perform simple activities around the house, concentrate on reading the newspaper or a book, complete forms, go for a walk without getting lost, and follow a map.

The *Katz Activities of Daily Living Evaluation* is widely used and consists of a simple six-item scale that ranks ability to complete various tasks.

The *Geriatric Depression Scale* is a more reliable measure than the doctor who wrote in his chart, "The patient is tearful and crying constantly. She also appears to be depressed." The answers to basic questions help evaluate a person's state of depression.

Behavioral Pathology in Alzheimer's Disease (BEHAVE-AD), a 25-item questionnaire, can be used when the disease has gone beyond the

early stages. Family members or caregivers fill it out. It is helpful
in determining the extent of the symptoms and providing guidelines for care. The questions determine sleep patterns, incidents
of delusion, and many other behavioral concerns.

Timed Up and Go is a test used most often with persons who have
become frail. It provides an impartial way to keep track of
progress or decline. The patient is asked to sit in a chair with
arms, get up, walk to a nine-foot mark, turn, return, and sit
down. Anyone able to do this in twenty seconds is probably
able to care for herself independently.

Physical Self-Maintenance Scale (PSMS) and the *FAST* scale were
both designed to help determine if placement outside the
home is necessary and the degree of care required.

Pittsburgh Agitation Scale and the *Disruptive Behavior Checklist*
provide information that addresses issues of quality of life
for the patient and helps determine services, set goals, and
specify needs.

Technologies

Just as our cameras now allow us to take pictures of a butterfly in
our garden and five minutes later send the photos across the Internet
to our grandchildren (God help those of us without fast connections!), the "cameras" used in medical technology have made major
advancements. Magnetic resonance imaging (MRI) can show if your
brain is shrinking. Positron-emission tomography (PET) reveals the
brain in action. It detects changes in the way the brain's glucose is
metabolized, pinpointing the parts most affected by AD.[4] PET has
demonstrated its ability to distinguish the specific type of AD from
depression, to identify very early evidence of neurodegenerative
diseases, and to predict conversion of mild cognitive impairment
(MCI) to AD, making it an invaluable tool. These neuroimaging
techniques are among the new technology using X rays, magnetic
fields, and/or radioisotopes to view three-dimensional slices of intact
living brains. The most exciting aspect is the fact that physicians

are now able to diagnose preclinical stages of Alzheimer's before damage becomes irreversible. While no one yet knows which comes first—the chicken or the egg conundrum—the question continues to be whether pathological stages appear years before symptoms or whether the risk factors culminate in disease pathology.

These detailed views into the living brain have revealed and confirmed that problems start in an area called the entorhinal cortex, the "gateway" to the hippocampus, the memory-processing center essential for making new memories and retrieving old ones. The entorhinal cortex registers the initial changes that initiate the development of Alzheimer's. Researchers have succeeded in tracing the disease progression through the brain.

A computer image similar to a black-and-white photo results from magnetic resonance imaging. An MRI's ability to measure brain volume, particularly the size of the hippocampus, has enabled the earliest detectable evidence of atrophy, which has been especially beneficial in uncovering MCI—considered a transitional phase into AD. An MRI is more sensitive than computerized tomography in its ability to detect tiny ruptured capillaries. Still, despite its marvelous capabilities, it must be considered in the context of a complete neurological evaluation before determining a person's problems are due to AD.

There is great variation between people in baseline MRI findings, so until more work is done, we don't as yet know the normal range. It may be that changes in an individual's results from one test to the next, spaced six months to a year apart, are better predictors of what is going on than a static baseline measurement. Changes in the brain appear to follow the same pattern whether or not they are due to an inherited form of AD or a random cause.[5]

Functional MRI (fMRI) uses a person's blood as a natural contrast agent to show changes in the intensity of signals when different areas of the brain are stimulated. The imagery of a light bulb to represent a good idea is accurate from what we have recently learned. The fMRI demonstrates that, literally, AD patients don't light up. This technique is able to detect neuronal damage before other methods but it is a very new technique, so its applications and accuracy are still being fleshed out. Newer still is magneto-encephalography (MEG), which allows study of the brain in real time. It directly measures nerve cell firing and may prove invaluable for detecting early stages of AD or MCI.

The CAT Scan (CT) has been around a long time and is essentially an enhanced X ray that can detect shrinkage, thinning of the neocortex, expansion of the brain's open spaces, the presence of neurofibrillary tangles, and amyloid plaques. Despite being older technology, CT allows technicians to diagnose AD with 90 percent accuracy and MCI with 80 percent accuracy. CT images can also detect evidence of tumors, strokes, blood clots, and hydrocephalus.

Biomarkers—the New Heralds

The job of a biomarker, like heralds of old, is to make sure information gets out. Biomarkers are useful because they let us know a disease is present or will soon be. There are many varieties including those revealed through neuroimaging, which we have just reviewed. Biomarkers can prove that a specific disease is linked to a biochemical process that has gone bad. For example, cerebrospinal fluid containing beta-amyloid and tau protein may have predictive value for the development of AD. There are obvious benefits to knowing that we are on the road to getting a disease or in its early stages. For researchers the value of early detection is that they have an opportunity to test medicines or techniques to learn whether or not they work to prevent, cure, or slow development. Here are a few biomarkers your physician may use now or in the near future to diagnose or predict your chance of developing AD.

- gene testing
- a blood test that picks up a protein called HO1, found in higher concentrations in the brains of AD sufferers
- testing the sense of smell—it has been noted that neurofibrillary tangles invade olfactory pathways early in the develop-

ment of AD, meaning an impaired sense of smell may be an early marker
- an EEG (electroencephalography)—reveals different brain waves are used, depending on damage and location

Thoughts on the Twilight Journey

I have a friend who celebrates getting older because his joints have become far more accurate in predicting the weather than the meteorologist on TV. It is difficult to keep a hopeful attitude when one has become a "slow-motion version of herself," as one woman with early Alzheimer's has shared. After years of effort to live in the now, we may find we have no option. The result may be that our lives will be less driven and that we increasingly treasure the good and simple things in life. Ronald Reagan ended his 1994 letter to the American people, announcing his Alzheimer's diagnosis, with "I now begin the journey into the sunset of my life." It was clear he had determined that his focus would not be the past. An Alzheimer's diagnosis demands that today become the priority. Loved ones can no longer expect a person with AD to be the person she was; expectations must accommodate the disease. Ultimately no one can completely understand how her life will be affected, and as comprehension diminishes there is even less chance for understanding. We are fortunate to live at a time when early diagnosis is possible. Unlike my mother's case, should my fears become a reality, timely awareness will offer me a chance to slow the process and smell a few more roses along the way.

Diagnosis must be multidisciplinary, involving medical, psychological, and environmental evaluation. There are physicians who won't reveal their suspicions or findings because they think nothing can be done or they don't want to deal with it. The official Alzheimer's Association position is that everyone has the right to know. You can count on follow-up services being poor after early diagnosis. This will change as the growing number of early-stage Alzheimer's patients find their voice. We need to be listening.

I believe in autopsy to confirm Alzheimer's. As was Mother, I am more than willing to donate my brain for AD research. I accept as true that in heaven I will receive another that will be much more efficient than my earthly model. It comforted me to know the exact state of Mother's physical condition when she died, and it was a gift to be reminded of the interventions that are apt to be uniquely important for me. I am sure Mother, who complained so often that something was wrong with her brain, would have been pleased that after her death it helped shed light on this horrible disease. There is no question that others will benefit.

While I am no more anxious to know definitively that I have AD than any other person would be, I nevertheless am convinced that early detection is to my advantage. It does not matter that the ultimate cure-all has not been found. There is much that can be done to maximize well-being, both personally and physically, while having the disease. There is nothing like a diagnostic wake-up call to motivate us. We have been there. We had been lulled into complacency when tests diminished the risk that my healthy-appearing husband would succumb to a genetic propensity for heart disease. Two years ago he almost died. Looking back, we can see the red flags and realize his risk could have been reduced. Fear, a physician who is not up to date, or inertia are not adequate excuses for avoiding diagnosis.

Brain Boosters

- Early diagnosis ensures control over your destiny.
- Denial and poor understanding of AD symptoms delay diagnosis.
- AD can be diagnosed with 80 to 90 percent accuracy.
- Cognitive testing provides a baseline from which decline or progress can be evaluated.
- Tests that measure activities of daily living (ADLs) are helpful in determining independent living capacity.
- Neuroimaging is a vital part of a complete diagnosis.
- Diagnosis of AD is multifaceted.

Six

A Rose by Any Other Name

Therefore do not worry about tomorrow, for tomorrow will worry about itself. Each day has enough trouble of its own.

Matthew 6:34

Mother's New Husband

Hallways extended from the nurse's station like arms of a starfish, giving nurses a clear view in every direction. This particular facility was one of the first with a wing solely designated for AD patients and the best I experienced through Mother's journey. Perhaps because it was new, the staff was enthusiastic about their undertaking; they tried to do what their mission statement declared. They were striving for a residence that treated patients and loved ones with dignity and without the sense of warehousing so common in most settings.

I had wept at the thought of bringing Mother to this facility, for it meant leaving behind the last remnants of her home. The bits and pieces that had decorated her apartment in the assisted-living facility were links to times when life was the way it was supposed to be. While the bright bedding, the small green violin-shaped vase that hung on the wall, the teak furniture she had lovingly oiled, were not valuable materially, they were priceless in that they attached Mother to past homes, holidays—and me. I cried; I mourned; I moaned. I was terrified to think of Mother's reaction. She entered her room and didn't miss a thing.

On one of my visits I tried unsuccessfully to push in the latest code to enter the Alzheimer's wing. The elaborate system, resembling something out of a Tom Cruise movie, was designed to ensure that no one left the wing who didn't have the wherewithal to function in the big bad world outside. It had failed, however, to stop Mother. Twice she was apprehended just before boarding a city bus for who knows where.

Once inside, I signed in at the nurse's station and steadied my nerves to hear the latest report on Mother's shenanigans since my last visit. Her favorite mischief was "refiling" patients' charts. How she removed them right under the nurse's watchful eye remained one of life's great mysteries. Single-handedly and with a brain half functioning, she had managed to shut down the whole wing on more than one occasion until the lost was found. While the nurses were never thrilled to find a chart missing, they did begrudgingly admire her stealth.

While Mother's chart habit proved an ongoing annoyance to the staff, my real fear was hearing that she had hit someone. The brainpower needed to formulate passive-aggressive schemes to get her way was now unavailable to her, so in her later years she had become a diminutive Mike Tyson. When I looked at the incidents from her perspective, they made perfect sense. No longer able to ask someone politely to get out of her way or to let her move something she was sure she owned, she hauled off and hit (and, yes, bit) whoever wouldn't take the time to see it her way.

I considered skipping the first family meeting for fear I would be ostracized for being the daughter of the powerhouse "puncher" from A wing. I cannot tell you how relieved I was when, after I apologized to anyone whom Mother had wronged, the whole room broke out in laughter while letting me know that Mother did not have a monopoly on strong right hooks and that, as she got used to the place, such incidents would diminish. Still, I remember several years later getting a call for the mandatory report of a "physical incident" and finding myself dancing through my tulips with the revelation that for once she was the "hit-tee" instead of the hitter. Only someone who has been in a similar situation could really understand such a perverse reaction.

As her stay extended, she developed routines that included the delusion that she had been hired to work there. When I would suggest we walk to the ice cream shop, she would check at the nurse's station first to see it they could spare her. At the last place she lived, a virtual hospital, frail as she was, she again thought she was employed. I begged the staff to let her help fold towels. She clearly enjoyed the task, having never lost her desire to fold laundry with all the precision of a watchmaker.

Mother's favorite activities remained eating dessert and going for ice cream, but she manifested a delusion that topped even those indulgences and that had the added benefit of her hanging up her boxing gloves. She located her last husband, Dr. Jimmy Stirrat—or at least a convincing facsimile. Apparently after traveling around the world, he had returned to her at this resort hotel and life was again good. The real miracle, however, is that an embodiment of her deceased spouse had found her. "New Jimmy" was no less convinced than Mother that fate had reunited them.

I have no idea how common or uncommon a shared delusion is. I suspect it doesn't happen often. Mother had found New Jimmy, and he was devoted to her. There was only one disturbing element to this wonderful love story. New Jimmy's real wife of more than fifty years visited him daily. She lived in the assisted-living section of the facility and spent hours attending to her husband's needs as well as those of many of the other patients. Her kindness, patience, and consistency clearly placed her in the category of unpaid staff. Despite her presence, New Jimmy found "new-old-wife," and they lived happily ever after—at least for a time.

Whatever his wife felt, she did not keep New Jimmy and Mary Jo from becoming an item. We used a great deal of cajoling and distraction to ensure that their delusions did not include conjugal visits. But their shared belief that they were husband and wife of a different time and place made my life much easier. Mother was contented, even happy. She stopped hitting. She was busy and preoccupied; after all, she had a husband to look after or, more accurately, who looked after her. They became inseparable, walking hand in hand and clearly appreciating and comforted by each other's company. Despite their obvious devotion, once they were separated, they seemed to forget the other existed. Fortunately it was easy to distract them on some pretense or another when my visits, other activities, or night-time demanded it.

New Jimmy's real wife was the stereotype of a kindly grand-mother. Pleasantly plump, extremely well dressed and mannered, she was a picture of calm. I often thought that the only thing missing was a halo sitting just above the crown of her beautiful white hair. I am ashamed to say that I never spoke to her directly. I was afraid it would be too painful for her and I didn't want to have to admit that I liked the arrangement. Looking back I wish I knew how she had managed to continue her loving care as her husband became increasingly enamored with what he saw as the "real" version of her. Did she cry when she returned to her room? Was she happy because he was happy? Intellectually understanding the disease process is different from accepting it emotionally. Had she managed to rise above what would be devastating to most of us? She continued to spend hours helping out in the AD wing, making sure her spouse was clean and well dressed and had everything he needed—even if it wasn't her. It was a lesson in loyalty, love, and dignity that I will never forget.

Unfortunately, like a Greek tragedy, New Jimmy and Mary Jo's romance was ill-fated. The lovers were separated when Mother threw a pitcher of water on a visitor who objected to her being in his mother's room and resolutely declaring his mother's robe was hers. Her aim was square, he was insistent, and I was given thirty days to find a new facility.

The Umbrella of Dementia

I have used the word *dementia* to denote decline in memory and other cognitive functions that affect daily life. There are distinct types of dementia, but the most common is Alzheimer's, which accounts for about two-thirds of all cases. So, should your memory begin to fail, a betting man would put his chips down on the square labeled AD.

Looking from the outside, categorizing diseases isn't easy because symptoms may seem similar. Researchers love that sort of challenge. Since different parts of the brain are affected in diverse ways and in varying order and the biochemical processes are singular, it is important to distinguish among types of dementia to ensure proper treatment and best understand the prognosis. The type of dementia affects length of life. Each responds best to specific medications and may have different responses to drugs coincidentally given for other health problems. But distinguishing one dementia from another does not reject the truth that there is considerable overlap among them. To those of us living with our afflicted loved ones, all roads lead to Rome, so to speak.

Besides Alzheimer's, there are three cousins: ischemic vascular dementia, accounting for a disputed percentage but considered the second or third most common dementia after AD; Lewy body dementias, diagnosed in approximately 25 percent of dementias; and frontal lobe dementia, more rare at 5 percent. Mary Jo, as the doctors at UCLA confirmed to Dr. Stirrat, had ischemic vascular dementia with its characteristic multiple small infarcts. Plaques and tangles noted on autopsy confirmed what is true for the vast majority of those similarly diagnosed, that AD was also at work.

The first symptom of an individual with AD or vascular dementia will likely be complaints about memory, someone with Lewy body dementia may first experience Parkinson-like problems and visual hallucinations, whereas the person with frontal lobe dementia may horrify or anger his loved ones by some act that shows a distinct loss of inhibition. Other types of dementias exist but are rare. About 25 percent of Parkinson's patients develop dementia and it occurs in combination with other diseases, such as HIV or hydrocephalus. As discussed in chapter 5, proper diagnosis is very important when concluding AD is the problem. A doctor must rule out diseases that mimic AD and treat all coexisting illnesses.

Lewy Body Dementia (LBD)

Lewy bodies are inclusions within neuronal cells. It is not unusual at autopsy to find Lewy bodies scattered throughout the outer part of the brain, intermingling with widely varying degrees of Alzheimer's pathology. The number of amyloid plaques and neurofibrillary tangles present determine if the diagnosis is that of Lewy body dementia or Alzheimer's with Lewy bodies. However, Lewy bodies alone can cause cognitive deficits, their density being significantly correlated with the degree of dementia. Warning signs can be confusing. A person may go to the doctor complaining of Parkinson-like symptoms and fluctuating cognitive problems that leave him lucid one day and confused the next. His movement disorder may be mild to severe with dementia usually beginning about the same time. Because the drugs that are used for Parkinson's disease can cause hallucinations in a person with Lewy bodies, it is important to make sure the diagnosis is accurate.

Visual hallucinations are not unusual with a diagnosis of LBD. Often they are of complex scenes of one's pets or other animals, children, or supernatural creatures frequently visualized in miniature. By contrast, it is unusual for persons with AD to experience visual hallucinations. The course of Lewy body dementia can fluctuate considerably. An afflicted person may have a little better memory than the average patient with AD but may be worse off physically. Spatial ability and word fluency can be particularly affected. Other symptoms like very low acetylcholine levels are shared with AD, but in Lewy body dementia the decline can be rapid. Cholinesterase inhibitors can be helpful in improving mental alertness and diminishing restlessness and agitation.

Frontal Lobe Dementia (FLD)

Frontal lobe dementia is rare, usually appearing before sixty-five years of age, with most people afflicted in their fifties. Fortunately neuroimaging techniques can make the distinction between AD and frontal lobe dementia. Otherwise it can be difficult to diagnose. It too has a lot of overlap with other degenerative diseases like AD, vascular dementia, and Lou Gehrig's disease (ALS). As the name implies, damage is done mostly in the frontal and anterior temporal lobes. The frontal lobes guide behavior, and when they are damaged, the person resembles a two-year-old who is controlled by his environment. Like the young and willful child, a person with FLD can get stuck in an activity and be unable to switch to another. A friend tells of her father-in-law, suffering from probable FLD, who refused to visit his critically ill wife because he couldn't or wouldn't leave his dog.

The sometimes bizarre conduct and inappropriate social and interpersonal behavior seems to come out of left field and can leave coworkers and loved ones completely confused and often angry. Such a person appears emotionally insensitive, which may reflect a major change in personality. The man who wouldn't leave his dog also showed little empathy or compassion for his wife when she was recuperating in a nursing home. He would go into her room, treat her like a stranger, and demand to go home minutes later. His children were outraged because their mother needed his support, and their father had always been her protector and best friend.

Afflicted people are described as being slightly off, not responding or engaging interpersonally as they used to or as you would expect from a healthy person. They may stare as if they are attending but emotionally are just not there. While mentally rigid, they are also distractible and unable to keep to a task. A particularly telling aspect relates to their concrete thinking and loss of insight, which would prevent them, for example, from giving meaning to a proverb such as "Don't cry over spilled milk."

There are three FLD subtypes of brain degeneration that result in slightly different symptoms. One is the opposite of the most common version, rendering a person meek and passive. The most widespread results in behavior that can be belligerent, crude, rude, withdrawn, or peculiarly ritualistic. Placing items in the mouth, constantly needing to munch on food or to chew on something like a pencil is common. Speech patterns can be altered and a person may develop an automated or hesitant cadence, talk fast, or stop talking altogether. You may have heard of people who become obsessed with winning the lottery, collecting cans, or, like a very wealthy lady in our area, buying houses, which she fills with hundreds of cats. People with these behaviors should be evaluated for FLD.

Needless to say such people can be very difficult to be around. When their coping skills and memory appear relatively intact, they are often not seen as having a cognitive problem. In this case low acetylcholine is not the problem, but low serotonin levels are. There are some patients with FLD whose behavior does not become outrageous but instead they are unresponsive and emotionally "blunt," dropping out of life instead of adopting new behaviors. There may be a genetic component to this type of dementia. People with frontal lobe dementia often decline rapidly.

Ischemic Vascular Dementia (VD)

The vast majority of people with ischemic vascular dementia also have the characteristic damage of Alzheimer's—plaques and tangles. There are a number of subtypes, which present differently. The most common are those caused by large or small strokes, or microvascular pathology. While Mother's gradual onset was typical of AD, her stair-step deterioration pattern was very characteristic of vascular dementia. Depending on the damage done by a stroke, symptoms can occur suddenly and commonly affect the ability to walk, causing unsteadiness and frequent falls. Early urological problems may present themselves. Personality and mood changes are common. A mental slowing may occur, which is different from the complete loss of memory. Organizational skills and the focus to complete complex tasks are reduced by executive dysfunction. Like Mother, delusional behavior may be a symptom. Fortunately for her, she remained physically healthy, but stroke damage leaves many having to contend simultaneously with physical and mental deterioration. Correlations exist between the severity of damage and certain behaviors, something researchers have not been able to definitively show with AD. Persons with vascular dementia are more likely to have a history or evidence of arteriosclerosis.

Mild Cognitive Impairment (MCI)

When I say I fear I am on the road to AD, I am worried about whether I have developed what is now considered a precursor to Alzheimer's, mild cognitive impairment. While I qualify for *impaired* on days when I'm tired or stressed, this is not enough to diagnose MCI. Ronald Peterson, director of the Mayo Clinic Alzheimer's Disease Center in Rochester, Minnesota, was the first to define a memory deficit that involved some forgetting, while the person maintained relatively normal functioning. He suspected a connection with Alzheimer's, and his suspicions were confirmed following a research study launched with the National Institute of Health. Whereas midlife conversion rates to AD would normally be 1 to 2 percent, it was confirmed that approximately 12 percent of persons with MCI progressed to Alzheimer's. After six years, 80 percent of people with MCI will have developed AD.

How realistic are my fears that I have MCI and how would I know for sure? Age-associated, normal memory loss, which involves those misplaced papers and keys or forgetting someone's name only to remember it after you have already ducked down a different aisle in the supermarket, are not what we are talking about. If you or I have MCI, our scores on memory tests will resemble those of a person with AD, but we will score like a normal person on cognitive tests that measure lack of orientation and confusion about routine activities. With MCI forgetting is frequent and involves relatively serious incidents, like missing appointments and delayed recall of information. Thus it is unlike the kind of forgetfulness a same-aged friend without MCI may have. While we may fear being diagnosed with MCI, it is a researcher's dream because it offers the opportunity to see if various interventions can prevent or delay the onset of AD.

Studies confirm that people with MCI are often well aware of subtle changes in memory. Technically a person with MCI is functioning okay in his daily life and does not meet clinical criteria for dementia.[1] Complaints of memory loss involving decreased retention of written materials, forgetting placement of valuable objects, decline in concentration, anxiety accompanying forgetfulness, and inability to work well in a demanding employment situation are prevalent. New neuroimaging techniques can reveal accompanying physical changes, chief among them brain volume and the size of the hippocampus. These changes have been confirmed by autopsies on people who died before they developed AD. A dinky hippocampus that doesn't measure up to your best friend's does not always indicate MCI. The condition can also be caused by a number of other illnesses.

Actual diagnosis of MCI must be made using a number of criteria:

- memory complaint
- abnormal memory for age and education
- normal activities of daily living
- normal general cognitive function
- not demented
- positive MRI results

Abnormal memory for age and education is not as vague as it sounds. It refers to problems with recent memory loss. This means that hints, which would help a normal person remember a list he or she has recently learned, provide no benefit to the person with MCI. Hints are not helpful to him because the information wasn't stored or was stored ineffectively. Because they retain the ability to think, understand, and make decisions, people with MCI are able to do what few with Alzheimer's can do—provide insight and information about memory changes while their mind can still register that changes are occurring. Awareness of what is happening to them and openness about it will help reduce the stigma of memory loss and result in new images of AD, other than those of the final stage, when communication, recognition of loved ones, and the means to do much on one's own are beyond one's capability.

While candidness will reduce our fear, it will also benefit the individual with MCI who complains of loneliness and exhaustion when the diagnosis must remain hidden—reducing feelings of competence and the ability to stay socially active. So how would anyone know if he has MCI? By remembering that it is normal to misplace keys and checkbooks, forget a name, and have increasing difficulty watching TV and reading, but it is not normal to be unable to learn new names, miss appointments, or forget things repeatedly. When these things happen, it is time to worry about MCI.

Alzheimer's Disease (AD)

"My mind goes to an empty and horrible place. When I come back from that place, I don't know where I am or who the people are who are with me," writes a fifty-nine-year-old early-stage Alzheimer's patient.

"My memory has changed but my love and appreciation of music, art, and nature haven't changed at all," says a woman with early-stage AD.

"If we go more slowly, our brains work better," according to a man with early-stage AD.

Imagine that you are seventy-three years old. You have just gotten out of bed, and absolutely nothing looks familiar to you. When you went to bed last night, you were thirty years old, visiting your folks, and spending the night in the room in which you grew up. You make your way down a strange hall and pass a mirror. Whose image is reflected back? He has white hair and wrinkles; you are blond and have a crew cut. A noise distracts you and with great trepidation you peek around a corner. That's not your mother . . . and where is your dad? Your heart begins to pound; you turn and make your way to a door that leads outside. Carefully you ease onto the porch making sure you aren't seen. You have to get away. You step down and begin to run; you fall and it's cold and you don't have a coat; your body aches. Someone is coming. You struggle to get up and hide in a grove of trees. Where are you? Where are your folks? And then you remember. You are supposed to pick up your wife. She'll be waiting in front of the school where she teaches. Where are your keys? Where is your car? You panic and have no idea what to do, where to go, where you are. You have AD.

If time is taken to gather a good history, evaluate mental status tests, order laboratory assessments, and obtain appropriate neuro-imaging scans, there is no reason an accurate diagnosis of Alzheimer's cannot be obtained. Most cases of this widespread dementia follow a recognizable pattern of insidious onset and gradual progression of mental and functional decline. Profound loss of memory is the hallmark symptom of AD. Accompanying evidence of outward physical deterioration may be completely missing. Depression, situational anxiety/agitation, delusions, and hallucinations are common but not universally experienced. Acetylcholine, the most important of the neurotransmitters, can be as much as 50 percent depleted. There is no doubt that AD increases mortality; only cancer is more lethal. AD causes deterioration at the same rate as cancer.

Unlike those with frontal lobe problems, people with AD tend to be friendly and try to cover their difficulties when with people. Mary Jo never stepped into a crowd without having something to say, and AD did not slow her down. Sensing a captive audience, she particularly liked to strike up conversations in elevators. She loved to talk to children, often beginning her conversation with,

"When I was a little boy about your age . . ." While most would look quizzically at this innocent but apparently crazy little grand-mother, the bravest would point out that she was a "girl." Without hesitation she would immediately reply, "Well, you are right but, when I was a little boy, I kissed my elbow and changed into a little girl." She told me the same story when I was small, which led to my considerable frustration at not being enough of a contortion-ist to make the switch and benefit from all the goodies I perceived were denied little girls growing up in the forties. Her "never met a stranger attitude" endeared her to many, most of whom had no idea of the extent of her memory problems.

That does not mean she didn't have her moments. Like most AD patients, she had her share of agitation and anxiety and problems that arose because of them. Failure of the staff at the assisted-living facility to produce her car keys or to call a taxi would leave her furious. While many professionals deny the effect of depression after AD is advanced, its presence makes perfect sense to me. It seems a normal response to waking up each day wondering where you are, having no control over your life, and perhaps seeing no familiar face.

Mother's Mike Tyson moods, like their namesake's behavior, were quick, dirty, and over almost as soon as they began. There were other times when she became so upset that calming her took time and finesse and left all involved exhausted. While many of these episodes were dismissed as "sundowning," some were undoubtedly incidents of delirium. Sundowning is a common phenomenon in which anxiety and confusion reign. Its name comes from the fact that by sundown the body is tired and light has grown dim, two factors increasing the chance of problems. A visit to almost any nursing home will find examples of patients whose behavior nega-tively shifts around dinnertime.

Delirium is not a normal stage of AD or any other dementia. AD can increase its incidence, however. A recognizable and distinct disorder, delirium is also known as acute confusional state. While its occurrence often increases in the late evening, it can come and go during the course of a day, sometimes dramatically. In most cases, delirium causes thinking to become even more disorganized and may include hallucinations. Such a patient cannot focus on an idea or task, so carrying on a conversation with him or trying to follow what he is saying is nearly impossible. Some individuals with delirium may become very drowsy instead of hyperalert.

It is important to understand the difference between AD behavior and delirium so that its causes can be appropriately addressed. Delirium should be suspected when the behavior represents a sudden shift from the person's previous course of dementia. Medication interaction or overdose should always be suspected, but too much stimulation and undiagnosed infections can all be triggers that need to be addressed.

Stages in Alzheimer's Disease

AD is being increasingly approached as if it were a chronic disease. Like other long-term illnesses, interventions are directed not just at a miracle cure but also at measures to alleviate pain and suffering and to slow the progress to more debilitating stages. The lifetime development of AD has been identified by phase. The latent phase is that in which we have greater or less propensity for developing AD due to our genetics, environment, and lifestyle. A preclinical phase follows when factors like head trauma, diabetes, cerebrovascular disease, stroke, or perhaps lack of certain vitamins or estrogen escalate our odds for developing AD. This moves us into a final clinical phase when symptoms appear and a diagnosis is made.

In a typical case onset to diagnosis averages between thirty-two and thirty-eight months; diagnosis to placement, twenty-one to fifty-six months; and placement to death, thirty-five to forty-five months. An Alzheimer's journey may vary from several months to an average of nine years. As I have shared, Mother's journey continued for more than twenty years. All people with Alzheimer's disease proceed through a definable pattern, frequently categorized as mild, moderate, and severe. They do not suddenly wake up one day with final-stage AD. Although there is some overlap, stages of the disease are well defined, and rate of progress from one stage to another will be different from person to person.

It is helpful to categorize persons with Alzheimer's as *fast* or *slow* decliners. Researchers have discovered that verbal memory tests and other cognitive measures can distinguish the two groups.[2] We can expect future research to provide us increasingly predictable and reliable information about the course of our individual disease process or that of a loved one. Such information is useful in making long-range plans and in adopting realistic expectations.

Mild-Stage Alzheimer's

The beginning stage of AD typically lasts two to four years. Forgetfulness occurs often enough to interfere with the ability to hold a job or complete household tasks. The person may struggle to remember common words like *bread* or *jacket*. Most begin to have trouble with numbers and handling finances even if working with them has been a lifelong occupation. Interest and initiative in activities and in life in general are diminished. Social behaviors are usually preserved and individuals can look and act quite normal, especially to those who didn't know them before. Since judgment and the ability to perform complex tasks are poor, others can easily take advantage of those in this stage of AD. Most people in this category experience a decreased knowledge of current events and ability to travel.

My friend Jane told me about the day her mother-in-law, Gladys, opened her wallet at the doctor's office to get her insurance card, and Jane noted that each pocket was labeled, "change," "key," "cash," "credit card," and so on. Surprised, she said to her, "Gosh, I didn't realize you were having such a problem remembering things."

Without missing a beat Gladys replied, "Oh, this is no problem. When I have to put a sign on my belly button 'Put underwear here,' that will be a problem!"

Moderate-Stage Alzheimer's

The intermediate stage of AD will range on average from two to eight years. Constant supervision is necessary because an individual with moderate AD may not be able to remember the name of his spouse or recognize close friends and family and can wander off and get lost. He may forget significant but recent family events, like a wedding or birthday. Confusion and episodes of anxiety increase and there can be personality changes. Common daily routines, like getting dressed or dressing appropriately, become difficult, as do activities like reading, writing, and any remaining skill at working with numbers. Delusions and insomnia add to an already confused state. Problems are obvious even to someone who doesn't know the person. Urinary incontinence may be present.

As Gladys's dementia shifted into the moderate stage, her personality and good sense of humor remained intact. One day her son broke the caregiver's cardinal rule when he took her shopping—he left her briefly at the cosmetics counter while he ran some packages out to the car. Mercifully, she was exactly where she was supposed to be when he returned, and she had completed her purchases. He was stunned when the salesgirl gave him the bill. His eighty-year-old mother had purchased a number of cosmetic items, including a one-ounce container of ninety-dollar wrinkle cream. Once the wrinkle cream was exchanged for a nice lotion, Gladys informed her son she needed a new pair of shoes. She had no trouble finding what she wanted and had no hesitation in ordering them in every color available. Her son's extraordinary negotiating skills enabled them to return home with money still in her account.

Severe-Stage Alzheimer's

On average the most severe and final stage of this progressive disease lasts approximately one to three years. It is the phase that comes to mind when we think of Alzheimer's. This final stage finds many victims unable to remember anything and lacking the ability to process new information. He no longer recognizes family and may be unable to understand words. Such a person is far from a vegetable, however, and is able to respond to music, touch, and eye contact. There are occasional lucid moments. In the end, difficulties with eating and swallowing may develop. Loss of the ability to control bladder and bowel movements is frequently accompanied by no longer being able to walk, maybe even sit up, and certainly to dress, bathe, and groom oneself. Physical impairment results in the person's becoming bedridden. There is a severe loss of speech and perhaps even the loss of the ability to smile—although there remains little for such an individual to smile about.

The usual difficulties of this final stage did not keep Gladys emotionally down for long. Although she was bedridden with complications of severe coronary disease, the family has many good memories, like the time she almost convinced her granddaughter that she (Gladys) was really the heir apparent to Universal Studios in Hollywood. Maybe that is why she needed all those pairs of shoes!

Thoughts on the Twilight Journey

My life would have been so much easier if I had understood more of what Mother was experiencing. Knowing that her behavior was a textbook case of someone whose brain is damaged by AD would have helped me maintain perspective. Today the Internet brings up a research study, "Treating Delusions of Theft in Alzheimer's Patients Can Reduce Caregiver Burden." No kidding! It speaks of such accusations being directed chiefly at caregivers. Really? It occurs more frequently in mild or moderate AD. Oh! Maybe I am not such a bad person; it is part of the disease process.

I'm sure New Jimmy's loving wife understood more than I. This disease has symptoms and varying progressions that make sense. So often the journey with Mother felt like I was in a rowboat that was being buffeted wildly by a storm. Maybe for my kids and me any such journey will feel more like an ocean cruise. We will all weather the storms without disaster or distress because they will be predicted. Once we have our "sea legs," we can look forward to cruising around the deck and enjoying the expansiveness of the ocean, the warmth of the sunshine, and the soothing rolling waters that lull us to sleep.

Brain Boosters

- Making an accurate distinction between dementias is important in understanding behavior, prognosis, and proper use of medication.
- Alzheimer's is typically categorized as mild, moderate, and severe.
- The rapidity of decline is very individualized, but predictive patterns exist.

Seven

What We Know We Did Not Know Thirty Minutes Ago

We should always presume the disease to be curable, until its own nature prove it otherwise.
The diagnosis of disease is often easy, often difficult, and often impossible.

Peter Mere Latham

Living on the Tilt

The call was left on my answering machine. "Mary Ann, when you come over to visit your mother today, would you drop by the office?" A cold numbness gripped my heart—the same awful feeling you get when someone from the school calls about your son or daughter. "Now what?" I mumbled out loud, knowing our welcome at the assisted-living facility was as fragile as the ice on a newly frozen pond. Was this the day the ice would crack and I would need to find a new facility? I grabbed my keys and my purse and for a brief moment contemplated erasing the message and "forgetting" about my visit. Maybe God would intervene. Searching for an alternative care facility had become my full-time job—one at which I was a decided failure.

I was greeted warmly by the manager at the one and only care facility in our small town. "What's the problem?" I asked, wasting no time but pulling up a chair just in case any pending news proved something that might knock me off my feet.

"Well . . . ," she hesitated as if searching for the right word, "Mary Jo was found on the second floor with only her blouse on."

"Did the aide not help her dress?" I asked.

"Oh, yes, she had her clothes on earlier," the manager said, obviously trying her best to stifle a giggle that was dying to get out.

The thought of Mother taking a tour of the facility in her birthday suit did provoke an amusing image. My mind wandered and I wondered what she might have said to those who found themselves on the elevator with her. She undoubtedly would have struck up a conversation; she always did.

Lest I relax and think the worst was over, the manager told me *the rest of the story.* "Actually, this isn't the first time. In the last couple of weeks she has taken off her clothes several times, but the aides have been able to catch her before she ventured too far."

I was puzzled. Mother did not have a background that included prancing au naturel. She was a modest woman. After her "flapper" days, she wore layers of underwear. There were the "room-to-move" panties under a layer of pantyhose, the "eighteen-hour bra" banished from sight by adding a camisole with wide shoulders designed to cover bra straps and made of opaque material to further conceal. If she wore slacks, she added a slack-slip, something that looked like long underwear and was designed to ensure the wearer a "smooth" line.

As I searched for some explanation, my first thought was that a lifetime of heaping on layers of undergarments had finally done her in. At seventy-seven she had contracted "undergarment overdose" and had become a free spirit. Or perhaps she had always been a free spirit. All those tales about her being the good daughter! Maybe my grandmother was justified in worrying about my mother's behavior. Whatever the cause, it further threatened her ability to stay put. One more foray on the wild side and she would be asked to leave. While I was grateful for the reprieve to continue the quest to find her next home, nonetheless, I remained confused. After all, my friends' mothers kept their clothes on. And then I remembered that my brother had told me about how I, as a three-year-old, had decided to run away from home and had discarded every item of my clothing in the middle of the street before taking off for points unknown. It hit me hard. I was doomed—it was genetic.

Several days later I received a call from a colleague, Dr. Dave Larson, with whom I was collaborating on a book. Dave immediately sensed something was wrong. When pressed, I told him about Mother's behavior and that any day I would be asked to move her. That God indeed works in strange ways was certainly true for me that day. Dave was one of a mere one thousand geriatric psychiatrists in the country at the time. A quick review of Mother's medications turned up the culprit. She was overdosed all right—just not on underwear. The side-effect profile of one of the medications was, you guessed it, disrobing. Who would have made such a connection? Her general practitioner certainly had not.

There were three times in Mother's journey when I was convinced she was dying. Each time her decline was the direct result of drug interactions, overdosing, or side effects. Sometimes she simply became quieter and more withdrawn. She would look at me with eyes that were devoid of hope, empty glazed orbs that no longer tried to connect. It was during one of those times that I took her to the mall to see the children and to sit on Santa's lap for a picture. Every Christmas I place that picture out for all to see. Her bright colored outfit and wild white hair catch the essence of her being. But the blank look and the drooping jaw do not. This did not have to be. Spending time in a mall, watching little children in their Christmas finery, and eating ice cream cones should have enlivened her—they were things she loved. But there she sat, dutifully propped up and held in place by a not-so-rotund Santa.

Sometimes overdose was signaled by a tilt. Off balance, she fell several times—unusual for a woman who could still touch her toes in her seventies. During our many walks through one of the facilities, my husband and I always found someone tilting. It was as if a wild, aberrant wind blew through the halls, knocking one person to the left, another to the right, while still others were teetering forward or back. Some individuals shook, like a quaking Colorado aspen. I am horrified as I reflect back on the number of men and women whose inability to walk, stand tall, or remain out of bed was more related to their medication than the stage of their disease. At the time I did not know this.

Today many of the drugs that were prescribed for Mother are clearly off-limits for an AD patient. Yet a number of friends report recent crises of drug overdose or misuse with their parents or grandparents. Some physicians appear woefully ignorant of appropriate drugs and oblivious to the quality-of-life issues that are allied with what they prescribe. In any care facility that is inadequately set up, understaffed, and employing poorly trained people, seeking order through sedation is often the chosen path. Sometimes the behavior the drugs trigger is the opposite of what was sought, causing grief for everyone. More drugs, fewer drugs, drugs to counteract the drugs, all result in weeks and months lost to an AD patient and his or her family. Enough is known today about appropriate medications that even with individual expression at work, category and levels should be arrived at without excessive trial and error. You cannot leave drug selection to the suggestions of the facility or the direction of the doctor without insisting on clear treatment goals, agreed upon risks, and the underlying concept that less is better, especially for behavioral and psychological symptoms.

A Devastating Condition with a Defined Pathology

Feeling scared and desperate about the prospects of spending my twilight journey on the same path as my mother is to a great extent connected to feelings of helplessness regarding available medical options. At the time I was caring for her, there were none. Any medications used were a best guess effort of selecting interventions that worked for similar symptoms caused by other disease processes. While I acknowledge I am not a stupid person, my husband is a physician, our life has been spent within the medical community, and we are not unaware of breakthroughs and everyday practicalities, my intervention choices were no more informed than those of the average person with no medical background. The science of Alzheimer's really commenced when the number of patients began to burgeon, and it kicked into high gear as a result of President Reagan's honesty about his plight. Advanced treatment concepts are barely ten years old. The paradigm shift began when it was realized that, since this is a disease that progresses over a long time and in a series of steps, possibilities exist for intervention at many places along the way.

For Mother, treatments were symptomatic. This is not a bad thing. Agitated behavior, wandering, and delusions, for instance, if left untreated can make it difficult for a person to remain at home and can exhaust caregivers. The armamentarium consists of drugs that affect the mind, collectively known as psychotropics. Specifically this classification includes drugs directed toward relieving problems with mood (antidepressants), the nervous system (neuroleptics), and agitation (anxiolytics). Some have proven effective for the AD patient while others create more problems. Today there is a much greater sophistication about which drugs can most appropriately be used with Alzheimer's patients. Their effect is to provide comfort and relief—palliative care—rather than to stave off the inevitable decline. Psychotropics have been the first, and for many in the past the only, medicine game in town for AD management.

In earlier treatment plans nonpharmacological therapies were simply given lip service or dismissed, but now research has confirmed or strongly supported their efficacy. For example, exercise has been shown to improve our overall health, not just our physical fitness. Not only does it reduce depression, lower blood pressure, and increase mental acuity, it actually staves off symptoms of dementia. And it is no longer just the "organic" crowd that touts the benefits of good nutrition and vitamins. The American Medical Association and *JAMA,* their journal, encourage folks to eat their vegetables *and* take vitamins. Indeed we now understand that what you eat can ultimately influence whether or not and when you begin an Alzheimer's journey. Equally important is the research that has uncovered the importance of humane and life-affirming psychological and social approaches for the AD patient. The mindset with which a patient is viewed can enrich or diminish her life and consequently affect those who care for her.

Mother did not have the options that a patient with AD would have today. There were no medicinal choices that interfered with the disease progression by modifying brain chemistry. Medications now exist to protect and increase the chemicals (neurotransmitters) that nerve cells use to pass messages from one cell to another. Drugs with such action are called cholinesterase inhibitors. While measurements of cognitive recovery have been minimal, behavioral changes with these drugs are recognized as significantly improving everyday living. For those who respond well or moderately to cholinesterase inhibitors, the disease process is altered and deterioration can be delayed from one to three years.

Another approach involves lessening the incidence of AD with anti-inflammatory medications that reduce nerve cell loss. Most physicians now recommend anti-inflammatory drugs for their older patients who can tolerate them. As we saw in previous chapters, studies have revealed that statins, currently used to lower cholesterol and reduce cardiovascular events, decrease the incidence of Alzheimer's. Research has verified the benefits of antioxidants and nerve growth factor modifiers and is exploring other potential neuroprotectors. Those of us who do not have dementia can look forward to new medications that interfere with the formation of those pesky plaques—actually modifying the mechanisms of the disease itself. Work continues on uncovering the why and how of

Current Treatments

For Alzheimer's disease: Exercise, proper nutrition, cholinesterase inhibitors, anti-inflammatory drugs, vitamin E

For Lewy body dementia: Exercise, proper nutrition, cholinesterase inhibitors, symptomatic use of antipsychotic and anti-parkinsonian medication

For frontal lobe dementia: Mostly palliative care

For vascular dementia: Management of vascular complications associated with medical conditions,[1] smoking cessation, anticoagulation agents

biochemical triggers, which will clarify the direction to explore and help identify treatments that may be most effective.

While new medications restore hope, the greatest gains impacting this disease come as the result of improvements in technology. Scientists are now able to observe the effects of AD on the brain. Imaging techniques enable doctors to track the disease before symptoms are evident. UCLA researchers have scanned people with minor memory problems and predicted with 95 percent accuracy who will have dementia within three and one-half years. While the machines they use to pinpoint the disease with such accuracy are currently rare and Medicare doesn't cover the tests, they do exist and will become increasingly accessible. Most communities have access to MRIs if not PET machines (see chapter 5). Mapping of degenerative patterns in a wide range of dementia and with varying severities means that ways to visually mark and evaluate the effects of new medications are now available.

Optimism lies in the realization of the brain's plasticity. Gone are the days when it was believed what you have is all you get. The brain is an active, dynamic entity that changes from moment to moment. Learning and remembering have an anatomical component. Giving your brain a workout actually changes its structure. It is the same principle as building muscle in your arm when you finally pick up those weights that have been sitting in the corner for six months. Increased strength and power result from exercising your arm or your brain. At the same time, the speed and efficiency with which you think is as dependent on chemistry as structure.

New drugs are not like the old ones that focused on helping people feel better by relieving symptoms; new drugs will be expected to prevent or delay progression of the disease itself. Once damage is severe, reversal is difficult if not impossible, so early treatment is very important in slowing down the disease. I suspect it won't be too long before our annual physical exam in our doctor's office will include monitors for measuring brain health similar to those now used for heart health. In the end, it will be a combination of factors that accurately forewarn us of our future. Researchers at Oregon Health Sciences University identified the eighty-year-olds who would develop dementia by timing a thirty-foot walk, giving a memory test, and using MRI results. The octogenarians who took two extra seconds on their walk, who lagged ever so slightly on memory tests, and who showed slight shrinkage of the hippocampus on the MRI developed dementia. A catastrophic outcome was correctly predicted from miniscule markers!

What We Have Now

Prescription pads are a good and bad thing. They are good when we have some acute illness or infection that is known to respond to the medication being prescribed. They are bad when the doctor decides that the quickest way to get you out of his or her office is by filling one out. Maybe you remind the doctor of Aunt Clara, the one who has asked every year since internship, "Are you going to start being a doctor soon or are you still practicing medicine?" Or it could be you are handed a prescription because there are fifty people in the waiting room. There are many pressures on physicians to prescribe rather than monitor and adjust treatment. Some

The Six Major Neurotransmitters or Neuropeptides

1. Acetylcholine: "The big gun" helps concentration and memory and is most abundant in the hippocampal area.

2. Norepinephrine: "The drama queen" is necessary for exciting and stressful events. It is vital for short-term storage and long-term conversion. Low levels can cause depression; too much results in starting a cascade of events that are bad for the body.

3. Dopamine: Helps control physical movement.

4. Serotonin: Helps us feel good and sleep well.

5. L-glutamate: Critical to laying down and recalling memories. Counteracts oversecretion of cortisol.

6. Gamma-aminobutric acid (GABA): Involved with relaxation and sleep.

are undoubtedly convinced that writing a prescription passes for having done something, especially if they do not plan to schedule a follow-up visit or provide counseling and evaluation because they fear the added expense of caring for someone with a chronic illness, in some cases a chronic illness they simply don't know how to treat.

Cholinesterase Inhibitors: The Best So Far

Cholinesterase inhibitors are the only drugs approved solely for Alzheimer's. As amyloid plaques build up, researchers have verified a reduction in levels of the primary neurotransmitter, acetylcholine. Cholinesterase inhibitors help by blocking the breakdown of acetylcholine. As we have discussed, neurotransmitters are the chemical messengers in the brain. Acetylcholine does its work in all regions of the brain and adequate amounts are vital for memory and learning. Reduced acetylcholine interferes with the transportation system that connects one neuron to another. Cholinergic mechanisms also play a major role in controlling cerebral blood flow. These mechanisms depend on adequate amounts of the neurotransmitter that acts to dilate or constrict blood vessels, depending on where it is released in the brain. A deficiency will prevent this vital regulatory process. Inadequate blood supply worsens AD.

As a class, cholinesterase inhibitors are far from being the solution to AD treatment, primarily because there is such a wide variation in individual response. However, they are proving beneficial in a way researchers had not originally anticipated but caregivers appreciate. For those who do respond to cholinesterase inhibitors, caregivers report improvement in orientation, ability to be left alone, improved appetite, reduction of nighttime behavior problems, lessening hallucinations and apathy, and better motor skills. They appear to have less impact on mood disorders, such as depression, agitation, and anxiety. For some, the important benefit is stabilization of dementia symptoms for one to three years, which can mean a delay in institutionalization.

As with all medications, there should be specific guidelines outlined to measure their effectiveness. Ask your doctor what changes are to be expected and how they will be measured. Evaluation of side effects should be made two weeks after the initial therapy is started. After four weeks a physician needs to repeat and compare tests of cognition and activities of daily living, comparing them with those given initially. Blood enzymes and other chemistries need to be checked every eight weeks and progress on ADLs monitored. There is anecdotal evidence that stopping treatment and starting it up again reduces efficacy. Remember, an individual may respond to one drug and not another. The principal side effects are gastrointestinal.

The Importance of Behaving Yourself

I am thrilled to see that more attention is being paid to nonpharmaceutical approaches when the behavior of a person with Alzheimer's is upsetting or disruptive. I was always able to quiet Mother by assessing the situation, staying calm on the outside (even if I was jumping up and down on the inside), and speaking to her with soothing and distracting words. Most of the time someone who had become frustrated with her had escalated problems to the point that she was seen as impossible to control. A war of wills would ensue and even though Mother was working with half her allotted neurons, her will remained intact! Medication for her behavior inevitably created more problems.

The current new and improved philosophy practiced by the most enlightened AD experts is that drugs should be used only when all else has failed. Research on what can appropriately be used to treat the AD patient for behavior and psychological issues is new. Many drugs are not approved for AD and are therefore used "off-label." Efficacy should be measured by clearly defining target symptoms. It is important to remember that behavior and psychological problems are just as much part of the disease as are cognitive difficulties. Additionally, they are often what lead to institutionalization—so a focus on their parameters is extremely beneficial.

The Dilemma of Estrogen

Research studies on estrogen's ability to prevent AD or improve its symptoms are currently all over the place. Some see estrogen as clearly protective of memory and some moderately so.[2] Still others declare no association.[3] Whether it is preventive or delays decline in those not cognitively impaired or merely slows the disease progression has been the focus of still other studies.[4]

In 2002 the National Institute of Environmental Health Sciences included estrogen on its list of carcinogens because of its role in slightly increasing the risk of breast cancer and its stronger connection with the risk of endometrial cancer. In July 2002 the government halted the portion of the Women's Health Initiative (WHI)—the estrogen/progestin phase—when guidelines that measured benefit compared to risk indicated that its use increased risk of cardiovascular disease, thrombosis/stroke, and breast cancer, while showing benefit for colon cancer and osteoporosis. This well-designed study on prevention was very large and concluded that, if estrogen/progestin are to be used at all, it should be for the shortest time possible (one to five years) for hot flashes and/or urovaginal atrophy after other avenues of treatment have been tried and failed. Women with risk for cardiovascular complications or breast cancer should not consider hormone replacement as an option. The study did not discontinue its estrogen-only phase, which is supposed to end in 2005, because so far the same levels of risk have not been seen.

Estrogen alters the production and balance of neurotransmitter systems and has a weak antioxidant and anti-inflammatory effect. It promotes neuronal connections while increasing blood flow to the brain and improving glucose metabolism. The result is improved verbal memory, vigilance, reasoning, and motor speed. But adding extra estrogen may not be a good thing.

In the spring of 2003, results from the Women's Health Initiative Memory Study (WHIM), an arm of the WHI, reported increased dementia (66 percent vs. 36 percent) in women aged 65–70 years old who had been taking estrogen/progestin compared to those on a placebo. Whether progestin was the culprit or an increase in the possibility of small strokes from the combination as reported in the WHI is at yet unknown—but at this juncture adding hormones to protect one's brain cannot be recommended. Whether just Premarin/Provera or any estrogen/progestogen combination is problematic is unanswered.[5]

Vitamin Research at Last

Vitamins help defend your memory, most significantly by protecting you from oxidative stress. Oxidation occurs when an electron in a cell moves from one oxygen molecule to another. An electron is very much like a two-year-old. Sometimes it simply takes off and does its own thing. Once on its own, the recalcitrant electron is known as a free radical. If no one grabs it by the collar and steers it back to where it is supposed to be, its free state is likely to go to its head. Left on its own, it proceeds to attack and oxidize everything from DNA to fat molecules in the bloodstream.

The brain is especially vulnerable to free radical damage because there is so much activity and it never stops working. Because of its need for a constant flow of blood and oxygen, biological oxidation occurs at a high rate, increasing the chance for free radicals to spin off and do their thing. Overproduction of free radicals causes inflammation, increasingly believed to be a major factor in the etiology of AD.

Antioxidants act essentially like the good parents of a two-year-old—rounding up, calming down, and converting free radicals into something worthwhile. There are many antioxidants, and inadequate intake has been linked to a number of chronic diseases.[6] Various research articles demonstrate a 43–70 percent lowered risk for developing AD for persons whose levels of antioxidants fall in the highest range.

The *Journal of the American Medical Association* recently published data on a significant five-year research study that involved more than five thousand subjects. The conclusion was that high dietary intake of the antioxidant vitamins C and E likely lowers dementia risk.[7] Vitamins C and E have been noted to be in short supply in the spinal fluid of dementia patients, perhaps because an AD patient produces so many free radicals they are depleted or the person simply consumes fewer antioxidants. Vitamin C boosts the effect of E, which is why studies consistently show greater cognitive decline is slowed with 800 to 2,000 IUs of vitamin E per day. Vitamin E has also been correlated with delays in the need for institutionalization and with longer life. Always consult a physician before taking vitamin E.

The controversy over whether additional supplements are needed to protect against AD and/or how effective they may be is still unresolved. No one disagrees with the importance of eating fresh fruits and vegetables of many colors and types. Most of us probably need to gain extra protection by adding a vitamin supplement. Physicians are beginning to recommend antioxidant supplementation with asymptomatic but high-risk patients who are likely to suffer from oxidative damage or carry the APOE-4 gene. At least nine vitamins, many of them antioxidants, are found to be in short supply among the elderly, vegans, those who are alcohol dependent, and patients with malabsorption problems.

The vitamin B complex is as busy as the proverbial bee maintaining brain health. Vitamin B1 (thiamin), B2 (riboflavin), B3 (niacin), B5 (pantothenic acid and pantethine), B6 (pyridoxine), B12 (cobalamin), and folate (folic acid) are all important for maintaining nerve and brain health.

In chapter 4 I listed herbs that seem to be somewhat successful in improving memory. The most effective is ginkgo biloba. Huperzine A, an herb derived from Chinese club moss and used in combination with ginkgo and vitamin E, is also used in China to treat memory problems. Oxidative damage has been reduced in mice made susceptible to AD by feeding them a curry spice, curcumin, the active ingredient in turmeric. Its potent antioxidant effect decreased beta-amyloid plaques 43–50 percent.[8] It has the added benefit of having an anti-inflammatory effect, which may make it an option for people who can't tolerate NSAIDs.

Never underestimate the importance of lifestyle and nutritional interventions. Preliminary research reveals a 50 percent reduction in risk for AD with these good health habits.

What Lies Ahead?

First, let me give a tribute to the little guy. Actually, this is an ode to mice. Considerable progress has been made on testing drugs because scientists have been able to breed mice that develop Alzheimer's-like processes that mirror the variations in the brain, behavioral changes, and neuroimaging abnormalities in humans. By producing a genetic strain that replicates human AD, we can now shed light on the genetic transmission factor. We must also pay homage to some of God's other creatures—fruit flies, sea slugs, snails, and flies that, despite their simplicity, have basic memory formations that are similar to processes found in humans.

By the time their conditions are recognized three out of four people ultimately diagnosed with Alzheimer's are past the moderate stage. There are many ethical decisions that must be made before deciding that an AD victim should participate in a research study. In the United States, research results are not given credence without a placebo comparison. But is it ethical to give some people a sugar pill when a drug being tested has some known efficacy? Before a drug is approved, the FDA requires Phase Three trials with humans which can last six months or longer—that might amount to a lifetime for someone with Alzheimer's. Here is another place I intend to be proactive and to let my children know my desires regarding my inclusion in a medical study.

I would hope that future annual exams, beginning at fifty, would routinely include a formal AD risk assessment. A history including the incidence of AD or other dementias would be fleshed out with a blood screen for relevant gene defects underlying AD, imaging for amyloid plaques and tau levels, and, when indicated, determination of cerebrospinal fluid levels of markers such as vitamins.

A summary of the future of Alzheimer's disease was beautifully expressed by Dr. Michael K. McCloud, director of Internal Medicine and Geriatrics Clinics at the University of California in Davis, California. His "Hope for the Future" was distributed during an educational series on Alzheimer's in 2001. In essence Dr. McCloud's analysis includes the following: A belief that there will be increased understanding of the distinctions between the various dementias. The discovery of the connection between AD and mild cognitive impairment (MCI) memory loss will provide an ideal group to study interventions that will delay or prevent AD. Alzheimer's will be increasingly considered a treatable disease. Some interventions will buy time until new breakthroughs are discovered, but many will improve the quality of life. There will be movement away from the use of antipsychotics for nonthreatening behavior problems. Early dementia support groups will be more readily available and reduce some of the fear, shame, and anxiety surrounding dementia. The development of upscale dementia assisted-living facilities will preserve dignity and quality of life and will provide therapeutic designs. All of these factors will work to ease the caregiver burden. Caregivers will be seen more in the role of care managers and will benefit from increased opportunity for respite and attention to personal health.

The Alzheimer's Society remains the number one source of updates on trends, services, medication, and research studies.

Thoughts on the Twilight Journey

The major complaint one hears from cancer patients is that there is so much information and there are so many opinions it is often difficult to know which treatment direction to take. I would have to say that when it comes to AD the opposite situation is true. Chances are the physician you are working with, after months or years of delaying a diagnosis when you have suspected AD, will tell you, "There is nothing we can do." Physicians who treated Mother bungled around for symptomatic control, throwing their armamentarium at the wall and hoping "something would stick." Little attention was given to side effects. In truth, sedation was the goal.

While it would be lovely to have a magic pill that would repair brain damage and restore memory, I'm pleased that at least today we have a focus on quality of life and reduction of anxiety through both improved medication and sociobehavioral techniques. While we wait for the big breakthrough, we all must live. We must hang on to the hope that someday we may actually improve! In the meantime

I am for anything that makes days brighter and against the things that make them duller.

The Internet provides a means for anyone to keep up on the very latest research. If you do not use a computer, assign the investigative role to a grandchild. When the day comes for me to have my memory evaluated, I will not use the latest self-test in a women's magazine. Probably I will not go to the physician down the block either. I will seek out the people who are on the cutting edge of new treatments, perhaps at a university or major medical center. If the diagnosis is Alzheimer's disease, there may be little time to waste.

Brain Boosters

- Always suspect the culprit is medication when new physical, mental, or social problems seem unaccounted for any other way.
- Drugs aimed at behavior should be used after social and behavioral interventions are tried first.
- Taking a good multivitamin that supplements a healthy diet is a safe and sane intervention.
- New discoveries are being introduced daily. It is our responsibility to be aware of them.

Eight

The Longing for Independence

It is not the disease but ignorance and neglect of the remedies that undermine a person's health.

Mark Percival, health coach

A Most Depressing Day

The landscape looked as desolate, stark, and strung out as I felt. There appeared to be no end to the eight serpentine lanes slithering across the desert floor toward Palm Springs, California—on and on they went, unrelenting, just like my situation. For a moment, the turnoff and a brief stint through small farms and ranches provided a distraction. Each small "ranchero," an oasis of life, clung futilely to its bit of open space. New housing nipped at its borders, poised to obliterate the last-ditch bloom of the desert.

Another miserable metaphor, I noted, exacerbating the pity party in which I had been wallowing since I had left home almost an hour before. The two-hour round-trip three to five times a week had to be squeezed between professional obligations, attention to two teenagers, and the busy life of my physician husband. I told myself it was a small price to pay for the promise that someone actually knew what to do with a seventy-eight-year-old whose body had gotten stuck in a time warp at fifty but whose mind got lost. It had to be worth it. Ahead was the trailer park, then the shopping center, loosely referred to as the mall by the locals. Finally, I drove into the steaming asphalt parking lot. It was too late to turn back, even though the worst part of the journey lay just ahead—walking through the door of the place I tried to pretend my mother called home.

The hacienda-style one-story facility looked friendly enough. As such places go, there were worse, and few as good. Still, I hated that Mother was there. Guilt oozed from some primordial place deep within me and no modern psychobabble could stop it. Good daughters did not put their mother in a nursing home. But I had, and whatever was left of her former life she carried within her. Five-four-two-one—this week's combination released the door. There she was, as usual, at the nurses' station, waiting for her opportunity to rearrange the nurses' charts.

This day a visit with Mother was only part of my agenda. I had been invited to attend a "Family and Friends" get-together. We were to meet and share something that would give others insight into our loved ones. As a writer, I was challenged and focused by the one-paragraph restriction and the request to squeeze my memory and a lifetime habit of Mother's into a succinct unit. Unfortunately, I was asked to go first.

This is what I shared: One of the fondest memories I have of my mother, Mary Jo, is of her taking care of any child that needed a "second" mom. My dad used to refer to her as "Mother Confessor." Her heart went out to every abused, neglected, or simply cold and hungry kid that crossed her path. I remember coming home in the dead of the Canadian winter to find her redressing, for the ump-teenth time, a toddler from a group whose mothers had sent them to play outside and who refused to answer the door for bathroom or hunger calls despite the below-zero weather. After dutifully peeling off the layers of clothing, mittens, and boots, one time too many, she looked up, her face reddened with effort, and said to me, "I think I know why their mothers don't let them come in."

And then the love stories began. Correctly, no one else limited the essence of his or her cherished one to a measly paragraph. Epics unfolded. The man who spent his days turning the pages of an empty scrapbook had been in the D day invasion. He had constructed and run an allied hospital under dangerous and daring circumstances. He was a colonel and a hero.

The "pretzel" woman whose defiant body refused to sit straight and whose communication was limited to the soulful repetition "Help me! Help me!" had helped many as a nurse during the war. She held one of the highest ranks achieved by a woman in World War II. Most days she sat buckled into a wheelchair, her cries inconsolable and disturbing. I remember the one day she said something else. The residents were having an afternoon social, and lively music filled the activity room. Thrusting her body out of her wheelchair with a mighty effort, she proclaimed, "I want to dance!" Startled, we rushed to steady her, just as she declared, "I can't dance," and collapsed into her familiar heap. One lucid moment replaced as quickly as it had come with "Help me! Help me!"

The tall, thin man who spent most hours mumbling an incomprehensible narrative had been a dentist and model railroad buff. Not just any weekend hobbyist, he had been president of the Model Railroad Association and proud owner of a meticulously converted basement that was a miniature railroad showplace.

Tiny, spunky Sharkey, whose real name was Sharon, was a mother of five, according to her friend. Joe and I had nicknamed her because of her habit of thrusting and sometimes twirling her false teeth in and out of her mouth. She and at least five others from the unit accompanied us when we took Mother for a walk through the halls of the facility. We were an interesting assortment. By comparison Mother looked like an Olympic contender, bound-

ing along, usually trying to take care of someone less agile. Sharkey
never missed the opportunity to join us, and with one or two in
wheelchairs and a handful of others in tow, we managed to make
a parade out of a walk.

The last to share was Mrs. Schultz, who spoke lovingly of her life
with Mr. Schultz and their family of three boys. If I had known he
would come to play an important role in Mother's life as the reincar-
nation of her last husband, I would have listened more closely. But
by the time I had heard about the outstanding achievements and fine
character of people I had only seen in the halls of an Alzheimer's wing
and Mrs. Schultz had finished with stories of such a devoted husband
and father, my mind was mush. The designated meeting time was
over. As the stories had unfolded, they fleshed out and restored per-
sonhood to the individuals who paced the halls, verbalized their own
language, and survived in a world of their own making. It seemed
each one had approached life with vitality, verve, and vigor. Yet the
current shell that was now the person gave few hints of the vibrancy
with which he or she had lived, loved, and laughed.

The goal of the meeting had been to allow family to reminisce
and think fondly of their loved one, while reminding others that
what we saw was not all there was. These weren't warehoused bodies;
they were individuals rich in history. The meeting helped me love
them more but at the same time it depressed me further. I registered
two emotions—despair and hopelessness. I was unable to ignore
what appeared to be the ugly reality. Being bright, lively, exceptional,
rich, successful, even heroic had not protected these dear people
from the ravages of losing their minds. From my perspective, they
had done the right things and it hadn't made a difference.

Any hope I had of a future that embraced the past was dashed.
The day would come, I was convinced, when I would be the subject
of a future "Family and Friends" meeting. No matter how I lived
my life, it seemed my prospects were sealed. The drive home proved
worse than the drive there. My body ached and my arms felt so heavy
I was surprised I could turn the steering wheel. A deep primeval

pain filled my being and I wept the whole way—for Mother, for all the individuals whom I now knew too well, and for myself.

A Letter for Joe and Malika

Dear Kids,

First, I love you. From The Time I cradled your Tiny bodies in my arms, my desire was To raise you in a way That you could become all That you dreamed. Admittedly and unintentionally, I have put up roadblocks To That process. It has been said, <u>Children begin by loving Their parents; as They grow older They judge Them; someTimes They forgive Them.</u>[1] I apologize and ask your forgiveness.

There will come a day when our roles will be reversed and you will Take on The unnaTural posiTion of parenTing your parent. The difference beTween my role and yours as "parent" is That you will know what I want my life To be when I grow <u>down</u> insTead of <u>up.</u>

Suddenly There is no Time To wasTe. It would be easy To look and act old. BuT The TruTh is I have received no signal That has convinced me iT is Time To check ouT of life. ThaT does noT mean That I am unwilling To accepT The facT ThaT in socieTy's eyes I am five years from being officially caTegorized as The real deal, "an old person." IT is True I may reverT To The same helpless sTaTe ThaT you were in when I firsT cared for you. I may someday be able To leT you know only ThaT I am hungry and weT and need To be held, buT Today I can do more. It is True I can'T remember how To puT picTures on The hard drive of

my computer, but I still have considerable control over
my long-term quality of life. It is driven neither by
fate nor genetic disposition but by the choices I make
now.

I want to make sure you know some of those
choices. It is well known that quality of life stems
from a sense of having control. Control is not
dependent on the state of one's body any more than
body image is tied to how a person looks. I intend to
communicate with you on an ongoing basis what is
important to me, and I will do so in a planned and
programmed way. I will try not to leave any necessary
thing undone. However, in areas where you are
unsure, keep in mind that the same things that
make life good when a person reaches her fifties
make it good well beyond fifty.

Please do not forget that although my journey may
share aspects with others, it remains unique. You
have known me for your lifetime. Trust that you
can stand up for me when my care involves a path
different from the well-worn one. So that others
won't ignore or dismiss me, remind them that I am
a person with a history. Don't forget that I may no
longer meet expectations of what I was, but I still
am. My desire is to be realistic and face impending
problems honestly.

If you ever feel stymied as to how to include
me in your lives, focus on my strengths. You know
I love people, hearing their stories and wondering
about why they make the choices they do. Take me
somewhere to watch people and talk with me about
what they might be feeling and how individuals are

related. Take me to museums and let's discuss what is going on in the pictures. We can visit displays of animals or presentations of nature's beauty and mysteries. Walk me through the vineyards and let me hear the birds. Spend time with me—Touch me. Sometimes cognition is overrated; there are other things in life.

Like everyone else, I need to be needed and to have purpose to my life. This is true whether I am diagnosed with Alzheimer's or any other debilitating illness or simply find my in-line skating days are over. That my presence makes a difference is something I must feel and that you must convey to me through your actions and words. Don't worry that I might embarrass you if you take me to visit, eat, or shop. Chances are my social graces will remain intact longer than I will.

However, if my behavior is bad or I seem anxious, take a walk in my shoes. Respond with life-affirming approaches that provide me the greatest opportunity and motivation to change my tune and straighten up and fly right, as Mother used to say. All of our lives will be enhanced when a battle is avoided. Anger and rage can be responses to a sense of loss of control, but they can also be part of the disease process. Don't take it personally; I need your empathy. Don't let me get bored; it puts anyone in a bad mood. Make choices that preserve my dignity. If I can still write, fill out my checks and let me sign them. See that my clothes are clean and, if I insist on wearing the same outfit, buy several just alike. Make sure my hair is not the cookie-cutter-

out-from-under-the-dryer style. Have someone paint
my toenails and draw flags on my fingernails for the
Fourth of July.

Remember, if I develop dementia, I can no longer
be rational, so don't argue with me. Ask me nicely
and don't order me around or use a condescending
tone; especially, don't tell me what I cannot do.
Offer a positive alternative if I insist on taking
off my clothes or tell you I'm leaving for a speaking
engagement that took place fifteen years ago. When
it is time, take my car away no matter how much I
protest. Don't ask me a lot of questions that depend
on memory and allow me graceful ways out when I
can't remember. And, please, don't talk about me like
I'm not there. Since my ability to understand may
vary from moment to moment, I may hear something
I don't need to hear.

If you must place me somewhere, make sure
everyone on the staff knows my life story; it will
affect the way they care for me. Don't put me
in a place that doesn't call people by their name.
Ask if they will be using a "friendship model" when
interacting with me. Take the time to learn about
this approach to interacting with those with memory
problems. It will help you know how to interact
with me, because there may come a day when I may
not recognize you as my son and daughter, but you
can always be my friend.

Forever and forever,
Your Mom

P.S. Don't ever leave me in the care of anyplace
or anyone that believes bingo is entertainment that
will contribute to my well-being.

Healthy Aging

I remember the day I realized that aging had less to do with age than neglect. A truth of aging is "Use it or lose it faster." My husband and I had been speaking to groups of people one might categorize as "health nuts," an activity for a doctor akin to a minister preaching to the choir. Hyperdiligence about their health and fitness left most of them looking and acting far younger than their chronological age. By contrast, the older most people get the weaker, more incapacitated, and diseased they become. Healthy aging clearly involves more than a fortuitous set of genes; it necessitates making a decision to be the best we can be. It rejects the stereotype of what aging is supposed to look like. By no means am I suggesting that we deny age. Like the people in other more enlightened countries, we should revere it. But we must accept that our "job description" as we age includes time devoted to maintaining our personal optimal health.

A mindset that says we must make healthy aging a priority is just as critical to success as what we actually do about it. For example, in chapter 4 I discussed the activities and nutrition that are most likely to maximize our cognitive function. We must figure out how to transfer those ideas from words on a page into our choices and activities. To quote Longfellow, "Life is real! Life is earnest! And the grave is not its goal."[2] Indeed, we have a calling and it is to live our entire life fully to the end, instead of to a certain point beyond which we sit quietly awaiting death.

Our problem lies not in the fact that we get diseases but that almost all of us contribute in some way to our inability to resist them. Living life in earnest occasionally necessitates adapting "the grand goal," which is then divided into smaller attainable targets. I remember when I was nearly incapacitated in my fifties. Once I managed to educate myself about what might be done to restore my health, a process that took a while, I made a mental plan (the grand goal) of how I would approach my getting better. It had taken years to get so sick; I had to acknowledge that it would take time, maybe years, to get better. I outlined a series of steps (small target goals), starting with the one that held the greatest hope for halting or slowing down my continued deterioration.

My expectations were realistic but hopeful. The steps to build up my compromised immunity took over a year. Five years passed before I succeeded in my last mini-goal, restoring reasonable exercise into my life. Periodic earlier attempts had failed. In the meantime, I continued to work on other things that improved my health. And then one day, exercise left me feeling restored rather than wiped out. Gradual improvement enabled me to start exercising regularly again with the result that at sixty I am in far better health, am stronger, and have more endurance than I did at fifty.

I'm not an exception; even the very old and frail can improve their health. For example, several research studies of eighty- and ninety-year-olds have shown that, even at an advanced age, the body can build muscle and strength as a result of a structured weight lifting program. In one study, strength was increased 175 percent in eight weeks and test scores of balance and walking speed were improved by 48 percent.[3]

Most of us do not plan to run the Boston Marathon. We want to get in and out of our car with ease, be able to garden, and rise from a chair without embarrassing ourselves with the struggle. And we want to remember we have done it! Our grand goals should be realistic. But setting a goal is not enough without determination to follow through. The truth is that you are not apt to work on improving your health because I said you should or even on the advice of your doctor. Motivation comes from believing you have the power to change and clarifying your own personal reasons as to why you will do so.

I have a friend who does motivational speaking for businesses. He has just *officially* reached "old age" (sixty-five). He related that he was speaking in a resort at which the main clientele consisted of retirees. As he was waiting for his meeting to start, he watched with horror the great difficulty the majority of guests had getting out of their chairs and simply moving about. On returning home, he couldn't get the picture of all those old people shuffling down the halls out of his mind. He determined his grand goal would be to do what he could to insure he would not join the "stiff and immobile" crowd.

His target goals included taking a yoga class as well as a comprehensive exploration of the specific benefits derived from various yoga approaches. He enthusiastically continued classes and within two years had acquired enough expertise to qualify for a teacher's certificate. He incorporated a new exercise program into his life while maintaining his usual schedule of speaking, several other business responsibilities, and his interest in art and travel. He is not a superman—he is an organized man, whose age has not limited his exploration of new ways to balance his life emotionally and physically. It is true that he can touch his toes and stand on his head, something he could not do a year ago, but the benefits of his commitment go beyond his body; they have had a ripple effect. He and his wife offered a very professional beginner's yoga program to their mostly Type A, fifty- and sixty-year-old friends. I confess to having benefited from their encouragement, diligence, and enthusiasm. Good health can be contagious.

Living Longer or Better?

A 2002 *Newsweek* poll on aging reported 43 percent of people forty and older are worried about getting Alzheimer's, while 54 percent fear a heart attack. Thirty-three percent say the worst thing about getting older is having more health problems, while 18 percent say it's having less energy. When asked how long they would want to live if a mechanical device replacing an organ would help them live longer, 45 percent said they weren't concerned with a longer life, while 27 percent replied they'd like to live as long as possible. Despite the fact that the majority of people would rather live healthier than longer, researchers continue to argue about the actual length of the human life span with some devoted to finding a way to make longer life possible.

Most scientists believe that embarking on a program to lengthen life probably won't accomplish much. Even if they eliminated the chief causes of death, such as heart attacks and cancer, they estimate life might be extended about fifteen years. The only known way to live longer is to radically cut back on calories and be a rat, monkey, or baker's yeast. Caloric restriction to extend life for humans has its advocates, however. The two humans (my estimate) in America who have stuck to such a limited diet for any period of time maintain it will lengthen life by preserving bone mass, skin thickness, brain function, and immunity. Specifically, the effort to reduce calories by fitting an entire meal onto a six-inch plate might actually increase one's resistance to toxic chemicals and traumatic injury. It is theorized that decreased production of free radicals that are behind the damage of many diseases, including those of the brain, in combination with reduction of glucose from an austere diet will extend life. Eating too much can result in high blood sugar, common with age and obesity. The increased insulin released when one has overeaten can result in insulin resistance, a condition that increases the chance of diabetes and heart disease. High blood sugar (glucose), unable to be properly utilized by the cells, joins with collagen and other proteins to damage nerves, organs, and blood vessels.

Another theory is that, since hormone levels wane as we age, antiaging is simply a matter of replacing hormones. Today someone you know is probably convinced human growth hormone, a pituitary protein that helps drive physical development, is the key to healthy aging. While the theory sounds good, evidence from several studies indicates a dangerous side effect profile that may include cancer—not known for its age-enhancing properties! Hormone replacement with estrogen or testosterone is also part of the agenda of those seeking the fountain of youth. But it is not the most fecund among us who live longest; not having children might actually lengthen life. The conclusion? Starving and castration may lead to longer life. However, I'm not convinced it will be a better one.

Providing Support for Health

If there are no real magic bullets to prevent aging, then we are forced to work with what we have. We cannot avoid getting old, but we can age in a healthy way. Our physicians don't always understand this. There is a subtle difference between disease prevention and support for health. If your doctor is truly concerned that you age well, he or she should provide for this by enhancing your immune system to ward off communicable diseases, like the flu, as well as noncommunicable ones, like allergies. Laboratory results that scream, "Oh, no, he's going to die! Get him out of the office quick!" are important, but a doctor should also be concerned with helping a patient maintain optimum health. More is at stake than avoiding the development of diabetes and coronary plaques.

When you go for a checkup, insist that your hearing and vision be tested. Make sure your dentist strives for superior oral health, not just repair of new or ongoing problems. For our children's sake, let's expect sociological research to address strengthening family and social networks, instead of focusing solely on dysfunction. Let's demand that geneticists studying chromosomal deviations look beyond the genetic bases of specific diseases, like AD, and expand their search to find connections to better health.

Healthy aging is possible in spite of physical and cognitive problems, but we must meet our challenge to actively pursue it. Take note that quality of life issues are not limited to improving the body. It is our mindset that might require the greatest intervention. Simply stated, optimism is good for your life and pessimism bad for your health. Pessimistic people tend to suffer higher blood pressure, weakened immune systems, and depression (which can increase the chance of AD), and they may even recover more slowly from surgery. On the other hand, optimists do not ignore or downplay real risks; instead, they think ahead, putting into place positive interventions that will benefit them long term. They don't panic but try to remain flexible and creative. They remain levelheadedly resilient, countering gloomy moods with action and seeking help through meaningful physical and mental activity.

We might say that optimists build up health reserves that enable them to cope with whatever environmental and diagnostic challenges may come their way. Reserve is necessary to live a passionate life. It is essential to keep perspective when the diagnosis is Alzheimer's disease. In the days when I was struggling with the guilt of placing Mother in a care facility and when I believed there was no hope for me, I had little reserve. Over the years I have moved from that place of despair and continue to work to replace it with an attitude of realistic respect for a disease to which I may or may not succumb. Developing a health reserve despite not knowing the outcome requires an expansion of the potential of life. I know for sure that I have this moment to embrace with joy.

A health reserve can be elusive. It is not approaching life as Polly-anna or with a "What-me-worry?" attitude. Building a health reserve requires a way of thinking that is life enhancing rather than passively reactive to external circumstances. It results in the wherewithal to live in the present and not long for the past or future. It requires paying attention to thoughts and attitudes and being willing to modify them to avoid living with fear, guilt, anger, resentment, or anxiety. We know we are building reserve when we willingly give our money, time, and talent from a sense of abundance, thus renewing and drawing support from nature, our connection to others, and God.

There are aspects of getting older that amplify the chance of finding joy beyond physical well-being. Living longer has a positive side. For the most part older people accept themselves. Often women cease competing and may for the first time fully appreciate the fullness of their being that the crises of chemistry and time have wrought. Men who can no longer beat their sons on the basketball court or who have stepped off the fast track at work find pleasure in the family they have launched and renewed appreciation for the wife they may have neglected. For some, the joy of parenting is experienced for the first time through grandchildren.

The good news is that it is never too late to begin a healthier lifestyle, increasing life expectancy and cognitive acuity and decreasing age-related disabilities. Besides, from the perspective of the optimist, things you buy now won't wear out! And think of all those years you invested in health insurance—your increased use of medical services means it is finally beginning to pay off!

The Problem of Where to Live

At fifty years old, Tim Brennan was diagnosed with Alzheimer's. He wrote a series of articles for the *St. Petersburg Times* about what it was like to have such a devastating disease at a young age. What follows is a portion of a letter that was published in the paper and then reprinted in the Greater San Francisco Bay Area Alzheimer's Association newsletter.

> My dear loved ones:
> . . . if I can no longer speak in the future, you must (know) that I would always want to be home, here with your mother, here with the love I have come to know and derive comfort from. And, yet even as you have known me, you must realize there are healthy concerns, which must be placed at a higher priority than love. . . .
> Please, place me in a long-term care facility when either of these two situations arise:
>
> 1. When you see stress building up in your mother. When you may observe signs that her mental and physical well-being are suffering because of the care she is trying her best to provide to me.
> 2. When my own physical and mental well-being dictates assistance provided to me beyond what any one person at home may be able to offer. . . .
>
> I . . . do not want my situation, which is something bad, to become something worse.[4]

This letter is signed, "Let me do the something I can still do." I too want to do "the something I can still do." That something includes making clear what my desires are regarding a care facility, should I need one. Doing so should help eliminate some of the stress my children are apt to be feeling as they wrestle with what to do with me. Of course, like Tim and almost anyone, my preference is to continue my life in my own home, coming and going as I please, eating what I want when I want it, and taking long leisurely bubble baths. But there may come a time when life's truths must override my desires. I may someday start forgetting to turn the stove off; I may quit sleeping through the night and leave the house to wander the countryside in the dark; I may forget my way home. Worse yet, I may no longer be able to get in my tub or it may start to look like a bottomless pit that I'm convinced will swallow me up. Should that happen, I may no longer be able to live at home. Unless I tell them, Joe and Malika have no way of knowing that my choice for that time does not include having a good-hearted companion live with me or moving in with them. They are busy parenting, and one parenting task at a time is enough.

Following Dr. Stirrat's death, there were few alternatives available when it became clear that living alone was not something Mother could manage. Of all the decisions I had to make throughout Mother's illness, none was more traumatic than deciding where she was to live. Each time it was requested she move, the same agonizing arguments raged in my head. Guilt was unremitting. Briefly I contemplated having her stay with us, but her penchant for getting up throughout the night and her level of agitation when any of us left the room caused us to reconsider. With an OB-GYN husband coming and going at all hours and a phone that never stopped ringing, we had all the chaos we could handle.

The difficulty of placing Mother lay in the fact that at the time there were few facilities that were designated for persons with Alzheimer's. Care facilities were not prepared to deal with relatively high functioning persons whose problems were cognitive. Many places insisted they were experienced in dealing with AD, but few actually were. Mother's behavior, or misbehavior, depending on your point of view, and the various facilities' lack of expertise necessitated the number of moves she ultimately made.

For instance, the manager of a highly recommended home in the area where my husband and I were to relocate maintained that her large, pleasant house was well equipped for an AD patient. I checked Mother in and went back to Southern California to finalize packing for our move a week later, only to receive a call with the news she was hospitalized after opening an unlocked door and falling down a flight of basement stairs. I stayed up nights berating myself for not noticing such a basic safety violation. This was the same facility that resolved Mother's penchant for wandering by convincing her doctor to medicate her into oblivion. When I put a stop to that, they informed me that I would be responsible for paying the police department to find her, since they simply couldn't go running after her—all the while assuring me they were experts in dealing with Alzheimer's patients.

Discovering the imprint of a hand across Mother's face resulted in my bringing her home. As I gathered her things, I was told I was the most "unreasonable" family member they had ever dealt with. Like many private care homes, they were torn between their income shortfall and being inadequately staffed and trained for AD care.

Still another facility, one that proudly advertised an AD wing with a low patient-staff ratio, continually pulled personnel from the AD unit to staff critical care. A recent government study confirmed that nine out of ten homes do not have the staff to provide residents with proper care.[5] When I complained, they replied, "The AD patients aren't dying." Somehow they couldn't see that they were "dying on the vine" as they roamed aimlessly throughout their little corner of what was a devoid and depressing world.

I have watched as friends have struggled to find the right fit for aging parents. Most begin by hiring someone to attend to or simply keep their loved one company. But juggling someone else's life in addition to their parents inevitably becomes unworkable. Eventually they turn to the ever-increasing range of facilities that have sprung up in the last few years. Independent-living, assisted-living, and Alzheimer's units have become available. Unfortunately many of these new concepts are undergirded by the same stale philosophy that was traditionally used in nursing homes.

In the past the focus of care for the elderly was on providing a hospital setting that ministered to the very ill, severely disabled, or dying. While new facilities have expanded their range of care, they continue to be built using blueprints drawn from stereotypes of what an aging person is like. Environments that enable a person to maintain an active interface with life have not been envisioned—protecting the elderly is the guiding principle. The focus is safety. This is not the approach used with disabled young people; no one suggests they should be placed in a sterile environment for their own protection. They are offered programs and facilities that mirror life in as normal and manageable a social setting as possible. Depending on their capability, they are placed in charge of many aspects of their care, sometimes even hiring, training, supervising, scheduling, and firing those they must work with. By contrast, older people are confined to a restricted space, and they are told it is for their own good. An attitude of "call us if you need us" is replaced with "let us do it for you." Such ageism means that the very people who are most affected have no voice.

Assisted-living arrangements theoretically distance themselves from the "warehouse for the elderly" or hospital option. Their popularity has resulted in some former facilities being converted to assisted living. Unfortunately many such conversions offer few homelike options and are essentially hospitals without medical care. Ironically the more the government is involved, the more even the most resourceful assisted-living facilities are pushed toward becoming glorified nursing homes. Medicaid sets the standard by paying enormous attention to medical interventions and keeping track of bedsores while ignoring quality of life. There are rules and regulations to cover every problematic event but none have been developed for measuring the misery quotient. Ageism keeps expectations low and is used to justify a focus mainly on health and safety. The reverse is needed, a focus on good quality of life consistent with the best health and safety outcomes.

The Basics of Quality Care

There is always a tension between safety and choice. Entering a care facility means giving up a lot of things, but a meaningful personal life should not be one of them. It can be challenging to find something that looks like ordinary life in a nursing home or AD facility. An individual's routine is surrendered to the facility's routine. Creative solutions for meeting needs without disconnecting a person from an active and vital life are not always sought and are often resoundingly rejected when recommended by a resident, family, or even an innovative staff. Given the option, what kind of facility do older people want? What do you want? That few researchers have bothered to ask this question probably does not surprise you. However, you may be taken aback to learn that, despite many older people's insistence that they would rather die than enter a care facility, residents reveal a generally high level of satisfaction.

Routines versus Flexibility

More often than not, control and choice of aspects of daily life are listed as being of primary importance to those facing living in a care facility. The opportunity to come and go, to leave the building and interact with others, is highly valued. Privacy is also at the top of most people's list—especially having one's own room and bath. In fact a majority of people report they would rather have a small space that is theirs alone than share a larger area. There is no reason to believe that these basic desires change as a person becomes more incapacitated.

Activities

Independent- and assisted-living facilities have all the options that are available to the general population when considering outings and arranging events that enrich life or are just plain fun. When ageist stereotypes are not at play, choices are endless. The resulting social interaction can bring new life to individuals who may have had fewer opportunities for getting out when living on their own. My aunt's facility offers daily trips to Wal-Mart and the grocery store, with only a rare outing that is more adventuresome—like a museum or a flower show. Activities that take residents into the world should also be open to the more incapacitated of the Alzheimer's wing. Anyone who has been on such a trip recognizes the pleasure and boost to the spirit an appropriately planned outing brings—even when it is remembered only during the experience. Living in the now is a goal for which we all need to strive and where joy can be found.

Daily activities for those unable to structure their own day are far superior and more reassuring than biding time waiting for the next meal. The most progressive care involves both group and individual activities. It's a good sign when a facility is sensitive to a person's background and former interests. On a recent visit to an AD facility, I saw a resident who had received a collection of rocks when it was discovered he was a geologist. He responded, "I've looked at rocks all my life, what I miss is my desk." The staff delivered an office desk to his room, and now he happily busies himself "at work" for a portion of each day. The same facility offers gardening to any resident and has made sure the woman whose love of gardening was a big part of her life has what she needs to continue her special interest.

Balloon volleyball for those in wheelchairs, various crafts, and even cooking, all have their place as long as they are not presented as means of filling time rather than with the expectation of creating intimacy and connection with others. A sensitive staff remains in tune with the changing mental and physical abilities of each individual. The ability to open doors and go outside, to enjoy a garden or an interesting patio, just to take a walk alone with unobtrusive safety measures in place give even the most cognitively impaired a sense of freedom and control.

Like most people, Mother enjoyed participating in everyday routines whether she was home or in a care facility. She liked setting the table or folding laundry, things she had often done in her past. The repetition of such activities provides structure, routine, and success. Reminiscing through scrapbooks, music, and old movies can be fun. My effort to keep Mother oriented with scrapbooks, however, was a total failure. I spent hours putting together a pictorial history of her family and another of times shared with her grandchildren and us. An apt historian in her younger days, she found my efforts completely boring. Several attempts to get her involved ended with the plaintive cry, reminiscent of a kid doing homework, "Can I go now?" As soon as I left, she would hide her scrapbooks. I was never sure whether it was for safekeeping or if she wanted to avoid what she saw as a mind-numbing activity.

Some homes recognize the value of pets. While dogs are the most interactive, cats and birds are sometimes easier to have on the property. Mother was never fond of dogs, but I would arrange to occasionally take my dog on our visits because it provided so much pleasure to so many residents. Even more fun are visits from children. There are a few facilities that house both elders and daycare for young children—a life-affirming combination for both.

Daily routines like bedtime and bath time are far from what individuals are likely to have experienced when they lived in their own homes. Many facilities expect residents to go to bed following supper. This often results in increased night wandering and early rising. So residents are given sleep medications, which create more problems. One concerned facility succeeded in getting 90 percent of the residents off nighttime sleep medications by providing stimulating fun and lively evening entertainment. Residents went to bed around 10:00 P.M. and slept through the night. That level of concern and sensitivity to creating normalcy should be looked for when deciding on where you or a loved one might spend his or her final years.

The Facility and the Staff

The success of promoting independence and not doing for residents what they can do for themselves, while helping them maintain a connection with life, depends on two things. First, there is an identifiable program or philosophy under which curriculums are designed and instituted. Second, there is a staff that genuinely cares about their residents, supports all programs and the philosophy behind them, and is trained regularly in the proclaimed agenda. A staff that turns over frequently is a poor indication that the focus will be on quality care. Only respected and fairly treated personnel can be expected to extend courtesy to those they care for. It is interesting to note that, while we may decry the low educational level of workers in such facilities, in many cases they are from cultures that place great value on older people. While American society sees their jobs as low on the totem pole, they are likely to view their responsibilities as having significance and worth, thus finding personal value and esteem by carrying out their responsibilities well.

Staff must be friendly, respectful, and optimistic—finding humor in the spontaneity of life. They must call the residents by name and make eye contact with them. Patience, flexibility, and a nonjudgmental attitude are reinforced when an effort has been made to learn the life stories of residents and use cues from them as guides for effective interventions. Such characteristics as competency, kindness, reliability, and trustworthiness are inevitably listed in surveys as important to the individual. People also want assurance that their concerns and desires will be taken seriously. A comprehensive approach to the use of medication, which encompasses an understanding that it is not the solution for all problems, should be spelled out in a care facility's philosophy. And, finally, the cleanliness and cheerfulness of a place and how it smells tell a lot about the kind of place it is.

Dealing with Behavior

Once I was told I had twenty-four hours to find a new place for Mother. This points out the importance of knowing the policy and circumstances under which someone can be asked to leave a care facility. An ombudsman for seniors later informed me that for Mother's offence she could not be forced out in less than thirty days. The criteria involved whether she was an immediate and ongoing danger to herself or others. She was to be ousted because a very impatient (and poorly trained) nurse inevitably managed to push what few buttons Mother had left. When asked by a new and hastily placed administrator what he could do to ensure that everything would run smoothly, Mother's nemesis did not have to be asked twice.

Their interactions had come to resemble a bullfight. Instead of a cape, the Nurse Toreador waved her med cart tantalizingly in front of the Mary Jo bull. "Get out of the way, Mary Jo," she would order. Mother would look slightly off to the side, as if she were planning to cooperate and then finesse a turn that would place her even more squarely in front of the cart. Nurse Toreador would try to stare her down, repeating a little louder, "I said, get out of the way!" The cart, like the cape, would be swished menacingly in front of Mary Jo, who had by then transformed into "raging bull." With eyes blazing she would muster all her strength and charge. Medicine would bounce out of their neatly assigned cups after which Nurse Toreador went in for the kill. That Mother, like her counterpart in the ring, was acting on sheer protective instinct did not matter. That she was unable to comprehend what was being asked of her or given time and help to comply were not considered.

When the new administrator called, he probably thought his request was simple enough, but my response was anything but. The first thing out of my mouth was a wail that echoed the cumulative effect of twenty-three years spent perilously pushing Mother on a twisting uphill road. I was almost at the top when his decree sent me tumbling down a ravine from which I would again have to fight to get both of us back on level ground. Another move would be terribly disruptive for my mother. For me, it would entail a frantic and probably futile scramble to find a place that could provide what her special needs required. The most realistic option was more than an hour away through a winding canyon road. I screamed and sobbed at the same time, "What do you mean I have twenty-four hours to move Mother? Don't you know I have exhausted all possibilities in our area? Do you know how disruptive this will be to her? How can you do this? Don't you understand—you are it; there is no option."

My pleas would have made more sense if his facility met the needs of a patient in the last stages of Alzheimer's. It was not where she needed to be, but it was what was available, and the nurses and staff had been cooperative in adapting to her needs—at least all but one. They had let her fold towels and join them in their break room, and she was able to roam in the rose garden.

The voice on the phone no longer sounded firm and in charge. The words, "I'll get back to you," stumbled out. A few hours later the admitting nurse called to say, "This is all a misunderstanding! We love Mary Jo; we are delighted to have her stay."

I was numb and unconvinced. "What if I get another call to move her tomorrow? I don't have the reserve to go through this again," I contended. I was reassured that the powers that be had experienced a remarkable conversion and that I was not to worry. As it turned out, Mother's bullfighting days were limited. Within a few months she became less mobile and after being bedridden for three weeks passed away in that same facility.

Somewhere along the road of Mother's illness I gave up trying to keep her oriented to the world as I knew it and entered her world. Life became much easier. Today there is a school of thought that redefines dementia to include a social definition that suggests it is an alternative but acceptable reality.[6] Behavior problems are considered as potentially making sense if seen from the perspective of the person with AD. In the past, as Nurse Toreador demonstrated, problems were automatically assumed to be bad behavior. It has taken a while for conduct to be looked at as a means of communication when needs cannot be expressed in the usual way. Mother's disease process and her past coping devices did not make her a pussycat, and it is estimated that at least 90 percent of persons diagnosed with dementia will have some behavior problems. In fact it is the most common reason for placement in a care facility. When evaluating a facility, ask how disruptive behavior is handled.

Problems can involve aggression, agitation, sleep disturbance, withdrawal, delusions, hallucinations, or misperception. Sometimes these behaviors are the result of progressive damage within the brain. Frequently they stem from medication problems. Troubles with hearing, sight, delirium, constipation, dehydration, infection, fatigue, and depression are also contributors. Undetected illness and physical discomfort should all be considered. Even the environment, like too much clutter, the overstimulation of a new place, or tasks that are too complicated can lead to outbursts. And always there is the possibility that efforts at communication have failed.

The British Alzheimer's Society announced in 2002 that it is launching a major research project to look at alternatives to the widespread use of tranquilizers to sedate people whose behavior is bad. While straitjackets are no longer used, such drugs are for all intents and purposes chemical straitjackets administered for their sedating side effect. It is easier to give a patient drugs than to do an evaluation, especially when staffing is short. While the short-term effect may be positive, if only for the facility, the side effects of excessive sedation can lead to increased confusion, tremors, and falls.

Good Food

When visiting my aunt at her assisted-living facility, our intention was to frequently eat in her dining room. We expected to at least have breakfast there. After three days, the mere thought of another undercooked egg, cold piece of toast, or a prune floating in a nondescript dish got us off to an early start searching for new and tastier options. While the food was aesthetically unappetizing and tasteless, it was undoubtedly lacking in nutritional value as well. Large-scale catering reduces nutrients that can be destroyed under heating lights or that are water-soluble. Living in a care facility puts you at risk for deficiency for a number of micronutrients including vitamin C, D, the B complex, and iron. Combined with the lack of exposure residents have to sunlight, vitamin D is commonly depleted.

Quality fish is needed as a source of essential fatty acids. I didn't see any "quality" fish at my aunt's facility. Fresh fruit can improve healing of pressure sores because it contains micronutrients that are not found in vitamin pills. Antioxidants, as I have noted in chapter 4, are vital for the prevention of many diseases, including AD, arthritis, cataracts, and heart disease. When an elderly person who lives in a care facility becomes sick, the likelihood of becoming severely malnourished is significantly increased, because the sick person tends not to eat well and the food he does eat is so devoid of healthful ingredients.

Deciding on Care Options

The problem with AD is that the downward course of the disease means that needs are apt to change rapidly. My discussion has focused on the use of a care facility, because moving into a care facility is often the most traumatic step an individual or family must take. But there are other options, especially in the early stages. The most common alternative is hiring someone to assist with care. This may prolong the time the loved one can stay at home. When you or a person you care for gets lost while walking or driving, forgets to turn off the oven, leaves the water on, or fails to secure the house at night or when going out, the option of hiring an in-home aide should be considered. If appearance and hygiene have deteriorated, meals are sporadic or poor, and there is doubt about the person's ability to handle an emergency, he should not be left to manage alone. Anyone who is losing track of bill paying or mishandling banking, who is having trouble buying groceries, let alone storing and cooking food correctly, and is not taking medication as scheduled is definitely in need of help.

While there are always job placement services advertised in the newspaper, on community bulletin boards, in churches, or at colleges, workers hired through them are not screened and may not be qualified. In some communities there are home care registries that assess needs and refer appropriate workers. You must choose and manage anyone you hire from their service. Home care agencies make life easier by providing and managing bonded employees, but you still must withhold social security payments, keep adequate records, and pay workman's compensation.

The Alzheimer's Association has phone numbers for adult day care or respite programs in your area. Adult day programs offer a break for the person with dementia and for anyone who is helping with his care. The concept is similar to that of day care for children but appropriately designed for adults. More will be said about respite care in chapter 9.

It is not unusual for care in the afflicted person's home to be a stopgap measure that eventually proves unworkable. At that point, the person is often moved into a relative's home. Anyone who feels at a loss to know how to best handle such a situation should remember that even social workers who have spent years learning how to make life rich for someone with AD don't have all the answers. When there are questions, take a trip to the library, local bookstore, or the computer and you will find excellent sources that address safety concerns and behavior problems. Don't assume that because you know this person well, you will automatically have the answers.

If you have been diagnosed with AD and plan to move in with your son or daughter, be proactive and provide him or her with a list of resources. Unfortunately most decisions on housing are made in crisis. Once you are sick or under stress, a good explanation of what you want may be difficult to express. Then it may be your family who decides for you, not knowing your desires.

Deciding what to do is always a conflicted decision. Internal storms within families can wash over dams that have kept them in check for years. Intake personnel at assisted-living and dementia units have horror stories of families who drop the resident off at the door and are never seen again. Others fuss and complain as the resident settles in and then seem to forget their loved one is there. Still others are never convinced the facility or the care measure up to their or their loved one's standards.

It's always best if we can make our own decision about entering a care facility. That means we can't wait for the crisis. Seeing the turmoil caused when a relative had to enter a nursing home after a severe illness, friends of mine determined they did not want to put their daughter in the difficult position of making the dreaded decision and complex arrangements. Without hesitation they listed their house with a real estate agent and within eight weeks had relocated to an assisted-living facility clear across the state.

A Model That Works

David Troxel is the author of two books, *Best Friend's Approach to Alzheimer's Care* and *Best Friend's Staff*. Caregivers and care facilities nationwide are adopting his concept of using a friendship model to undergird Alzheimer's care.[7] How does the concept of friendship provide a model for good AD treatment? Think about your best friend. He or she knows your history and understands your quirky personality but is still willing to do things with you. At the heart of any friendship is the ability to communicate—often nonverbally. Friends build each other up; they laugh together and sometimes at each other. Friends are equals, demonstrating love and affection despite societal barriers.

Within the framework of a care facility, this means that if the staff is to be my friend, they must take the time to know who I am. I am known when effort is spent on activities, chores, and special occasions that tie into my skills and interests. Troxel insists that every person who works at a care facility, from janitor to CEO, should adopt a "best friend" with whom he or she will spend one hour per week. The facility provides to the best friend and other staff extensive background information, likes and dislikes, and other pertinent matters. The information is updated regularly. The worker acts as a true friend because time is spent listening to what is meaningful to the resident. He or she becomes his cheerleader and sometimes his protector, spending time learning how best to deal with him, preserving his dignity, and allowing him to save face. The staff member is a friend who gives attention, affection, and respect, despite the resident's baggage, traditions, or religion.

The friendship concept for care works for patient and staff. It is a good program with its philosophy outlined in the "Alzheimer's Disease Bill of Rights."[8] Every person diagnosed with Alzheimer's disease or a related disorder deserves:

- To be informed of his diagnosis
- To have appropriate, ongoing medical care
- To be productive in work and play as long as possible
- To be treated like an adult, not a child
- To have expressed feelings taken seriously
- To be free from psychotropic medications if at all possible
- To live in a safe, structured, and predictable environment
- To enjoy meaningful activities to fill each day
- To be out-of-doors on a regular basis
- To have physical contact, including hugging, caressing, and hand-holding
- To be with persons who know his life story, including cultural and religious traditions
- To be cared for by individuals well trained in dementia care

Thoughts on the Twilight Journey

I am pleased to report that the despair I felt so long ago does not occupy me today. So much has been learned since the days when I struggled to find an appropriate setting for Mother. Despite my good intentions, the promises of cure, safety, or dignity were inevitably empty, and my choices resulted in a less than desirable quality of life for her. Since Mother's death, new facilities have managed to better assess the needs and put into operation much more realistic and hopeful settings. If nothing else does it, hope for the future lies in sheer numbers. When seniors outnumber teenagers, our society will shift its priorities. This realignment is already true in Italy.

There is no easy way to determine the best situation for every individual or family facing Alzheimer's. Finding a place that fulfills individual sensitivities, even educating oneself on options and what kind of care is needed are best decided over time. Few people do the work necessary to smooth the way. You may protest that spending the time to investigate alternatives and doing the soul searching necessary to determine a plan is a waste of time if you never need to use it. But the numbers indicate that someone you are close to will need advice and benefit from your expertise sometime in the future. We are our brothers' and sisters' keepers.

Today I celebrate the fact that Alzheimer's is considered a treatable disease and that there are more options available than when my mother needed care. There are services that enable an individual with AD to stay at home longer, providing more years of laughter, love, and learning. There is an ever-increasing diversity in care facilities, many with a graduated care plan that eliminates the necessity of several moves.

I know now that I will not go from a diagnosis to a nursing home. There are many stops along the way. I do, however, remain convinced that the itinerary for my own twilight journey must be clearly mapped before crisis is the driving force. I am simultaneously dreaming about trips to dude ranches, the seashore, and "hup—hup—hupping" around the vineyards with grandchildren for many more years. I am working hard to physically and mentally stay in good enough shape to get on a horse, crawl over a fence, read a book, and tag along with the next generation! I'm daring to dream two trips with paths that cross much more than I once anticipated. If I never take the route to a care facility, I will still have learned from the planning how to more fully savor the road remaining.

Brain Boosters

- Clarify your desires should you need to leave your home for care elsewhere.
- Discuss living with family before it becomes a necessity.
- Maximize your mental and physical health.
- Remain flexible. It is a sign of good health.
- Be realistic about your ability to remain independent.

Nine

Bless the Daughters

We are all in the gutter, but some of us are looking at stars.

Oscar Wilde

The Christmas Present

A few years after Mother's marriage to Dr. Stirrat, our family had long passed the stage when anyone needed another pair of slippers or a new robe for Christmas. My efforts at finding a replacement for the red sweater, the one Mother would go to her grave thinking I had stolen, were over. We had no choice except to be creative. Joe had no trouble deciding what to do in lieu of gifts; he would take our teenage son, Mother's husband (Dr. Stirrat), and his physician dad to a hockey game in Los Angeles. To make it special he appealed to a friend who could provide tickets for the team owner's box. The experience was a thrill for each of them—a once-in-a-lifetime moment that would be replayed and perhaps get better with the retelling.

I decided to give our young teenage daughter, Mother, and my mother-in-law, Frances, a day at a spa. The guys could root and rout all they wanted—we would relax! Reservations were made at Elizabeth Arden's Red Door Spa. For me, the thought of a day of pure pampering was a great Christmas present. My days were hectic and stressed. I was increasingly concerned about Mother's condition. Two teenagers in the home and two professional careers rounded out a lifestyle that kept all of us busy. A day of doing nothing but enjoy coddling was the kind of gift I needed. Sharing it with my family and especially my daughter, who was steeling herself for her first massage, was going to make it a day to remember—and it was, just not in the way I imagined.

Getting Mother to remember changes in her morning routine had begun to be a problem, so I made sure I called early to remind her that I would be picking her up for our special day. Then we were on our way, heading down the eight-lane Southern California freeway to Rodeo Drive in Beverly Hills and "movie star" treatment.

Relations between Frances and my mother were cordial despite some early discord and Frances's fear that Mother's problems with memory might somehow stray her way. She knew they couldn't, but Mother's forgetfulness (and I think her efforts to save face and cover up her "glitches") made Frances uncomfortable. One can hardly blame her. Her own brother had died quickly from early-onset AD.

We were no more than twenty minutes from home when Mother began to share that she had received a phone call that very morning telling her that I had been working behind her back to take her farm. Perhaps my early call had triggered what is called a misattribution, and she had combined a real event with details that were not accurate.

Whatever had set Mother off, she was adamant. Nothing any of us said or did could distract her. "This person clearly cares for me," she insisted.

I countered, "Mother, I'm not trying to take what is yours. Just who is this person anyway?"

"It's somebody that is sweet and is trying to warn me. They didn't say their name," she replied.

"But Mother, if someone really cares about you, why wouldn't they say who they were?" I asked.

"They've called before. They care about me. They are trying to warn me that Mary Ann is trying to take everything," she replied, becoming more animated and angry.

Frances could stand it no more. "Mary Jo, you mean you would trust an anonymous voice over the phone rather than your own daughter?"

I was not prepared for her reply. "Yes," she shot back without a moment's hesitation.

My foot hit the gas and the speedometer hit ninety. The car began to wobble. My daughter's eyes got very big, and Frances pleaded from the backseat, "Let's just go back. Let's just go home."

My immediate response was anger flamed with hurt. I struggled to gain some control and to decide what to do. "No," I insisted, tears pouring down my face, "we are *going* to the spa."

"Well, at least slow down" was the plaintive request from an equally shaken Frances.

Mother sat quietly, directly behind me. I caught glimpses of her in the mirror. Her jaw was set and it was clear she believed everything she had just said. That moment registered as one of the most painful in my twilight journey with Mother. It was made so by the fact that my daughter heard it all. What must her young mind be thinking? How could I explain something that made no sense to me? Mother's insistence that the phone calls had occurred and that someone out there loved her and was looking out for her was so convincing it was hard not to believe her. I felt helpless. In my mind I ran through a list of anyone who might be calling. I questioned any financial decisions that had been made. Had I inadvertently done something that was viewed as unethical or greedy?

Oblivious to the emotional bomb she had just detonated, Mother mumbled, more to herself than us, "I think it's Sondra Kay. She is such a sweet girl. I think it's her." Sondra Kay was my cousin, my father's sister's only daughter. I had not seen her since I was a child and I was sure neither had Mother. I could not say another word. My hands gripped the steering wheel and every muscle throughout my body was on high alert. I turned on the radio and spent the next fifty miles silently filtering through the thoughts exploding in my head.

The juxtaposition of a spa day and hearing that your mother's opinion of you lay somewhere between a bank robber and a sociopath might have been funny if I had been able to muster up the courage to laugh. As we walked through that big red door and entered the spa, I fully expected my mother, sensing a new audience, to begin again. "Hi," she would say. "This is my daughter. This day at the spa is a mere ruse to cover up the fact that she is stealing everything I have. I'm fortunate, though. Someone else *truly* cares for me and is letting me know what is really going on."

I need not have worried. Mother docilely followed her masseuse, had her fingernails painted, ate her spa lunch, and had her hair done. At the end of the day, she felt relaxed and refreshed and enthusiastically reported what a great day it had been—hadn't I enjoyed it too? she asked.

I do not know how Malika and Frances really felt. They said the day had been wonderful and the treatments relaxing. As for me, all the primping and pounding had not made a dent in the shell that had formed around me. It was not helpful that the masseuse had given me an account of every knotted part of my body. "Do you not understand the value of breathing?" she asked. "Surely you realize that your shoulders are not supposed to be by your ears." She sighed, clicked her tongue, and issued more sanguine diatribes as she discovered some new area of my body that could sue me for neglect. Her comments proved as regular and predictable as the Southern California traffic reports.

The makeup artist determined I needed color; the hairdresser, a short bob to help me look perky. I'm sure they all went home with headaches realizing that, despite all their efforts, I emerged relatively unmoved and as tightly wound as when I walked through that red door six hours earlier.

Our drive home was mellow; my three passengers appeared lulled by the rhythm of the road. I managed to get us home safely—within the speed limit.

There was a second time when Mother expressed an opinion of me that had the potential, if not for God's grace, to be my undoing. In my profession as a therapist, I was required to keep my skills honed and meet state licensing requirements through continuing education classes and seminars. On one occasion, years before the incident on the way to the spa, I attended a retreat called "Healing the Mother Void" at a Vineyard church. I went as an observer, expecting only to fulfill my licensing requirements. I soon discovered, however, that if I didn't participate, I would have to leave.

During the day a wonderful woman guitarist, whose repertoire consisted mostly of using her melodious voice to sing Scripture, set the mood. At the retreat's culmination, with Psalm 139 being sung softly in the background, we were to imagine ourselves on the day of our birth—actually visualizing being born. In the process, I saw myself poised to leave the birth canal but with no one present to catch me. The realization that I was not wanted washed over me. As you might expect, it filled me with the most profound sense of sadness. And then a figure appeared, reached out his hands, tenderly brought me into this world, and held me protectively in his arms. "I wanted you," God said. In an instant my feelings of abandonment evaporated as my need for perfect parental love was met. The imagery of God attending my birth provided reassurance that my life had meaning and purpose. I was wanted.

For you created my inmost being; you knit me together in my mother's womb. I praise you because I am fearfully and wonderfully made; your works are wonderful, I know that full well. My frame was not hidden from you when I was made in the secret place. When I was woven together in the depths of the earth, your eyes saw my unformed body. All the days ordained for me were written in your book before one of them came to be.

Psalm 139:13–16

As I contemplated and prayed about such a profound revelation, I came to terms with my father's desire for a boy and my mother's motivation to fulfill her wifely duty and produce a child for her new husband. I acknowledged that despite their expectations, my parents genuinely loved me. And I accepted God's love for me, always difficult for a perfectionist who is convinced she will not measure up. It would be years later, however, before I would realize everything this experience was to mean.

I had flown to Canada because Dr. Stirrat had been admitted to the hospital with a unique form of leukemia prevalent among pathologists, triggered by years of working around formaldehyde. He was not expected to recover. One day on the way to the hospital, we stopped for gas. I sat behind Mother in the backseat of Dr. Stirrat's lovely vintage auto while his daughter, Marjorie Anne, filled the tank. Mother was humming softly and for some reason I was prompted to ask her why she had risked marrying three men who drank heavily. The only thing I remember after that was her saying, "I never wanted another baby."

I swallowed hard and managed to ask, "Why did you decide to have Mary Ann?"

"Oh, I didn't want to," she said. "I did everything I could to miscarry—I even beat on my stomach."

Now, as you have probably surmised, I have never had a problem crying. This time, however, not a tear was shed. It was as if we were talking about someone else. I sat there in the Canadian cold and thought what an awful but wonderful thing had just happened. My own mother had revealed something that I never imagined and that no child would ever want to hear. But I had simultaneously been flooded with the same imagery I had seen years before. There was the figure, reaching out for me, gathering me tightly to his chest. God had known this moment would come. He had prepared me for it. My awareness of his grace was palpable and his abundant love resulted in that moment being more miraculous than sad. Mother's words were mere confirmation of what I already knew.

There was no reason to fall apart; it had been taken care of. My life had meaning and purpose. I was wanted.

Marjorie Anne popped back in the car, and I was left with my thoughts. Nothing had changed but perspective. After that, the three of us did what we could to provide comfort and express love to husband, father, and stepfather.

After Dr. Stirrat's death, I prepared myself for the task of taking Mother back to California. Would she go with me? Would she remember that Dr. Stirrat had died? What would I tell her about her new apartment? Should I tell her? Would she grieve? Just what did she understand? There was much to think about.

Who Will Be There for Us?

For any of you who have shouldered the responsibility of caring for a parent or loved one, you know that it is never easy—even if done with a willing heart. Something akin to a father's anxiety over a daughter's first date lies just under the surface. Are you doing enough? Are you doing it right? Is there a better way? Are you really helping or are you getting in the way? Should you let go or hold on tighter? The strain of this care has led some of our friends to talk about "the little red pill," something they fantasize will speed their demise and ensure that no one will be placed in a position of seeing that they get to the bathroom on time or having to play airplane to get them to eat their carrots. Such is the concern about end-of-life care. It is not just getting feeble that is the fear; it is getting feeble and needing help.

Options are not plentiful, but needs are. By age eighty-five, 50 percent of the elderly require daily personal care. A survey of Baby Boomers conducted in 1999 revealed that, although 40 percent worried they would run out of money after they retired, 75 percent had not set up any type of retirement plan and, of course, had no plan for long-term care. It is estimated that the cost of a nursing facility ranges from forty to eighty thousand dollars annually. By the year 2030, if the rate increase continues, it will top ninety-seven thousand dollars per year. Medicare, supplemental insurance, or major health insurance provided by most employers does not necessarily cover long-term care. The question of who will care for us is complicated by the fact that we will probably live six to fifteen years longer than our parents.

The prospect of care provided by family is equally bleak. With the changes in family structure (divorce, cohabitation, remarriage, and more never-marrieds), the reserve of children available to care for aging parents is shrinking. There are more people without children than at any other time in our nation's history—19 percent (almost one-fifth) of women in the United States in their forties are childless. While people living now average 2.5 living biological children, by 2030 that figure will drop to 1.5. The number of grandchildren will be reduced from 4 to 2.5. We might expect that stepchildren would provide some care, but research does not hold out much hope. Stepkids may be willing to send you tickets to a concert, but they are less likely to be there when you need help cleaning up after soiling yourself. Divorce and blended families tend to weaken ties between generations, especially between a dad and his children. It has also been shown that when children have several sets of grandparents, they have less commitment and/or sense of obligation to the extended family.

While 60 percent of U.S. citizens expect to be a caregiver—the one responsible for meeting the needs of a relative or parent, perhaps in light of the cost of placement outside the home or hiring someone to come to the home—in most situations it is a daughter, or at least a woman, who takes on the role. Seventy-five percent of caregivers are women. It is estimated that fifty million Baby Boomers will enter menopause in the next few years (4,900 per day), the group most likely to be caregivers of elderly parents. One-quarter of these women are simultaneously caring for teens and elders (and in some cases toddlers), in the role of primary caregiver. Currently it is estimated that there are twenty-five million caregivers in the United States, accounting for more than 23 percent of American households. And the demand for caregivers is not going to lessen.

As people age, almost all—85 percent—want to stay in their own home, according to a 1999 survey conducted by the American Association of Retired Persons (AARP). The expense of care and the toll on women in particular translate into a serious societal problem.

Life as a Caregiver

Caregiving is not a one-way street to misery. There are aspects of it that are positive and enjoyable, despite the emotional ups and downs. When Mother died, I missed her. I celebrated the whole, restored body she had and her renewed mind, but I longed for her presence. The unrelenting responsibility for over twenty years and the constant second-guessing of what the best care might be had been part of our relationship, not its totality. Those who seek to avoid caring for a loved one risk missing an experience that has the potential to heal, teach, and satisfy.

It should be noted that caregiving is not the exclusive domain of women. While females take on the role more readily than males, they are not inherently better at it. Sometimes the choice is made by default when a husband or brother seems hesitant to assume care. He should be encouraged and allowed to be involved so that his life is meaningfully impacted in ways never imagined before the experience. Today for instance most men would resent being left out of bonding and nurturing opportunities with their children. They should be equally upset if prevented from providing personal care for aging parents or other loved ones. It is incorrect to view this role as inappropriate for males or beyond their abilities.

Men or women who find meaning in their responsibilities grow emotionally and spiritually. The key to coping has much to do with being able to discover the positives in the negatives. The ability of a caregiver to see alternatives, to open a new door when an old one is closed, provides impetus to continue doing what needs to be done. In other words, remaining hopeful despite the circumstances

preserves mind and mindfulness. Often the ability to hope is connected to faith.

By contrast, hopelessness results in powerlessness and a sense of
not being in control. Feelings of being swept along by each turn of
life's events leads to despair. Such a person is convinced that nothing can be done to make the situation better—or more tolerable.
Inability to see alternatives—the sense of being trapped—results
in nothing changing. If change is risked, it is not pursued with
hope. It is rather like the bottle thrown into the sea containing a
note pleading for rescue that immediately sinks to the bottom. The
despair that follows makes matters worse.

Eighty percent of caregivers report high levels of stress and
stress-related illness. Fifty percent acknowledge being depressed.
A caregiver without hope suffers intensified stress and increases his
or her chance of mental and physical illness—and premature death.
Those most susceptible to a negative experience are individuals who
struggle to cope with unresolved relationship changes and losses.
My mother is a good example. Undeniably, her years of caring for
her mother, whose love she sought as payback, right on the heels
of grieving the death of her husband contributed to her own final
illness. A combination of helplessness and hopelessness sets up a
negative emotional spiral that makes it difficult for a caregiver to
reach out to others for support—or even to God.

The Problem Is Remembering

I was my mother's caregiver when she lived on her own and after
she moved into a care facility. The role of caregiver must change,
depending on the setting and the disease progression. I spent years
not understanding what was happening. I assumed Mother suffered
from Alzheimer's, but no one confirmed it. For a while I thought
she was depressed and that being nurtured under the wing of my
husband and me, along with being in the company of her grandchildren, would make her better. The doctors at UCLA said she
suffered from a few small strokes. Dr. Stirrat refused to consider

AD. Today an MRI or PET scan in combination with laboratory and memory tests would have defined with 90 percent accuracy what was going on.

Knowing would have made a difference. We might have spoken more openly about what was happening. Together we could have faced the reality and made long-range plans. I think Mother would have been relieved to know that she was correct when she insisted, "Something is wrong with my brain." Sadly, even today the majority of AD patients are still not diagnosed until the disease has progressed to a stage when reasoning and problem-solving abilities are affected. Until a diagnosis, many family members will be in denial, with acceptance of the reality occurring one step at a time.

When my husband and I began to recognize what we thought were clear flags signaling AD in his mother, Frances, his older sister still believed all was fine. Our experience with Mother and the fact that we saw Frances on a regular basis made for different conclusions about the meaning and significance of subtle changes. As her symptoms worsened and she moved closer to her daughters, they acknowledged reluctantly that something out of the ordinary was going on.

It is not unusual for a crisis to occur before families finally talk and come to an agreement. Even when dementia is acknowledged, each family member is likely to see the consequences of that admission differently. For all, the guiding principle of any future decisions should be how do we make the AD person's life better? This is the basic tenet on which family members can agree.

No family member should be excluded from a family meeting, even if that person feels he or she has little to offer. With some creativity a task can be found for each member. One person may handle finances, while another researches medication, and still another takes responsibility for finding a care facility or at-home options. Not everyone is suited for hands-on, day-by-day care, although all should be willing to provide relief as needed. There are no exclusions from the business of supporting the primary caregiver, the one who has the most direct responsibility. Ideally the broader and longer the view the family takes, the better the overall plan. But looking long term and facing what is coming is not easy to do. Most families or individuals make decisions about their loved one in increments, and, only when pressed, will they make the next decision.

With doctors' growing confidence in making a diagnosis of Alzheimer's disease, more people are aware of what they face. A very early diagnosis may mean years will go by with few adjustments other than coming to terms with a progressive disease. This was true of Mother. Protracted but subtle deterioration enabled her to continue to live independently and limit our intervention to help with finances and medical oversight, while she participated in family activities and trips.

It must be remembered that this disease is not about intelligence; it is about remembering. People with AD are not suddenly stupid. No matter what the stage of the disease, we must encourage and allow the person to do for herself whatever she can.

Mild-Stage AD

While maintaining a delicate balance between overprotection and independence, we as caregivers must resist the temptation to take over the AD victim's life. Still, concerns for safety and well-being will require intervention. Early on, our loved one will mourn and may resent the restraint of her independence, but this should not deter us from keeping an eye on her comings and goings.

If the person with AD drives, she must be careful to stick to familiar routes and keep maps and notes for orientation. Some new cars have a Global Satellite Positioning device that, with the push of a button, will locate the driver and supply directions home or even to the nearest gas station, restaurant, or police station. A connection is made directly to an operator who can assess the situation, has emergency contacts on file, and is available to send help and make phone calls, as the situation requires. It is the best of "big brother" and a perfect solution for a person with early AD who wishes to extend his or her independence.

As the disease progresses, the AD person's driving often becomes a nightmare for friends and relatives and getting the keys away from an impaired driver sometimes requires a covert operation. When the problem is addressed early, a sense of personal control is maintained when the diagnosed person, understanding the danger, voluntarily surrenders her keys. California law requires that physicians who make a diagnosis of dementia report their findings to the Department of Health Services, which in turn informs the Department of Motor Vehicles. Your state may have similar requirements.

When an early-stage patient is open with acquaintances about her diagnosis, there are many advantages. Honesty enables her to relax and feel less stressed about memory deficits. There is no need to try to cover up. The biggest bonus lies in the fact that paranoia is reduced because friends and family do not have to work behind the person's back to resolve problems or safety issues. Instead, they can openly keep an eye out and be helpful.

Early-stage support groups for patients and those caring for them can be immensely beneficial. While no such groups existed when Mother and I were struggling to figure out what was happening and what to do, I remember how much my aunt's collaboration meant to me when she happened to be visiting and I faced moving Mother to another facility. Having her share in the decision making and knowing I had her support made a difficult decision less so and easier to bear than those I had made alone.

Moderate-Stage AD

It is a different story when an AD person's function diminishes to the moderate stage. Looking back, I believe Mother was already at this level when she married Dr. Stirrat. For seven years his loving care and their travels kept me from having to make a decision about someone living with her, bringing her home to live with us, or moving her into a care facility. The extent of her dementia the last year of their life together must have made his days extremely difficult, especially since he was suffering from his own medical problems. But like the majority of caregivers, he never complained and did not ask for help as they shuttled every six months between California and Alberta, Canada.

Moderate-stage AD necessitates changes in the environment and supervision, and it increases safety concerns—especially if the individual is to remain at home. Mother once left her toaster oven on for over a day. I discovered it just before the cabinet above began to burn. The temperature of her hot water was a concern due to the sensory loss that often accompanies AD, so we lowered the thermostat on her hot water heater.

Mail began to pile up or turn up in the most unlikely places. I have already mentioned the proliferation of notes she wrote to herself. I tried to help by giving her every conceivable variety of calendar—big, little, paper, magnetic. She was not interested in any of them. But she was pleased when we installed an enormous bulletin board in her bedroom on which she pinned pictures of the family, friends, and grandchildren. She saw it as decorative; my motive was to keep her oriented. Mother reached a point when she was no longer able to pick the kids up at school. She could find our home from her condo because it was a straight route, but stopping by the schools along the way became too confusing and too difficult for her to remember.

At the assisted-living facility, we made sure her sliding door could not be opened. We eliminated throw rugs and maintained clear pathways to lessen the chance of a fall. There were safety grab bars in appropriate places, and we added nightlights and increased the daytime lighting. We paid for an aide to help Mother dress and bring her medication each day. We could no longer trust that she would remember it and feared she might take her allotted dose several times. Although her room had a kitchenette, we found we had to remove the knobs to her stove. Since Mother never liked to cook, she loved the idea.

Unlike the era during which Mother was ill, there are now wonderful books brimming with information to improve the life of a person with AD and that of her caregiver. The most frequent suggestion is the need to simplify both the environment and life in general. You have probably done it before. It is the same principle you adopted when you had your first baby and for safety and sanity cleared the decks, literally and figuratively, of anything extraneous. Despite my protestations over the bleakness of the hospital-like settings where Mother stayed, their simplicity made daily decisions easier for her.

When we were trying to look out for the needs of two sets of parents, we found we had to streamline our lives as well. For just that season of our lives, we pared down our activities as much as possible. We did not, however, eliminate our lifelong commitment of spending at least one night a week on a personal and private date. The benefit of simplification was increased calm. With less stress I was able to be more patient, especially with the endless repetitive questions and plaintive, "Where are you?" that inevitably trailed after us when we left the room.

Severe-Stage AD

As dementia worsens there is increasing danger of wandering and getting lost. A tottering elder can be surprisingly nimble when she decides to see just exactly what is around that next corner! Most of the places Mother stayed had elaborate lock systems or attentive people who prevented her from taking off on her own. This was not true of the facility she lived in following our move to Northern California. Despite being overmedicated, tilting, and moving like a snail, she wandered away several times, once making it to the Russian River, a mile from her residence. Alert police brought her back.

If she were alive today, I would make sure that she was registered with the Alzheimer's Association's "Safe Return" program. It is an inexpensive, nationwide identification, support, and registration

The popular AD "bible" *The 36-Hour Day* suggests handling problems of behavior with a six-stage intervention:

1. Restrict, if necessary, behavior that is causing a problem.

2. Reassess what is going on.

3. Reconsider how the person with AD is seeing what is happening.

4. Rechannel the behavior to a less disruptive model if the person cannot seem to give it up.

5. Reassure the person.

6. Review which actions were effective to learn the most effective interventions.[1]

program that is available twenty-four hours a day, every day. A "safe return" bracelet or necklace is imprinted with a toll-free number that can be called should anyone find a person wearing it who is lost. If needed, the organization can fax a person's identification to police. The jewelry is also recommended for caregivers who are responsible for someone not safe on her own. If, for instance, a caregiver were in an accident, someone would be notified to ensure care is provided for the person with AD.

Other devices can make life easier and safer. Photodial phones have a place to insert a picture, which, when pushed, automatically dials that person. A waterwand is available to turn off faucet water automatically. There is even an automatic flush system that also acts as a bidet to help with hygiene. Catalogues are generally the best source for such devices.

A facility with poorly trained staff or a home that considers TV watching as mental stimulation can be deadening to both the spirit and the body of someone with AD. Invigorating mental and physical workouts that are not frustrating or overwhelming are possible, and many books on caregiving are filled with suggestions. Mind, mood, and body benefit from visits with children, grandchildren, and pets. Mother was also a good caregiver. Her nurturing nature led her to look after those she frequently saw as less fortunate. While her efforts were sometimes unwelcome, it remained important to validate ways she chose to stay connected that were in keeping with her character.

In comparison to my mother-in-law, Mother behaved poorly. Her behavior, while frequently fun and funny, did not always endear her to staff and fellow residents. She was not alone, however. At least 60 percent of those diagnosed with AD have episodes of disruptive behavior. Looking back, I believe the vast majority of Mother's "misbehaviors" were intensified by someone who tried to deal with her using their reality rather than hers. Often a caregiver spoke to her like a child, and no adult wants to be spoken to like a child, even one with dementia.

When orienting Mother to the present became an exercise in futility, I increasingly entered her world. I talked to her as if she made perfect sense. When she said she had to check with the nurses to see if she could get off work to go for ice cream, I never reminded her she did not have a job in the facility. I told her instead that it seemed like a responsible thing to do. When she worried that New Jimmy might be missing her, I suggested to her that he was taking a nap. "Aren't we lucky to have this time together, so he can have a little peace and quiet?"

There were times her behavior became very violent. The worst occasion was at the end of our long flight home from Canada. Mother was tired. I had no idea how much Dr. Stirrat's death had impacted her or what she remembered. To my great relief, she had given me no trouble getting on the plane and had not questioned why her husband was not with us. She thoroughly enjoyed the flight, her food, and visiting with the flight attendants. Throughout the flight I had wrestled with how much I should tell her about the fact that she would be going to a new apartment instead of to her condo. My husband picked us up and drove us directly to her new accommodation.

Two of my friends had reconstructed her decor, using the items I had deemed most meaningful to her and had frantically set aside before leaving to bring her home. They had done a great job. The room looked like Mother. Her oak table, the one she had sat at for years drinking her coffee and eating her beloved cookies, took a prominent place. But to Mother it was less than inviting. She took one look and let out a screech. Suddenly her mind was working better than it had for months. "I'm not staying here," she screamed. "You take me to my home."

"Mother, with Jimmy gone, you can't live alone. This is a nice place. You will have friends to visit and best of all, you won't have to cook." Even that ploy failed to work. Mother yelled and began to cry. She spun around like a wild animal desperately looking for a way to escape. Joe decided to bring out our last big gun—a pint of chocolate ice cream we had made sure was in her small refrigerator.

"Here, Mary Jo, let's take a minute, have some ice cream, and relax," he said as kindly as he could.

She grabbed the container and he handed her a spoon. She shoveled the rich, cold ice cream into her mouth. For a minute it looked as if the magic tranquilizer had been found. And then the wild animal, revived and renewed, apparently by the cold and the sugar, pounced again. "I will not stay here. Take me home," she said, turning and attacking me with all the skill of a lioness. Her blows hit with much more force than one could imagine from such a little lady, especially one holding a container of ice cream. Her eyes were focused and they radiated what looked to me like pure hate. I stood there unable to move.

To protect me, my husband stepped between us and grabbed her arm, pulling the forearm to her eye level. Caught off guard, she looked over, stared at her arm, and blurted, "Look what you did to me. You hurt me. I'm hurt. I'm bleeding."

No one moved. Sure enough, there on her arm were nasty looking brown marks. It was not clear whether they were bruises or blood. My husband's look reflected the horror he felt at having hurt his elderly mother-in-law. He let go of her arm. I grabbed it and looked more closely, my already guilty conscience about to collapse with the thought that we had committed elder abuse. And then I saw clearly what had happened. "Mother," I said, stifling a laugh welling up as much from nerves as relief, "you are not hurt. This is ice cream. See, I can rub it off. You're fine," I added, wishing I believed it.

Now some of you who read this might be saying to yourself we deserved her reaction. After all, I had clearly mishandled the whole situation and ought to have known better. You are right. In hindsight, I can see any number of options that would have been easier on all of us. At the time, I did consult with several people on how to handle this move to an assisted-living setting. No one knew what to do. The lesson learned is that decisions made in crisis are rarely good ones.

Sometimes disruptive behavior occurs at specific times or around certain people. The possibility of physical problems should always be checked out. A person with AD may no longer be able to share that something hurts or that she is uncomfortable in some way. When behavior becomes psychotic and includes serious hallucinations, such as the fear she is in danger, medication may be necessary. There is always the chance of overstimulation. Ironically, repetitive behavior that may or may not be disruptive can result from understimulation. I think back to the man who constantly turned pages in an empty scrapbook day after day.

Not uncommonly AD triggers behaviors that are not disruptive but are unusual. Someone with dementia may decide an activity is important and insist on doing it. My friend's mother-in-law, Gladys, could not be persuaded she would not need every pair of shoes she owned when she went on a visit. (As the heir to Universal Studios, at least in her mind, perhaps she thought she would be going to a lot of parties!) Hoarding and hiding habits are common. Mother would hide her hearing aid, denture piece, and purse almost daily.

While we began to hone in on her favorite spots, occasionally her inventiveness would take several days of sleuthing to uncover the missing items. And then there were the spoons. When I was first moved to write about Alzheimer's, I joked that I would title any such book "Please Shoot Me before I Start Hiding My Spoons."

"Here, Mother, let me take your purse. I'll carry it for a while." My mother, a frail and tiny version of her former self, handed me what had become her symbol of normalcy and activity. The days when her purse was her passport to life for driving, purchasing, identifying her as the active mother of two, wife of Wilburn, citizen of Texas were long gone. Still, the need for the purse continued, like a trusted companion whom one wouldn't think of leaving behind. While Mother remembered little of the usual routines of life, she never forgot to take her purse, even though she continually forgot where she had put it. "Mother!" I exclaimed. "What in the world do you have in here? It weighs a ton!" I quickly began a search of the multiple caverns that contained the treasures she had deemed necessary for our venture out. Bolts of Kleenex, a lone lipstick, dental floss, her aqua-rimmed, rhinestone-studded sunglasses, an empty coin purse—and two carefully wrapped sets of spoons! "Mother, what are you doing with all these spoons in your purse?" I queried, immediately sorry I had asked. Blushing slightly, she stumbled for an explanation. "Well, you never know when you might need them," she replied defensively. "Besides, Jimmy needs them to stir his martini when we go to dinner." I thought of Dr. Stirrat, the patient loving physician who had married Mother knowing Alzheimer's disease had already begun to chip away her reality. He had died the year before.[2]

Of all the behaviors that are common to AD, the habit of constantly repeating the same question is one that requires Herculean patience on the part of caregivers and loved ones. When the question remains around the same theme, it is sometimes possible to deal with the anxiety that is inherent in the question. In the end most people must fall back on the old standby: counting to ten, distracting, leaving for a while, recognizing the battle is not worth it, and taking a few deep breaths.

Caretaking during late-stage AD is focused on safety, but the real goal for caring at the end of the AD journey is providing comfort. Since considerable help with daily activities is needed, the demands are often beyond the scope of what can be offered at home, at least without additional help. As at all levels, there must be sensitivity to the person's abilities and even at this stage encouragement to remain as active as possible. Not allowing a person to stay in bed or eat her meals there is a sign of a good facility.

The Challenge of the Long Haul

Once the commitment is made to become a caregiver, most people try to do their job without help from anyone else. One of the most difficult challenges is learning when to take action and when to let go. My efforts to ensure my mother dressed with the flavor she had throughout her life fell into that category. She rarely bought expensive clothes; she was a mix-and-match-polyester queen, who nevertheless always looked neat, tailored, and pretty well put together. She accessorized most often with turquoise Southwestern jewelry and ankle-high beaded Indian moccasins. I worked hard to see to it that she continued to look the same. I told myself it was important for her dignity, but I'm sure her familiar veneer signaled to me that in some way she was still the mother I remembered. It helped me hold on to what was left.

As her dementia worsened, it became increasingly difficult to keep her neatly coifed, with fingernails the flaming orange color she loved, and dressed in the choices she would have made when healthy. It was easy to blame the care facility. Regulations that required all laundry be washed in extremely hot water with bleach left clothes mere shadows of their former selves. The fact that a whole wing of AD patients does more clothes swapping than fourteen-year-old girls at a slumber party meant keeping matching pieces together was as difficult as reassembling a five-hundred-piece puzzle.

"What happened to this?" I would demand, holding up some remnant of clothing that had changed from turquoise to gray-blue.

"This size sixteen isn't Mother's. She is just over five feet tall and barely tips the hundred-pound mark." "Where did this pink thing come from? Mother hates pink. Her mother made her wear pink when she was little because her sister had red hair and couldn't wear it." "What happened to her hair? She looks like a bag lady," I would complain, making myself thoroughly unpopular with the overworked aides.

Finally, I gave up. I discovered interchangeable fleece tops and bottoms somehow managed to look neat no matter how they were laundered or mismatched. I chose tops that had pictures on them, because people would stop Mother and comment about them. I accepted the reality that she could not sit long enough to paint her nails or have her hair rolled. It took a while but I did learn that when a person has Alzheimer's, we must continually reevaluate what is important. Ultimately some things really do not matter. Cleanliness, comfort, and kindness always do. For us to share an enjoyable now, I had to let go of how it used to be.

If a caregiver is to go the distance, some care must be directed to himself or herself. My one bit of advice is that, if you decide on a spa—go by yourself. The difficulty of maintaining balance in one's life is another of the reasons I do not want my children to look after me in their home. There is no doubt that life is much more bearable when one manages to squeak out some quiet or find time for personal pursuits, but it is very hard to do when caring for someone with AD. Even now I have *The Art of Doing Nothing* sitting by my bed unread. Putting energy into self requires a discipline that responsible, compassionate people do not exercise with enough regularity.

It Takes a Village to Care for an AD Person

Some people find their days go better when they get up early and have a quiet time to organize. Plan ahead, anticipate problems, and take precautions, like storing your keys and checkbook in safe places, to prevent crises and reduce stress. Delegating some responsibilities to others can bring some relief, but you need to have ready a list of things others can help you with should they ask.

Hopefully, before you reach a stage when it is no longer clear exactly which of you is the one with dementia, you will have discovered restorative activities that work for you. To have the time to participate, you may need to consider respite care or what is often referred to as day care. Since "day care" sounds a little too much like a place you leave a three-year-old, I prefer to call it day socials. Mother certainly experienced them as "social." She began participating not because in my wisdom I knew they would be good for her, but as a result of the manager of the assisted-living facility informing me that Mother was taking up too much staff time. I would have to move her if we did not work something out. After carefully checking out the only place in town offering adult day socials, attending a function, observing the staff-patient ratio, and assuring myself that Mother would be safe, we visited together and signed her up for twice-a-week attendance. On those two days, the activities kept her safe and occupied.

Day socials ultimately worked for Mother but in the end provided little respite for me. Getting her there required every ounce of psychological expertise I could muster—more than I ever learned in graduate school. Her excuses for not wanting to go were plentiful. She was tired. She hated it. Someone was coming over to drink coffee with her. She would not go. Once there, she did not want to get out of the car. Finally, she would agree to walk in with me. "But I won't stay," she would quickly add. This scenario was repeated every single visit. Once inside, the loving attendants greeted her warmly and swept her into the activities. She would barely notice when I left. When I picked her up, she rarely stopped talking about her day. Frequently, according to her blow-by-blow description, she had been to "a family reunion." I would hear all the latest gossip and how great it had been to see everyone. But when it was time to return, I would be met with, "I'm too tired. I don't want to go." Each time it was emotionally draining for me.

For many caregivers socials a few times a week offer the needed break to regroup and deal with other issues in life besides their aging parent or relative. There may be times when longer care is needed, and in most cities there are respite centers that offer care for a weekend or other short-term stay.

While we have to face the fact that Alzheimer's is not curable, we caregivers can still have a positive attitude. When the American Association for Retired Persons (AARP) surveyed how caregivers cope, their study, conducted in 2002, reported that 62 percent of caregivers relied on their faith, 42 percent on a religious organization, 47 percent on siblings, 30 percent on other relatives, 30 percent on adult children and neighbors, and 8 percent on employees. Educational and professional support for caregivers delays the loved one's institutionalization and reduces caregiver depression. It is okay to admit that it is impossible to stay hopeful every minute. The rules of the game are to *hope for the best but plan for the worst.*

Caregivers report that the loss of friends and other supportive people is one of the most difficult aspects of caregiving. Support groups and the companionship of loyal friends, neighbors, and coworkers are lifelines to maintaining perspective. Yet it is not difficult to understand why people pull away. Many find facing the disease fearful and the related behavior simply too much to handle. There are some people who feel they cannot bear to see their former friend being robbed of so much of who she was. Others simply feel inadequate and thus incapable of dealing with someone with AD, or they feel rebuffed by a caregiver who will not accept offers of help. It is especially important to nurture those friends who are good listeners. Caregiving for adults is as stressful or more so than for children. If you want to stay the course, you must share the load.

The Problem of Overcaring

There were periods in my mother's illness when I was probably guilty of what is known professionally as *overcaring*—although it never felt like it was a problem when I was in the midst of it. Like other caregivers, I was often frustrated by my inability to keep on top of everything. Feeling one is on an emotional roller coaster is normal. It is also common to be angry, to feel trapped, and to be frustrated by people full of advice who do not know what they are talking about. For example, with the best of intentions, people would tell me not to be so conscientious about visiting Mother. "She no longer knows if you visit or not," they would insist. While that was technically true, I knew that my visits made a difference. When she saw me, her face would flood with life. True, she did not know who I was or would only fleetingly make the connection, but she knew someone she liked was present. The importance of my visit had to do with that connection, not whether she knew who I was or remembered it any longer than it took for me to walk out the door.

Finding balance without sacrificing family, personal renewal, and professional responsibilities is a delicate operation. Someone who is guilty of overcaring is no longer capable of analyzing his or her situation objectively. It is not unusual to find that the person's actions are directed by promises he or she made to the loved one. Caregivers who operate under directives like, "Promise me you will never send me to a care facility," are unable to look dispassionately at the situation and determine what is best. Realistically, any pledge we make should be to do what we can, for as long as we can. It should never be to do everything and to do it forever.

Dr. Carol Farran, an Alzheimer's disease researcher, suggests that caregivers must come to a place, much like the alcoholic, when they admit they are helpless in their attempt to handle everything themselves. Such a task is impossible without calling on and enlisting help beyond themselves.[3] Along with colleagues, she has developed a course that is essentially a twelve-step program for caregivers. The curriculum is undergirded with the belief that caregivers must be realistic, which includes being able to separate the disease from the person.

Losing perspective can also be the result of sibling rivalry and other dysfunctions that characterize a family. Codependent personalities may blame themselves for everything and become angry and hurt with other family members. Victims of abuse, whether sexual, physical, or emotional, can feel a lot of guilt. It is common for such people to feel ashamed of who they are or harbor feelings of not measuring up. One way to ensure that their lives have meaning is to prove they are good enough by unselfishly caring for someone else. However, their care goes beyond what the individual requires or becomes detrimental to the caregivers.

Besides being exhausted and depressed, how would people know they are overcaring? Here are some guidelines that should set off an alarm.

- Insistence on calling or visiting a loved one or the facility daily
- Constant effort expended to find a new specialist or facility that will provide improved care or outcome
- Arguments among family and/or unresolved guilt over placement
- Having no time for self, children, or other family members, sacrificing job or educational opportunities, or doing one's job poorly
- Inability to accept help
- Foreseeing nothing but disaster when looking ahead six months
- Others' comments that you are stressed or doing too much

Caregiving from Afar

Sometimes it seems as stressful to be away from someone needing care as it is to directly care for him or her. And a few who live far away may feel guilty about being grateful for the distance! More than a third of adult children live at least one hundred miles from their parents; one-quarter of those visit several times a year. Almost 61 percent of children of aging parents have contact from once a day to several times a month. Whatever your circumstances, if you are unsure about how your parent is doing, you will find it of value to visit and participate in a full assessment. Some employers have benefits through the Family and Medical Leave Act that give an employee the right to take up to twelve weeks of unpaid leave to attend to family business. You can check to see if such benefits are available in your state.

Once there, it will become clear how your parent is doing. Check out whether there is adequate food (and if it is fresh) and if the person (or couple) is eating regularly. Is the home or apartment being kept in a manner close to the way it has always been? Are bills being paid? Is mail accumulating that is unopened or scattered in unusual places? Is there a social life? Does the person look okay or have grooming patterns changed? Is she driving safely? Frances Mayo used to stop in the middle of intersections and spend time making decisions about which way to go while her passengers contemplated whether last rites were in order! We began to liken an outing with her as equivalent to Disney's *Mr. Toad's Wild Ride,* because of all the sudden stops and changes of direction.

Make appointments with your parent's doctor, lawyer, and financial advisor. Do not hesitate to contact neighbors and friends and get their feedback. Do some quiet activities that give you a chance to renew a personal connection with your loved one. If you are not the primary caregiver, it is necessary to do all you can to support the caregiver and plan periodic visits to allow for a break. Make plans for emergencies. Stay in close touch and do what you can from afar, such as handling bills, filling out insurance forms, making phone calls, and investigating services. Help the person who is giving hands-on care be successful.

If a change must be made or considered, it is best if all family members are present. There is a role for everyone. Priorities and plans can be agreed on, even if there is dissention to be resolved. The first priority is concern over health and safety; then issues of personal assistance can be addressed. The aid of professional help can resolve issues and present solutions that may seem more doable when suggested by a third party. The Alzheimer's Association has eldercare locators for local adult day programs, respite care, and protective agencies. The local Agency on Aging or senior citizen's center has a list of services. It may be that relatives, neighbors, fellow church members, or community organizations can help. The Internet is a resource. Recommendations may also come from hospital social workers or elder law attorneys.

When there are disagreements or confusion over the best course of action or when a person is unable to visit personally, professional care managers can be utilized to assess an older person's needs and situation. They are sometimes more successful at encouraging a person to accept help than family. Their proposal should include a detailed plan of care with specific recommendations. Some will find and secure services, such as legal counsel, home care, nursing care, and home maintenance. Not all are licensed.

An organization called National Geriatric Care Managers is seeking to standardize and upgrade members' credentials so that recommendations are professional and dependable. A care manager should have a license and a degree or experience in gerontology and human services. They should also have references, which most definitely should be called. It is important to know the personal philosophy of anyone you are working with. Some care managers may recommend that a person should be at home no matter what; others may believe everyone should be hospitalized. Make sure you clarify the range of services and cost since it can get expensive, although a family may save money by becoming aware of options they did not know about. Contact www.caremanager.org, 520-881-8008.

To Stay at Home or Not

Our choices for care are never perfect. Moving a parent into a care facility may be the most loving thing we can do—it just never feels that way. Deciding if it is time for a person to leave her home or move out of a relative's home is generally emotionally devastating for all concerned. It is often mentioned as the most difficult and conflicted decision a person looking after someone must make. Intake personnel at care facilities report that family reactions are all over the board. Some sleep on the floor next to their loved one's bed. Others drop the person off and leave faster than a bank robber determined to escape capture. They are sometimes never seen again—apparently it happens all the time. Because the decision may make you feel guilty, you will need to tell yourself several times a day, *My mother's disease process put her in the nursing home, not me.*

Occasionally the decision is tentative, a small step is taken, two or three options are considered, and the "toe is placed in the water." Or, commonly, as in my case, a crisis results in decision making that is hurried and flawed.

There are advantages to keeping the person where she is—the environment is familiar and you have more control over care and perhaps you will be honoring promises. The companionship and pleasure derived from a caregiver's satisfaction in the role need to be considered. It avoids having to come to terms with feelings like *You didn't give up on me. I can't give up on you.* It eliminates a sense of failure that a caregiver may experience following the placement of the loved one.

Avoiding placement, however, by moving someone into a family member's home, for example, has its own set of concerns. Does the person want to move in? Is the home equipped for safety and space? Can someone be home with the person? What is going on with the rest of the family? How will job, family, and finances be affected? Are there respite opportunities?

Since relief help is not always reliable and may be difficult to obtain, a move is inevitable when a caregiver is exhausted or has become ill. Sometimes the person with AD has become violent or wanders. Sometimes what needs to be done is clear, but the afflicted person is resistant to any intervention. While one can legally apply for conservatorship, this is a costly and emotional last resort. Analyzing the source of the resistance can uncover anything from fear to stubborn pride. When my mother reacted so strongly to entering the assisted-living facility, we found that acknowledging her concerns and the help the staff offered eventually calmed Mother. By the next day she was making friends and had forgotten the trauma of the day before. A helpful resource is *Moving a Relative with Memory Loss: A Family Caregiver's Guide.*[4] Always present options calmly to the person who needs care, and, as much as possible, seek her input.

Care outside the home falls generally into the following categories.

1. Residential care homes for the elderly are designed to supply nonmedical care and provide assistance with activities of daily living. They are also called assisted-living facilities.
2. Board and care homes are smaller (and sometimes cheaper).
3. Skilled nursing facilities (SNFs) offer twenty-four-hour nursing care and may have special AD facilities.

Last week I read in the newspaper that a ninety-one-year-old man jumped off a bridge rather than enter a nursing home when he was released from prison. He had begged the judge not to release him because he would rather "die than go to a nursing home." He meant it. What he did not know is that, although there are plenty of facilities that match the stereotype he carried in his head, there are also some wonderful places. Talking to a professional can help clarify, shed light, and sort truth from fiction. To compare nursing homes anywhere in the country, go to www.medicare.gov.

How Do We Pay for This?

Medicare does not pay for long-term care, and Medicaid isn't available until assets amount to no more than two thousand dollars. A person who is single or widowed may find she has to give up her home, whereas a remaining spouse may be able to keep a home, car, and other assets amounting to no more than $90,660. Planning done to shelter or preserve assets must start early, including the appropriateness of spending down an estate through gifting. Regulations change frequently and there are variations from state to state. It is vital to obtain advice from an attorney specializing in elder law or others with financial expertise. As of the summer of 2002, Medicare now covers "evaluation, management visits, as well as therapeutic services for those needing care." Payment of medical services will for the first time be based on the ability to respond to treatment rather than denied because of a primary diagnosis of AD. It will now be illegal to deny service based solely on the fact a person has Alzheimer's. In California, as of January 2001, changes were made that enable a family to deduct some expenses incurred by taking care of a loved one that were not allowed before. Consultation with a tax expert is advised.

A financial expert must be consulted for specific advice on the best course of action to ensure a person does not outlive her income and the options for full-time care. About one-sixth of Americans who reach age sixty-five will spend an average of two and one-half years in a nursing home. Women are twice as likely to do so as men. A majority simply need supplemental help at home. Increasingly, long-term care insurance is paying for such services. Adaptations to the home that are needed to make such care possible, such as grab bars, aides, and even caregiver training, are covered. And more long-term care policies are expanding coverage to include therapeutic, rehabilitative, or personal care whether delivered at home, in a community-based setting, or in a facility.

Deciding what you can afford requires expert help. A general rule of thumb is that long-term care insurance purchased to increase your options for care and to preserve some of your estate may be feasible if the premium is less than 7 percent of your gross income and you have assets of at least seventy-five thousand dollars, excluding home and car, and an income of twenty-five to thirty-five thousand dollars per year. Depending on the extent of coverage and age, long-term care insurance can be very expensive. It is best to purchase it as a fifty- or sixty-year-old for lower monthly premiums. A person with

Alzheimer's, Parkinson's, or other existing health problems that will likely require long-term care may not qualify.

You will want to ask if a policy's benefits increase with the inflation rate, if only care in nursing homes is covered, or if there is also coverage for day care, respite care, or at-home care. You need to know how long benefits last, if coverage is limited to Medicare-certified facilities only, if a hospital stay is required before benefits are available, if annual rates will increase, and the daily benefit rate. Financial planners, your local Health Insurance Counseling and Advocacy Program, or a local Agency on Aging can provide more information and help you evaluate an insurance plan.

Thoughts on the Twilight Journey

"If you only knew the half of it," I might say to you if you were to comment on my caregiving stories. There were so many, it was difficult to decide which to share. Anyone who has taken on a caregiving role has his or her own stockpile of stories that, with the passage of time, move from "that was the worst day of my life" to "actually, it was kind of funny." I am convinced that such a transition takes place as a result of miraculous intervention, the grace of God. I realize that my desire to prearrange my care so that someday I do not oust one of my grandchildren from his or her room may deprive the family of "Nonna stories," but I can live with that. And I am convinced it will be a lot better for them.

I do want us to have fun and make lovely memories. As long as I can, I want to travel with our children and visit in their homes. I will even eat breakfast in a Waffle House in North Carolina, as long as it is shared with them. I do not wish to have included in my obituary: "She drove her kids to their emotional edge, but she did not mean to." And I do not want them to feel guilty, except if they do something they should feel guilty about, like planning a visit and not coming or giving me a housecat for a present.

There is a lot of living to do with or without AD. The secret of survival lies in not letting expectations of what might, should, or "oughta" be ruin what we actually can count on any given day.

Most likely there will come a time when our roles will reverse and my children will be placed in the unnatural position of parenting me—but through the grace of God even that can have its own beauty. I believe such a transition is expressed best in the children's book *Love You Forever* by Robert Munsch. Here is the refrain, repeated as a mother's child grows from babe in arms to manhood:

And while she rocked him she sang:
I'll love you forever, I'll like you for always, As long as I'm living my baby you'll be.

At the end, the son is seen singing the same song to his new daughter, having returned home after receiving a call from his mother:

"You'd better come see me because I'm very old and sick." . . . When he came in the door she tried to sing the song. She sang: I'll love you forever, I'll like you for always . . . But she couldn't finish. . . .

The son went to his mother. He picked her up and rocked her back and forth, back and forth, back and forth. And he sang this song: I'll love you forever, I'll like you for always, As long as I'm living my Mommy you'll be.[5]

Brain Boosters

- Caregiving is not the exclusive domain of women.
- Caregiving can have rewarding and joyous moments.
- There is a caregiving role for every willing family member and/or friend.
- Well-trained caregivers maximize a person's function and quality of life.
- No one person alone can take care of someone with AD.

- It is easy to lose perspective, become depressed, or overcare unless restorative breaks and activities are incorporated into the routine.
- Care managers help make caring from afar manageable.
- Long-term financial planning eases caregiver burden.
- Faith can make the demands of caregiving bearable.

Ten

Life in the Long Run

I give you peace, the kind of peace that only I can give. It isn't like the peace that this world can give. So don't be worried or afraid.

John 14:27 CEV

He will wipe all tears from their eyes, and there will be no more death, suffering, crying, or pain. These things of the past are gone forever. . . . I am making everything new.

Revelation 21:4–5 CEV

Those who were lame will leap around like deer; tongues once silent will begin to shout.

Isaiah 35:6 CEV

Our dead and decaying bodies will be changed into bodies that won't die or decay. The bodies we now have are weak and can die. But they will be changed into bodies that are eternal.

1 Corinthians 15:53–54 CEV

Our Lord Jesus Christ has power over everything, and he will make these poor bodies of ours like his own glorious body.

Philippians 3:20–21 CEV

There are many rooms in my Father's house. I wouldn't tell you
this, unless it was true. I am going there to prepare a place for each
of you.

John 14: 2 CEV

Welcome Home

"Welcome, Mary Jo. I heard from Number One you've been waiting quite a while to get here. We're so glad you made it; we're ready
for you. Maybe you heard the lyres and the singing? There was
quite a celebration when it was announced you were on your way.
Somebody said your daughter came in when you were getting your
preliminary peek—and she asked if you were seeing heaven. She
really did? Well, don't worry about spilling the beans and telling
her yes. It's hard to keep your face from showing it when you get a
glimpse of what awaits you.

"Do you have everything you need? How about that crystal
toothbrush! This is paradise you know. If you need anything, it's
yours. Looks like you got outfitted just fine. There was quite a rush
last week—I tell you, if this weren't heaven, it could get depressing.
What? You were surprised to find your moccasins? Well, we aim to
please. And, by the way, that turquoise necklace is your color.

"Oh, in case you're wondering, your room is prepared for you.
I can run you by to see it now or we can get you straight to the
reunion. The choice is yours. What's that you say? You want to go
straight to the reunion? How did I know! You always were a people
person—Mother Confessor, isn't that what they called you? There
are a lot of loved ones waiting to welcome you—all set to partee.
Just remember, this is your first day. You don't have to do everything.
You have an eternity.

"Day after tomorrow I'll pick you up for the New Jerusalem
tour. You'll love it! Pure gold, mind you, and walls of jasper. You
know how you loved picking up and collecting rocks—just wait
till you see what we have here! A little bird told me your daughter
loves pearls. Let me tell you, when she gets a load of the solid pearl

gates, they will blow her mind! Did I tell you the streets are paved with gold?

"Whoops, careful, a glorified body takes a bit of getting used to, but the benefits are great. You won't ever have to open a door or fiddle with a lock again. You'll get the hang of it. As promised, it is the same glorious model as our Lord's. In case you're worried, remember—and I hope you've noticed that you can—there is no more decay or dying here. Put that restored mind at ease. That business with the plaques and tangles—that happened in your earthly life. It could never happen here, not here, not ever. You want to know if you will have an opportunity to tell God thanks? You bet you will. A private audience. He's just like the rest of us—he loves to hear praise.

"Well here we are—your reunion. What? Oh no, don't worry about not being recognized. Don't give it a thought. Sure, you'll know them. No, no, needn't worry about bitterness or disappointments or unmet expectations—this isn't like Thanksgiving dinner on earth. All those burdens got deposited at the gate. Now, you go in and have a great time. And, by the way, dessert first is no problem—it's no sin here!"

In Search of a Good Death

Unlike generations that came before, 78 percent of us will live past our sixty-fifth birthday. That is the good news. The bad news is that three-fourths of us who make it to that magical marker for old age will have to contend with cancer, stroke, heart disease, lung disease, or dementia during our last year. Eventually, whatever the cause, we are going to die. Even those who have given little thought to that eventuality, if pressed, probably have an opinion as to how they prefer their death scene to play out. But the reality is that what we want and what we get are not always the same. We can count on a disparity if we fail to let anyone know what our wishes are.

The goal is not that we pursue a particular death but that we define for ourselves and clarify for others what our particular death should look like. It is analogous to a woman giving birth. Some are anxious to experience every twitch and refuse medication or anything that will distract from the intensity of the experience. Others ask to be knocked out and awakened when it is all over. Some seek to share the event and seek the input and desires of the father, whereas others, distracted by the effort, would prefer he wait in the car.

Anyone who is planning for something simple—the drop-dead approach—has a 90 percent chance of not getting what he or she wants. A less desirable process is likely. Almost 50 percent of conscious hospitalized patients, for instance, have serious pain in the days before death.[1]

While we often look to physicians to help us predict the time of death, the truth is they are, for the most part, no better than the rest of us at forecasting demise. There is a general clue that is predictive, however. When multiple organ systems (lungs, heart, kidneys) begin to fail, they become too weak to support the processes necessary to keep us alive. An individual with dementia can continue functioning until the damage to the brain begins to affect the normal function of other vital systems and the body shuts down. Without input from the individual or family, a physician is likely to feel obliged to provide life-sustaining treatment. With multiple system failure, however, it is time to be realistic regarding the purpose of any intervention.

When people who are terminally ill are interviewed, their concerns lie more in how they will die rather than the fact that their death is imminent. Only a small number want to be drugged and miss the entire process. Thirty years ago, as a result of new technology, almost every dying hospital patient endured resuscitation efforts. Today many people die at home and/or under the care of a hospice program, which offers end-of-life care that is designed to provide comfort—palliative care. Some use the term *palliative care* more narrowly to mean the art of balancing medication to provide relief from pain, discomfort, and suffering during the time preceding death. Most people want to be as alert as possible, aware of the process, and able to experience closure with loved ones.

Designing the Care You Want

It was not until the mid-fifties that doctors developed the technology needed to extend life and prolong dying. As a result, if you want to ensure that you die with anything short of being the recipient of every death-prolonging method known to modern medicine, you must officially say so. The method of doing this is called an advance directive, which consists of your rules regarding the conditions under which you want life-sustaining treatment continued or ended. It is used when you are near death and cannot make your will known. There are several varieties to cover both medical and financial concerns. A "living will," as it is frequently called, details your desire for treatment if death is imminent. Since you are unlikely to know all the possibilities that might surround your death, a second document called a durable power of attorney for healthcare designates someone you trust to make decisions for you that you would have made were you able. It generally includes your specific requests as well as more general guidelines for decision making. In some states you can write your own directive, but others require a specific form. Without a directive, a hospital is legally bound to do all it can to prolong your life—or death, depending on how you look at it. Neither form is used if you are able to make your own decisions.

All states and the District of Columbia have regulations concerning the use of advance directives. Your right to accept or refuse treatment is protected by both common and constitutional law. A "do not resuscitate" order, for example, means that extraordinary means are not to be used to revive you, should you be near death with no promise of quality of life. While many feel strongly about what they want, in most crisis situations, if there is a form, it cannot be located. It must be in the hands of emergency personnel, hospital staff, or a physician, or extraordinary efforts are always called for, including life support. Some people carry the directive in a wallet, keep a copy in their car, or file it at any hospital they are likely to enter. Again, you can always override directives as long as you are capable of saying what you want.

No one desires, when final days are reached, to be alone . . . in pain . . . in a hospital. Almost everybody (90 percent) wants to be comfortable at home. Insurance policies and government programs do not support the home care necessary for this to happen. Currently only about 20 percent of Americans actually die at home. To ensure that your personal twilight journey is the trip you planned, it must be organized like any other. There are details to attend to. And the truth is, no one else can know exactly what will make your journey *your* journey. Ask yourself, *What do others need to know about the things that make me comfortable—a special blanket, setting, music? How can this journey be paid for? What aspects of dignity am I most concerned with? What unresolved issue of forgiveness or unspoken word is left to say? Is there peace in my spiritual life?* While there are no laws regarding these details, there is no good reason to avoid making your wishes known.

We are a country evenly divided on whether a person can choose to end his or her life because illness makes continuing to live seem untenable. At this writing, Oregon is the only state to have an assisted-suicide law on the books. It's interesting that few people have actually taken advantage of Oregon's option. Those who express such a desire often change their mind when their reasons are delineated and they receive assistance in making their life better, such as reducing pain or relieving depression.

Whatever route we take, failure to make our desired direction known can result in our dying being painful, prolonged, and taking an additional emotional toll on family and friends. The desire to have things resolved as a family is consistently listed as important to the terminally ill—just after the desire to die in comfort.

Other countries do death better. We in the United States live with a longing for perpetual youth and longer life—not the concept of a celebration of a life well lived. Our physicians tend to view death as a personal defeat or professional failure. They are not trained to deal with the spiritual questions and high emotions surrounding it. And like the rest of us, doctors do not escape our society's desire to hide death and pretend it is not a part of life.[2]

Hospice

Woody Allen said, "I'm not afraid to die. I just don't want to be there when it happens." Even Woody would have to agree that hospice programs have reduced the sting of death. They first appeared in the late 1970s. In 1982 they received a boost when Medicare was expanded to cover enrollees with a prognosis of less than six months to live. All but six states cover hospice through Medicaid. Although programs are growing, the vast majority of Americans still do not benefit from all they offer. In fact only 40 percent of cancer patients are ever referred to hospice, according to 1999 statistics. When hospice is suggested, it is often too late for the dying individual to receive all the potential benefits. In 1998 the median care was for fewer than twenty days with more than one-fifth of patients dying within a week.

Hospice care can be provided in a hospice facility, hospital, care home, or at home. It is actually many services. A nurse is designated to act as a care manager. He or she supervises medication used for pain relief and individualized comfort and coordinates all care with the physician in charge. Equipment to ease pain and relieve symptoms is available through hospice, along with home care aides for personal care and dietary, spiritual, and other counseling. Volunteers are trained as counselors and support personnel, while professionals may be hired to help with new disabilities. Counselors and social workers provide support, including respite care when needed and bereavement support for up to a year following a loved one's death.

The goal of hospice is caring not curing. The name is derived from the medieval practice of providing pilgrims a place of rest on their journey. Once hospice is accepted, the patient must waive his or her right to curative treatment for the terminal illness. But new Medicare regulations are more flexible, allowing for two ninety-day periods in hospice care, with an unlimited number of sixty-day periods as long as the person is eligible. Since it is sometimes very difficult to ascertain when the end is near with a person suffering from late-stage Alzheimer's, this is helpful. The real advantage of hospice is that it offers those who choose to die at home the opportunity to do so, encircled by family, friends, and familiar surroundings. Families are allowed to participate in care and are educated at a level that is comfortable for them. The aim is to ensure a final twilight journey that diminishes fear and stress for all involved.

You're Starving Your Mother

Getting "three squares" a day is not the primary thing on a terminally ill person's mind. That is a difficult concept for us to accept because it is so often on our mind. My husband and I fed Mother a thick vanilla milkshake daily the last week of her life. Delivering each spoonful down to the last melted droplet was a long, drawn-out process, but she found pleasure in each creamy mouthful. Was it a medically sound thing to do? No. Any physician who looked at her chart would agree it was not, but it fed her soul and nourished ours. There was no doubt about the pleasure Mother derived from being fed something so exquisite or in the act itself, so connected with life's primeval circle—a mother nursing a child, an old woman being fed by a grown child. As with the babe, the sustenance supplied love and comfort, the fuel necessary to pursue the journey of life. In Mother's case, it was the final twilight journey.

When it became apparent the end was near, Mother was not interested in eating her peas. The facility's solution was to puree them and, if that wasn't successful, I was told they would insert a tube down her throat to ensure she would be nourished. "Oh no," I recoiled, "I don't want you to do that!"

The nurse's response was quick, "Mrs. Mayo, I'll tell you right now this facility will have no part in your *killing* your mother. If that is your choice, you will have to move her to another place." I was stunned but I made no reply.

Back at our medical office, my mood shifting between anger and revulsion, I demanded, "Am I killing Mother if I refuse to let them put in a feeding tube?" To ease our minds, we immediately consulted with several physician friends who had more experience dealing with dying patients. One had recently lost his mother. They reassured us that Mother's need for peas (or any other food) was miniscule and that refusal to allow a feeding tube was not an inhumane choice. In fact, if a tube were placed through her nose and down her throat and she lived beyond a few weeks, a permanent tube would then be inserted in her stomach, necessitating a surgical procedure. Without the tube, if the care facility insisted that Mother eat something, it could cause choking and pooling of fluids in her lungs known as aspiration pneumonia. To me, both options seemed inhumane.

Our friends said we need not be concerned about dehydration. Ice chips or sips of water could be given if desired. Without either food or water, they insisted, Mother would fall into a sleep and die within days or weeks. While a person with dementia may be unable to share his experience, patients with cancer report that going without food in their last days is not difficult and if they did experience hunger it was briefly in the very beginning. The same was true of water, a little was fine. Refusal to eat in the last days of life becomes protective because it triggers the release of endorphins that enhance a sense of well-being. Dehydration can be protective for the same reason.

If a person with AD is not eating, there could be various explanations. For instance, the possibility of overmedication should always be taken into account. Any drugs that interfere with attention, appetite, or salivation should be discontinued. Appetite stimulants such as megestrol acetate have resulted in death in demented persons. Depression must be considered. Sometimes a change in the food offered (like ice cream?) is a solution.

In final-stage Alzheimer's, a clear goal must be defined before the insertion of a feeding tube. Ultimately, is life or death being prolonged? The truth is, most people feel uncertain about the correct choice for their loved one. Research, however, confirms essentially no survival benefits or evidence that suffering is alleviated through tube feeding a person with final-stage dementia. Confusion is rampant due to poor feeding tube information and consent procedures, but no major studies demonstrate any clear advantages to using a feeding tube at this stage,[3] and certain problems with it are common. There is a 2 percent death rate with insertion. Keeping a person from pulling a tube out sometimes requires use of restraints, which, one must assume, aren't pleasant. Studies that sought measurements of improvement of pressure ulcers, reduction of infection, and improved function did not show tube feeding helped but did detect a possible negative association, especially with regard to risk of infection. Two studies demonstrated careful hand feeding resulted in good survival in comparison to inserting a tube.

What is your chance of having a feeding tube inserted if you are demented? It may depend on the color of your skin, where you live, and if you have signed a paper that effectively blocks such a choice. A survey of nursing homes in four states showed a difference in using tubes ranging from 7.5 percent in Maine to 40.1 percent in Mississippi.

Pain Management

A survey of what is important to those who are terminally ill revealed pain and symptom management was their number one concern. While comfort is increasingly becoming a goal to doctors, many are slow to get the message. This remains a great country in which to have an acute illness but a lousy one to have a chronic disease or to be in pain. Doctors still worry they will create addicts, despite evidence that the additional pain relief medicine used to treat serious pain is less likely to be addictive. Besides, should the fear of addiction be the overriding concern at the end of life? Pain management experts have noted that depression can prevent pain medication from working well and that antidepressant drugs can help with pain.

Doctors are often ignorant of the many advances of palliative care. If pain is an issue, insistence on consultation with one of the new palliative care specialists can remarkably impact quality of life. In California, as of 2002, physicians are required to take a continuing education class on pain management to renew their license.

Ideally, when a person is terminally ill, his comfort should be measured along with blood pressure and temperature. Pain is quantified on a scale of one to ten, but medication is given always with an eye on helping the patient remain as alert as possible. Often nurses are more sensitive to the comfort level of the patient, especially someone with dementia, than is his physician and can be called on to help communicate with the physician. When a person has dementia, administering pain medication to him is especially challenging, due to the erratic response resulting from a fragile body combined with respiratory difficulties. Often the best pain management comes under hospice care.

When the End Is Near

Seeing the drawn look on my face as I left Mother's room, the new male nurse made an effort to head my way and, clasping my arm gently said, "I know you are worried, but I think your mother is getting better. I think in a few days this crisis will have passed and she will be fine."

Too tired for niceties, I looked him straight in the eye. "No, she won't," I said. "She's dying, but it's okay." I felt bad that I could not respond differently to his message of hope or at least his effort, however misguided, to comfort me. Mother was tired, she was ready for a new body, and I knew I had to let her go. There had been other occasions when I thought the end was near and I had not been as calm. In those incidences overmedication was the culprit. But this was different; there was evidence that one by one her vital systems were shutting down. It was time.

While Mother had long since passed the point when she could talk about the process, others who are terminally ill remark on how their ideas change as to what makes life worth living. As the illness progresses, the list becomes very short. When the end is near, it is common for people to begin to withdraw from this world as they prepare for a final release from their earthly life. I have seen cases where such a transition is delayed until the family can give assurance that they will be all right and permission for their loved one to continue his twilight journey to its culmination is expressed.

Generally a person near death becomes more fatigued and sleeping increases. Some people become disoriented and may hallucinate. Body temperature changes can be observed; he may lose bladder and bowel control. Reports of people having periods of increased lucidity or improved motor function are not uncommon. Most distressing to those observing the process are changes in breathing. Irregular or long spaces without a breath occur because of decreased oxygen in the blood and poor circulation due to a failing heart. The agitation and restlessness, moaning and groaning that is known as terminal delirium does not necessarily signal the person is registering pain, since consciousness is markedly decreased. Even though an individual may appear unarousable, hearing is one of the last senses to go, so both watching what you say and continuing to talk is important.

What can a physician promise as far as how your loved one's last days are managed? He or she should be able to keep the person comfortable. You have a right to know the pace and prognosis of the illness and any changes that occur. All care should be aimed at helping improve function and survival—not making the patient more sick and/or debilitated. The doctor should be able to promise that care will be coordinated and your loved one will not be avoided or neglected, that consideration will be given to personal finances, and most important, that everything will be done to make the best of each precious day.[4]

The Emotional Challenge

While pain is mentioned as the thing the terminally ill fear most, the emotional pain that comes from grieving the loss of earthly reality can be enormous. For many it means letting go of the known for an unknowable destiny; to others it signals leaving one realm of existence for another. Some people, including those with AD, are able to make the most of the life they have at that particular moment. Most terminally ill patients have a sense of what is happening. They may say to their doctor, "I don't think I'm getting better." If their physician is sensitive, he or she can use the opportunity to be honest, allowing time for processing what is shared and understanding there may be a time when knowing more is important. There is no pattern that is right for everyone.

The stages of grieving defined by the author Elisabeth Kübler-Ross—denial, anger, bargaining, depression, and acceptance[5]—are experienced in any order from day-to-day or even hour-to-hour by caregivers and patients alike. When the process is drawn out, as it is in AD, the anticipatory loss may involve more grieving than what actually comes after the loved one's death. As the moment of death approaches, conversation will depend on the person and his awareness; you cannot fix the past or argue him out of his current mindset. Humor is appropriate. Asking whom you should contact, reflecting, remembering, and saying that you care promote closure. So does just sitting silently and holding hands.

There are some people who honestly relish knowing it is their final pass at life, and they find pleasure in and appreciate everything. Apparently good manners remain very important too. It has been said that such moments, what might be called the *glory* moments that accompany death, are too often buried in the mundane. I was amazed to watch Dr. Stirrat's efforts to make sure he was not improperly exposed when he seemed aware of little else. I marveled as Mother attempted to press a napkin to her mouth to catch an escaping bit of ice cream. So much was gone but not the need for dignity. The human spirit far outlasts the body.

For me, taking my mother's ashes to be buried beside my dad in Texas was the last difficult journey we shared. As I checked in at the airport, I discovered I could not bear to have her remains scoot through the X-ray machines like a piece of baggage. Compassion prevailed, and since it was before 9/11, she sat on my lap throughout the journey until we reached her earthly resting place.

Doing What Has to Be Done

I hope that you have grasped the importance of planning your final twilight journey to ensure it is, as much as possible, to your liking. While we have no one to blame but ourselves if we fail to take such steps, it is difficult to encourage our parents to do the same. Adult children are often hesitant to ask about their parents' finances, desires, and many of the concerns of aging. Doing so places them in a position in which their motives may be suspect. They feel as if they are violating their parents' privacy or they look like they are in a hurry for them to pass on.

A recent study reported that 30 percent of adult children do not know the location of their parents' important papers. Besides the durable power of attorney for healthcare, there is also a need for a durable power of attorney for assets. This is a legal document that enables someone you choose to take care of any financial decisions, should you be unable to make them yourself. Without this document your family may have to go to court to get permission to use your resources to pay for hospital or other costs or to carry on your business. Having this document is far superior to having to petition for conservatorship, which incidentally strips you of any rights. A durable power of attorney should be on file with financial institutions you do business with. Some banks and title companies prefer their own papers but by law they must honor a legally drawn up and validated document. Always have an attorney prepare a durable power of attorney for you.

It goes without saying that preparation of a will or trust is important unless you like wasting lots of money. A will must go through a court procedure called probate to determine how assets are to be distributed. A trust is a document that decides how assets will be managed and who will manage them in life and after death. A trust does not have to go through probate and thus avoids the court arbitrarily making sales, investments, accounting, and distribution decisions. If your estate warrants it, a trust can save time, money, and taxes. A financial planner, accountant, or lawyer can advise you on an estate plan that ensures your wishes will be carried out in a financially sound fashion. Generally, advance directives or living wills are prepared at the same time as wills and trusts.

In the lists that follow, I have identified areas that you will need to think about so that you have in writing the things that are important for others to know when you are no longer able to communicate. Adapt them to your own individual needs. Unless my husband had specifically told me, I would never have known he is adamant about having his high school song, "Here's a Tiger to Tooele High" be the anchor of his music selection at his funeral—just after a rendition of "Through the Years." And who would have guessed that barn buster hymn "There Is a Balm in Gilead" is scheduled to escort me on my way.

If you want people to know you really died, write down that you want an open casket, or, if the thought of friends declaring how "real" you look is likely to send you to an early grave, ask that it be closed. Finally, do they know you hate carnations? Write it down!

Give the location of documents, instructions, contact person, and any personal thoughts for the following:

Funeral
- dispensation of the body
- plot/deed particulars
- service
- obituary

Medical
- list of medicines (prescribed by whom?)
- durable power of attorney for healthcare

- living will; do not resuscitate form (distribute copies to doctor, care facility, local hospital, and keep a personal copy)
- care preferences
- autopsy
- organ transplant
- research (organ donation)
- life support

Business/Financial

- bank accounts and account numbers
- safety deposit box, number and key
- insurance policy number (life, long-term care, auto, other)
- insurance policy beneficiaries
- deeds/titles (house, vacation home, rental property)
- will/trust
- annuities
- employer/retirement pension
- liabilities (loans, liens)
- assets (real estate, bonds, stocks, other)
- mortgages
- credit card numbers
- tax report/property tax
- important contacts (accountant, broker, lawyer, financial planner)

Everyday Concerns

- house maintenance (contracts, utilities)
- pets
- household contracts
- location of jewelry and other valuables
- personal safe, combination number

Family Documentation

- name, birth certificate, Social Security number, Medicare number
- spouse's name, birth certificate, Social Security number, Medicare number
- children's names, places of birth
- death certificates
- divorce decree/prenuptial agreement
- citizenship
- military service
- parents' names and birth dates
- mother's maiden name
- people to notify (relatives, friends, clergy, business associates, other)
- miscellaneous information (keys to house, cars)

Faith

There is much research that attests to the fact that faith in a power beyond ourselves provides comfort and strength as we face death. A problem with dying is that we generally do not know just how long we have left to live. It is not until the end seems near that we exercise the choice to live like each day will be our last. A number of my closest women friends have died at a relatively early age of cancer and, this last year, as a result of a car accident. I still long to share family news with them; there are empty spaces where each took a little something away. Miriam Hanson died January 4, 1996. She was a pastor's wife and the illustrator of two children's books I wrote. She specifically requested that I tell people what she learned about living from dying. What follows is an excerpt from the eulogy I shared January 7, 1996 at her funeral.

We thank our precious Lord today . . . because Miriam Hanson
was healed. It is obvious the healing wasn't physical, but it was no
less a healing. In the last two years of her life . . . two years by all
scientific reasoning she shouldn't have had—given the diagnosis and
virulence of her cancer—Miriam experienced a level of emotional
and spiritual honesty that brought clarity and peace to her and
amazement and admiration to those in her presence.

I could do the usual and list all the wonderful traits and talents
of my friend but those here today already know them. Instead, I
would like to share with you, in her own words and with as much
accuracy as I, in my human frailty, can muster. Most of what I'm
about to say comes from notes I made at Miriam's request, on
September 10 of last year and three weeks ago when, for much of
the day, our communication was sitting on her bed, holding hands,
as she slept. Of course, you do remember her hands, exquisite and
long, and reflective of the beauty she could create with them.

With your indulgence, I'll speak in the first person.

"Mary Ann," she said, "I have only one request for you. Write
about what I have learned about living from dying.

"Mary Ann, C. S. Lewis was right. We live in a 'Shadowland'—reality is coming. A shadow is a reflection of what is real
but it lacks color, dimension, detail. Our existence, even at its most
magnificent—intriguing and entrancing as life as we know it is—is
a mere reflection of the majesty that is to come. When I was in the
hospital, it was so evident to me who consciously or unconsciously
knew this. Those who knew which was real and which was a shadow
world were much more willing to let go.

"Let me tell you about things given to me through life, starting
with my two most precious times with the Lord. The first occurred
many years ago. I was separated from my husband at the time, so
I was alone. My neighbor, a sweet Christian woman, called in the
middle of the night and asked if I would come over and wait with
her until the coroner came. Her husband had died and was lying
on the floor of their bedroom. Of course, I went, but I was uneasy.
The thought of being with a dead person was frightening. We
weren't being particularly spiritual or saying much, just sitting in
her bedroom with the body of her husband, but I became aware of
God coming through the household and leaving a trail of love. Love
was dripping off everything and was only confined by the walls. I
experienced such peace.

"The second perfect time with the Lord was when my mother was dying and I was holding her hand. Without a shadow of a doubt, I became aware of total overwhelming love and of the Lord lifting our hands and brushing love through. You see, God sweeping down and taking a soul away is the real thing; afterward we go back into the 'Shadowland.' Death enables us to peek through the door and glimpse reality. When death comes, everything here appears to come to a standstill and feels unreal. It enables us to balance what we should know and to live for a moment in his reality."

She went on . . .

"When I was around thirty-five years old, I was lying in bed reading Revelation 19 concerning the second coming of the Lord riding a white horse. I could not envision Christ's face and I began to pray. Unexpectedly, I felt myself being physically pulled out of bed . . . rising . . . looking down . . . seeing my husband and myself in bed and the baby in the next room. I rose through the ceiling into a formal garden where I saw a person walking. I knew immediately it was Christ. I saw the back of his head and I knew I was going to see his face. I was overwhelmed with guilt and condemnation. I felt ashamed and sorry for all I hadn't accomplished. I listed one thousand things I hadn't done and berated myself for them. Suddenly, a scythe cut across my list. The meaning was immediately clear. There is no condemnation in Christ. It didn't matter what I did. I was saved. He just wanted me and I wanted him —and I knew this was real and the rest didn't count.

"I said, 'I want to be with you.' But he said, 'Not yet.' I dropped back.

Mary Ann, this is my life Scripture: 'There is no condemnation . . . in Christ' (Romans 8:1 NIV). Therefore, I can no longer condemn anyone."

There were other visions she shared; their themes intertwined and repeated themselves. They added clarity to her truth of no condemnation. They reinforced that this life is not reality; this is "Shadowland." She recognized that Christ put us here to learn what he himself demonstrated by his life, that eternity is possible because he brings a glimpse of "reality" through his life, death, and resurrection. She added she had also learned that sometimes we see clearest during life's darkest moments.

Miriam's healing necessitated being brutally honest with herself. She reflected on her marriage and what she felt was her biggest personal failure, not recognizing the Lord had his own thing for her to accomplish. Instead, she had tried to live through another. . . .

Like most of us, Miriam said she always lamented that life here in "Shadowland" could not be perfect, but she understood that a perfect life is found only in the cross.

She told me about a time she was at the church praying. "I repeated my prayer many times and I saw myself at the base of a cross, touching the wood, experiencing its roughness, knowing Christ was hanging from the cross. I had a speck of blood on me that stayed red only an instant and then was clear. I stood up and put my back on the cross. Wherever I looked was illuminated; everyplace else was dark. I got it. The truth of God flows through the cross, through us, and through the world, to illuminate the darkness."

The Episcopal *Book of Common Prayer* states Miriam's revelation this way: "Almighty God, whose Son our Savior Jesus Christ is the light of the world; Grant that your people, illumined by your Word and Sacraments, may shine with the radiance of Christ's glory, that he may be known, worshiped and obeyed to the ends of the earth; through Jesus Christ our Lord, who with you and the Holy Spirit lives and reigns, one God, now and forever."

Three weeks ago Miriam shared with me that the sicker she had become—the closer she came to seeing firsthand the perfection that was Christ—the more aware she was of the enormity of his sacrifice for us—and how unworthy she felt herself to be.

I reminded her of two things. First, the more we grow in holiness, the more conscious we are of our remaining faults, and, second, the Lord is not through with her yet. In heaven, this very day, Miriam has her own ministry to take care of.

For those of us left mired in "Shadowland," who struggle with discerning the real from its reflection, it may be difficult to find much comfort in thinking about that, especially on this day when we mourn the earthly loss of our lovely friend. Just be aware that Miriam will.

There is a joyful noise in heaven this week, because Miriam Hanson has moved into her mansion. She is probably organizing a garage sale. I'm sure she is drawing one of her incredible masterpieces—probably of a white horse. We know she is experiencing God's unfathomable love. Miriam, we join with the heavenly chorus in exclaiming, "Well done, good and faithful servant—you learned what was real about living, from dying."

Thoughts on the Twilight Journey

Miriam was indeed a spiritual person. There is no question in my mind that the beautiful and reverent observations she made about life were truths she held in her heart that found utterance because she was open to learning about "living from dying." But in that mix that makes us human, she was also a flawed person. After discovering a breast lump, she delayed seeing a physician for months until her husband set up a brief visit to our town, enabling us to literally place her in the car and drive her to an oncologist friend's office.

The news was brutal: the mass, even without further tests, was almost assuredly malignant. I drove her back to her San Francisco hotel, making sure her husband was forewarned that the prognosis was not good. Later that day she received a call that her daughter, after months of denial, was to enter a drug rehabilitation facility. Days later she discovered her husband had been unfaithful. Two weeks later, while she was still groggy and being wheeled down the hall following removal of one of her breasts, he asked her to sign divorce papers that included a settlement written in his favor.

We talked almost daily, but I failed to hear much about lifestyle changes that would maximize her chance for a quality life in the time she had remaining. Once she told me, "I have friends in *low* places. I'm drinking too much, dancing too much, and I don't want to change." But she did. She endured pain with dignity. A relationship with her daughter was restored and she lived to see her granddaughter's first birthday.

In the last months of her life, she was at peace, and she surrounded herself with those who cherished her talent and were inspired by her composure. The sense of hopelessness and despair that led her to a period of denial was replaced by serenity and grace. There was a lot to grieve—the death of what might have been, the demise of a marriage, an old age never experienced. Her comfort lay in the new life that was beckoning, enticing her with its possibilities. There was no longer need or purpose to focus on what was being left behind.

Mother too found peace as she glimpsed what lay ahead. As I entered her room that last day, the look on her face caused me to grasp my chest and feel as if the room had been drained of all of its air. There was a slight smile breaking free from around her lips. Her eyes—those eyes that had become dull—had a vibrancy I had not seen for years. Her face glowed, her smooth skin appeared translucent. This ethereal glow left her stunningly beautiful. It seemed the most natural thing in the world to ask if she was seeing heaven.

The woman, who had been too weak to talk, responded with a clear "Yes."

"Is it beautiful?" I asked.

She nodded slightly.

"It's all right to go, Mother," I managed to say, for once holding back the tears.

Mary Jo Manahan died early the next morning, just as I was preparing to get up and go be with her. She is waiting for me to join her—and we will shout, dance, and leap like deer, and all things will be new.

Brain Boosters

- Bring death into your life; clarify your preferences.
- Prepare advance directives.
- Call on your faith.

Appendix A

Treatments for Dementia

Drugs Currently in Use

Aricept (donepezil): An average of 23 percent of people show measurable improvement in a mental status exam score with some functional improvement and stabilization of daily activity. It is given once a day and has mild side effects. For some, agitation is increased. It is best given during the day to avoid sleep problems. Currently (2002) it is the most commonly prescribed cholinesterase inhibitor.

Exelon (rivastigmine): An average of 25 percent improvement is achieved in mental status. Considerable improvement in behavior and other areas of function was noted. In one study improvements in behavior were seen from the baseline after fifty-two weeks—a period of time in which decline would normally have occurred. Use of Exelon enables many patients on antipsychotic medications, which can have very negative side effects, to quit taking them. It is best given with food twice a day, with the dosage being increased very slowly. Weight loss is an issue for some. One study in the *Archives of Neurology* noted that the greatest response was found among those with rapidly progressing disease. Because of its short half-life and the fact it bypasses the liver, it has fewer drug interactions with antidepressants.

Reminyl (galantamine): An average of 37 percent improvement in mental function and the only cholinesterase inhibitor shown to delay cognitive decline for a full year. Improvements in function are also significant. Bathing, dressing, eating, and interaction with others are improved. Its mechanism is slightly different from the other AD approved drugs. It too enhances the release of acetylcholine but also protects other neurotransmitters that influence behavior, such as agitation. It is well tolerated.

Cognex (tacrine): This was the original drug in this class. It is no longer used as a first choice because of severe gastrointestinal side effects and liver toxicity.[1]

Memantine: A new medicine currently being evaluated by the FDA and slated for approval in 2004, memantine is the first to show evidence of slowing the disease among severely ill patients.

Anxiolytics (benzodiazepines) reduce anxiety, usually with the side effects of sedation and withdrawal. But an AD patient may experience increased distress. Use should be short term because of the possibility of further motor and cognitive impairment and the difficulty of getting a person off the drug. Side effects include falls, cognitive impairment, disinhibition, and irritability.

Buspar (Buspirone) has an advantage of being an antidepressant and anxiolytic. It is nonsedating and has minimal risk for motor problems.

Anti-convulsants are used for agitation. Drugs like Valproic Acid and Depakote are choices for a variety of impulsive/aggressive behaviors.

Beta-blockers for agitation should be used only when all else has failed. They are difficult to balance, interact with many other drugs, and can trigger delirium.

Selegiline may improve cognitive function, behavioral disturbance, and mood without a lot of adverse effects. However, serious side effects can occur when taken with tricyclics and seratonin reuptake inhibitors (SRI). Selegiline is believed to enhance neurotransmitters. Overdose with SRIs can lead to increased agitation, insomnia, confusion, and even death. They can be particularly problematic with frontal lobe dementia. Problems often result from use with other medications. An advantage of SRIs is that they help depression without sedating. Citalopram is the cheapest SRI and has no significant drug interactions.

Antidepressants are often prescribed because behavior problems can be an indication of depression: Zoloft (sertraline), Paxil (paroxetine), and selegiline in low doses enhance cognition, especially during mild stages of AD. Trazodone is the most widely used antidepressant but causes sedation and requires frequent dosing. It has a low addictive potential.

In general antidepressants like tricyclics can cause everything from urinary retention to decreased GI motility, memory impairment, sedation, falls, and worsened dementia. They should not be used with the AD patient. Use is especially discouraged with people who also have cardiac disease.

Antipsychotics are the most common class of medications used for behavior and psychological problems with AD. They are most often recommended when delusions, hallucination, or paranoia are present. The lowest dose (initially one-third to one-half the usual dose) should be used to minimize sedation.

The norepinephrine reuptake inhibitor Reboxetine is new and appears to have a low potential for drug interaction. It shows good promise in treating apathy in dementia.

Psychostimulants like Dexedrine, Cylert, and Ritalin can get a quick response for an AD patient who is jittery and needs more energy.

Antidepressants that are bad for cognitive function are Imipramine, Clomipramine, Amitriptyline, Doxepin, Trazodone in high doses, and Nortiptyline.

Research

A Cortex Pharmaceutical drug, CX516, magnifies signals from other brain cells and is now being tested with humans.

GlaxoSmithKline's SB271046 blocks a serotonin receptor that is prevalent in the hippocampus. Human trials are just starting.

Progress has been made in keeping cultures of neurons alive in the laboratory from brains of AD patients. This gives scientists a chance to view how aging and disease is occurring and what various interventions might accomplish.

The first preliminary work utilizing natural antibodies to treat AD is being done at the Indiana University School of Medicine. Antibodies are reduced in the AD patient.

Stem cells are hot news. A four-day-old human embryo is a miniscule hollow ball of cells but its inner layer contains the embryonic stem cells that are at the heart of a controversy over their ethical use. In the United States no new cells from human embryos can be used for research—just those that have already been harvested. The gathering of stem cells from adults is possible but is more of a challenge. However, other countries are continuing to harvest stem cells from embryos. The value of stem cells is that they have not yet decided what they want to be when they grow up. Consequently, they can be influenced to develop into any cell the genes it contains prompt it to. It wasn't until 1998 that scientists first learned how to get cells to reproduce and yet remain neutral, so research using these cells is very new. The prospect of generating cells to replace damaged ones in various tissues and organs, including the brain, is called regenerative medicine.

Patients with severe dementia that causes sleep problems can benefit greatly from a simple procedure. Exposure to bright light every morning can keep them sleeping rather than wandering throughout the night and may prevent some from entering a care facility. Light boxes are available for times when bright sunlight is not available.

Another simple but effective intervention for ministering to a person with AD is music. If our children don't know what kind of music we find exhilarating or comforting, we should make a list because it has been shown to powerfully transform and heal. Listening to music can lower blood pressure by as much as ten points. Stroke victims who exercise to music are better able to coordinate movements. Even memory is improved! The concept of music as healing is not new. Chanting, singing, and drumming were used to heal pain in ancient Greece, Rome, and Egypt. King Saul requested that David play the harp to assuage his melancholy moods. Dr. Oliver Saks, the author of the book *Awakenings,* which was made into a film starring Robin Williams, still actively incorporates music in therapy with his Alzheimer's patients.

Increasingly it is being recognized that genes cause extra production of amyloid plaques, but scientists are beginning to understand the nongenetic factors that somehow cause the clearance mechanism that normally shuttles A-beta out of the body to work poorly.

To be able to look inside the brain and see how much healthy tissue plaques and tangles have replaced requires an exquisitely tiny probe. But such probes are being developed. Along the same line, researchers at Brigham and Women's Hospital are also developing a process wherein tiny lipid bubbles injected into the bloodstream gather at the brain. When zapped with ultrasound, they burst and provide an opening through which a probe could be placed.

A flow-regulated cerebrospinal fluid shunt is currently being studied as a treatment for AD. The hypothesis is you drain off fluid that may be stagnant and contain toxic proteins and inflammatory mediators that play a part in developing AD. I don't know whether this sounds more like the medieval practices of attaching leeches or getting an oil change, but scientists who know what they are doing swear it has promise.

Neurotrophins are a group of proteins whose job it is to keep neural networks up and running and prevent their death. Nerve growth factor (NGF) is the most extensively studied neurotrophin. It is known to reduce damage to neurons from toxic material. But the NGF molecule is too big to pass through the blood-brain barrier, so researchers are looking for a small synthetic molecular substitute that will mimic crucial parts of the NGF protein, enabling it to do its work. A similar concept has been used with insulin.

Accumulation of metals like copper, zinc, iron, manganese, and cadmium may reach carcinogenic or damaging levels as we age. Researchers are looking for ways to reduce any overabundance and the damage they do to the brain.

Swedish researchers have found a defect in the blood-brain barrier, the job of which is to keep most substances out of the brain. Certain proteins that are responsible are found more abundantly in patients with AD. At the moment scientists are not clear which came first, the proteins or the AD.

Potential Help for the Brain

Fighting Beta-Amyloid Formation

Beta-amyloid is actually a chip off a larger normal protein located in the outer membranes of brain cells. This amyloid precursor protein is commonly referred to as APP. The problem with APP lies in its structure. It has little extensions, sometimes likened to a worm with its head in an apple. Little warriors, enzymes known as secretases, cut off the end of the "worm," leaving it unattached and drifting away from the cell membrane. The little snippet of APP out on its own is called A-beta. Most of the A-beta on the loose is dissolved into the brain fluid and its remnants are sent packing. A few of the hardiest A-betas hang around, grab a few other lonely A-betas, and cluster together to form fibrils. Six different drug makers are developing drugs that may prevent the secretase warriors from hacking off APP extensions and some are being tested on animals. So far secretase inhibitors have caused other problems like damaging bone marrow and digestive tissue.

Stemming Fibril Formation

Those A-beta fibrils that bind together form sheetlike structures that become larger and stronger masses. They become less soluble and more difficult for the body to excrete by combining with a protein known as serum amyloid protein (SAP). An international research team is studying SAP in hopes of finding a way of preventing it from combining with fibril structures. A "small molecule" drug called CPHPC interferes with SAP's ability to bind with amyloid fibrils and leads to their rapid clearance by the liver. So far, both SAP and fibrils have been reduced without negative side effects. Human trials are just beginning. A second approach involves development of beta-sheet blockers that latch on to the roving A-beta pieces and help them maintain their shape so they are less apt to join with other A-betas to form sheets of fibrils. The delay gives the body a greater chance to clear A-beta from the brain. Two drugs with this in mind are currently in development.

Reducing Plaque Formation

Clusters of A-beta fibrils bind together to produce large plaques, sometimes the size of BBs, capable of displacing healthy brain cells and eventually killing them. As AD progresses, more plaques create greater damage. Concentration of tough insoluble beta-amyloid plaques results in the brain losing its ability to produce acetylcholine, the neurotransmitter most critical to memory and cognition. Beta-amyloid plaques may also disrupt channels that carry sodium, potassium, and calcium—essential nutrients for producing electric charges that must fire regularly for signals to pass from one nerve cell to another. Research is directed at using the immune system to mark plaques for destruction and attacking them with antibodies.

There was great excitement several years ago when antibodies were found to improve memory in mice. Elan pharmaceuticals, an Irish company, developed an amyloid vaccine that attacked plaques. Vaccinated mice cleared out 96 percent of their plaques within three months. Trials with humans were discontinued when the vaccine attacked normal tissue, causing inflammation of the brain and surrounding membranes. Elan and Eli Lilly are continuing to work on developing ready-made antibodies that will be more specific in targeting only plaque.

Eliminating Neurofibrillary Tangles

The branches that sprout from brain cells house microtubules that are vital for many brain functions. Every microtubule holds its shape because it contains tau proteins that are like the wooden ties of a railroad track. When the brain is healthy, tau lines up neatly and does its job of maintaining the shape of the microtubule, sometimes called a neurite. When enzymes loosen tau as a result of AD, the ties of tau begin to tangle and the microtubules are damaged. When that happens the whole neuron shrinks and dies. Some believe that it is a mutated form of tau protein that blocks the activity of normal tau in the assembly of a healthy microtubule structure. The neurofibrillary tangles that result are most frequently noted in the hippocampus. There is great debate among scientists over which comes first—amyloid plaques or tau damage. Which are most important in the development of Alzheimer's—the plaques that litter spaces between nerve cells or the stringy tangles that erupt from within?

Preventing Neuron Death

Plaques and tangles are the force behind the death of brain cells. Inflammation, oxidative stress, and neurotransmitter loss are driven by the havoc the plaques and tangles cause. But the brain chemical glutamate does its share of harm as well. As amyloid plaques increase, so does the concentration of glutamate in the brain. This neurotransmitter locks in memories when released in short bursts but kills neurons when chronically elevated. Neurons of people with AD become insensitive to glutamate. A new drug that allows glutamate to flow into cells but that does not block the spurts that are necessary for learning and memory has been approved in Europe.

Notes

Chapter 1 Make Me a Child Again

1. "What Is Alzheimer's Disease?" at http://content.health.msn.com/printing/dmk/dmk_article_3961782 (2 November 2002).

2. R. Katzman, "Epidemiology of Alzheimer's Disease," *Neurobiology of Aging* 21 (2000) (suppl 1):S1, Abstract 1:1.

3. "Statistics about Alzheimer's Disease," at www.alz.org/AboutAD/Statistics.htm.

4. Ibid.

5. Wolfson et al., "A Reevaluation of the Duration of Survival after the Onset of Dementia," *New England Journal of Medicine* 344, no. 15 (12 April 2001): 1111–16.

6. Wolfson et al., "Early Alzheimer's Disease: Recognition and Assessment" (U.S. Department of Health and Human Services, Agency for Health Care Policy and Research: publication no. 97-R123, September 1996): 5.

7. Wolfson et al., "Cognition Deteriorates, but Emotion Remains", *American Journal of Alzheimer's Disease* (study conducted by Florida Atlantic University and Miami VA Hospital as reported in Alzheimers.com NewsFlash section, 10 November 1998).

8. Quoted in R. Langreth, "Viagra for the Brain," *Forbes,* 4 February 2002, 46–52.

9. S. Herbert, "Losing Your Mind," *U.S. News & World Report*, 26 July 1999, 45–51.

10. J. S. Goodwin, "Geriatrics and the Limits of Modern Medicine," *New England Journal of Medicine* 340, no. 16 (22 April 1999): 1283–85.

11. M. von Faber, A. Bootsma-vander Wiel et al., "Successful Aging in the Oldest Old: Who Can Be Characterized as Successfully Aged," *Archives of Internal Medicine* 161 (2001): 2694–2700.

Chapter 2 Get Me to the Church on Time

1. Neurons, the brain cells through which all this activity takes place can, with a little imagination, be likened to trees. If the nucleus of the cell is seen as the foundation, trunks called axons end in branches, called dendrites. The more dendrites available, the greater the chance of neuron to neuron connections. Unfortunately dendrites are reduced with age. Axons, through which electrical impulses travel, become less efficient when the myelin sheath they are wrapped in deteriorates, weakening the signal. Fewer dendrites and less efficient axons result in a slowdown in our thinking that becomes apparent somewhere around our fortieth birthday.

The electrical impulse that travels up the axon of the neuron and branches out among the dendrites must be converted into a new form to navigate the space between brain cells, called a synapse. It is transformed most often into a neurotransmitter or sometimes an endorphinlike hormone. Once the synaptic gap is crossed, the dendrites of the adjoining neuron convert the signal back to an electrical impulse. Strong synapses result in good learning and remembering—neurotransmitters are essential fundamentals for memory. If their concentration is below par, so is thinking. It is theorized that memories are stored in the neuron as coded proteins and the RNA found in the cell nucleus and cytoplasm surrounding it helps create those proteins. See Dharma Singh Khalsa with Cameron Stauth, *Brain Longevity* (New York: Warner Books, 1997).

2. I have stated that normal changes of an aging brain include shrinkage, reduction of dendrites, and deterioration of axons. Performance is also affected by a decline in neurotransmitters, which influence the capacity for complex thought, focus, and multitasking. The rate of deterioration or brain aging can, to a degree, be influenced by factors that are within and out of our control.

Cortisol is a stress hormone released by the adrenal gland that in moderation is beneficial but when overproduced over a long period of time can have deleterious effects on brain function and memory. For example, excessive cortisol is known to interfere with the glucose supply needed by neurotrans-mitters. It allows calcium into brain cells—one process among many that creates free radicals. Free radicals are unstable molecules that attach to and alter chemicals needed for healthy brain function. This hormone-gone-wild affects the sleep cycle and other biological rhythms that directly and indirectly affect memory and learning. Most significantly, years of taking a bath in excess cortisol damages the hippocampus. Over time the hippocampus can lose its ability to exert any control over cortisol production.

Chapter 3 Don't Worry—Be Happy

1. Z. Guo, L. A. Cupples, A. Kurz et al., "Head Injury and the Risk of Alzheimer's Disease in the MIRAGE Study," *Neurology* 54 (2000): 1316–23.

2. While new genetic connections are being uncovered, it is the apoli-poprotein or "APOE" gene we hear most about. For years it was known to be a risk for heart disease. Its main jobs are to facilitate repair of nerve cells and transport cholesterol. APOE comes in three versions and you inherit one version from each parent. Your parents deserve kudos if they gave you two APOE-2s, which will protect you from AD or at least lower your risk. The news is not so good if you carry two APOE-4s. While people known to have this gene combination have lived into their nineties without developing AD, it does significantly increase your risk, one APOE-4 accounting for a threefold, and two, an eightfold increase. Additionally, an APOE-4 puts you at greater risk after a stroke and more susceptible to brain damage during cardiovascular surgery or following traumatic head injury. Twenty percent of those diagnosed with vascular dementia carry APOE-4. The good news is that only 2 percent of the population carries two APOE-4s. The most com-mon gene combination is APOE-3. APOE-4 combined with APOE-2 or 3 results in an intermediate AD risk.

What is known so far is that amyloid plaques and tau tangles are found in the brains of persons with Alzheimer's. APOE affects the balance between production and elimination of amyloid. Genes involved with early-onset AD trigger an over-production of beta-amyloid while those associated with the most common type of AD may send faulty orders that don't effectively remove beta-amyloid plaques. Amyloid plaques are formed on the outside of brain cells. Once they have gained a foothold, they become very dense, causing an inflammatory reaction that can eventually kill the nerve cell. Because of its waxy nature, beta-amyloid kept melting in the laboratory and was difficult to study until, in 1960, it was finally isolated.

Additionally, tau protein, a molecule that helps support the tail structure of the nerve cell, can literally lie down on the job, allowing the inner structure of the cell to collapse and tangle. The cell becomes vulnerable to inflammation processes causing it to shrink and die. APOE-3, the most common form of the gene, prevents these tangles from forming while APOE-4 provides no protection.

3. S. Gao, H. Hendrie et al., "The Relationships between Age, Sex, and the Incidence of Dementia and Alzheimer's Disease: A Meta-Analysis," *Archives of General Psychiatry* 55 (1998): 809–15.

4. J. T. Moroney, M. Tang, L. Berglund et al., "Low-Density Lipoprotein Cholesterol and the Risk of Dementia with Stroke," *Journal of the American Medical Association* 282 (1999): 254–60.

5. D. Snowdon, *Aging with Grace* (New York: Bantam Books, 2001), 156.

6. M. X. Tang et al., "The APOE-4 Allele and the Risk of Alzheimer's Disease among African-Americans, Whites and Hispanics," *Journal of the American Medical Association* 279, no. 10 (1998): 751–55.

7. L. A. Farrer, "Intercontinental Epidemiology of Alzheimer's Disease," *Journal of the American Medical Association* 285, no. 6 (14 February 2001): 796–98.

8. W. A. Kukall et al., "Solvent Exposure as a Risk Factor for Alzheimer's Disease: A Case-Control Study," *American Journal of Epidemiology* 141, no. 11 (1995): 1059–71.

9. Simon James, "Highlights of the Twelfth Annual Meeting of the North American Menopause Society" (October 2001, San Francisco), report on an article by Sano et al., "Mood and Cognitive Changes in Menopause."

10. S. Kalmijn et al., "Dietary Fat Intake and the Risk of Incident Dementia in the Rotterdam Study," *Annals of Neurology* 42 (1997): 776–82.

11. V. M. Moceri, "Early-Life Risk Factors and the Development of Alzheimer's Disease," *Neurology* 54, no. 2 (25 January 2000): 415–20.

12. Snowdon, *Aging with Grace,* 114.

13. Ibid., 59.

Chapter 4 Staving Off the Beast

1. J. S. Bland, "The Use of Complementary Medicine for Healthy Aging," *Alternative Therapies* 4, no. 4 (July 1998): 42–48.

2. Ibid., 44.

3. C. J. L. Murray, A. D. Lopez, "Alternative Projections of Mortality by Cause 1990–2020: Global Burden of Disease," *Lancet* 349 (1997): 1498–1504.

4. K. J. Joshipura, A. Ascherio, J. E. Manson et al., "Fruit and Vegetable Intake in Relation to Risk of Ischemic Stroke," *Journal of the American Medical Association* 282, no. 13 (1999): 1233–39.

5. D. Laurin, R. Verreault et al., "Physical Activity and Risk of Cognitive Impairment and Dementia in Elderly Persons," *Archives of Neurology* 58 (2001): 498–504.

6. Khalsa, *Brain Longevity*, 9.

7. L. Yochum, A. Folsom, and L. Kushi, "Intake of Antioxidant Vitamins and Risk of Death from Stroke in Postmenopausal Women," *American Journal of Clinical Nutrition* 72, no. 2 (August 2000): 476–83.

8. D. A. Snowdon, C. I. Tully et al., "Serum Folate and the Severity of Atrophy of the Neocortex in Alzheimer's Disease: Findings from the Nun Study," *American Journal of Clinical Nutrition* 71, no. 4 (April 2000): 993–98.

9. P. Le Bars, M. Kieser et al., "A 26-Week Analysis of a Double-Blind Placebo Controlled Trial of the Ginkgo Biloba Extract EGb 761 in Dementia," *Dementia and Geriatric Cognitive Disorders* 11, no. 4 (2000): 230–37.

10. P. Le Bars, M. Kieser et al., "Lipid-Lowering Drugs Reduce Dementia Risk; Statins Lower Cerebrosterol," *Archives of Neurology* 59 (2002): 213–16, 223–27.

11. B. Wolozin, W. Kellman, P. Rousseau et al., "Decreased Prevalence of Alzheimer's Disease Associated with 3-Hydroxy-3-Merhyglutaryl Coenzyme A Reductase Inhibitors," *Archives of Neurology* 57 (October 2000): 1439–43. J. H. Zomberg, S. S. Jick et al., "Statins and the Risk of Dementia," *Lancet* 356 (2000): 1627–31.

12. Wolozin et al., "Decreased Prevalence of Alzheimer's Disease," 1441. The statins most effective in reducing AD appear to be lovastatin, pravastatin sodium, and lovastatin plus pravastatin. Less effective was simvastatin.

13. R. Wison, D. E. Mendes, C. Leon et al., "Participation in Cognitively Stimulating Activities and Risk of Incident Alzheimer's Disease," *Journal of the American Medical Association* 287, no. 6: 742–48.

14. It wasn't until 1998 when Fred H. Gage, a professor at the Salk Institute in La Jolla, California, reported finding new cells in the hippocampus of five terminally ill cancer patients that we knew humans could grow new brain cells. Such a discovery has enormous repercussions.

15. See Gary W. Small, *The Memory Bible: An Innovative Strategy for Keeping Your Brain Young* (New York: Hyperion, 2002).

16. S. J. Kiraly, "Risperidone: Treatment Response in Adult and Geriatric Patients," *The International Journal of Psychiatry in Medicine* 28, no. 2 (1998): 159–63.

17. K. S. Kendler, C. O. Gardner et al., "Religion, Psychopathology, and Substance Use and Abuse: A Multimeasure Genetic-Epidemiologic Study," *American Journal of Psychiatry* 154 (1997): 322–29.

Chapter 5 Distant Early Warning Signs

1. Daniel Kuhn, *Alzheimer's Early Stages* (Berkeley, Calif.: Hunter House, 1999).

2. Laboratory tests for an Alzheimer's diagnosis include complete blood count with differential, C-reactive protein; a chemistry screen for glucose, electrolytes, liver and renal function; cholesterol/triglycerides; total serum protein; albumin and albumin/globulin ratio; tests for phosphorus and calcium and uric acid; thyroid profile TSH; free T4, folate, and vitamin B12 levels; urinalysis; electrocardiogram; brain imaging (computerized tomography without contrast usually suffices); and syphilis serology (RPR).

3. Signs of a drug overdose are memory problems, a change in overall health, fatigue, constipation, diarrhea, anorexia, confusion, incontinence, falls, depression, weakness or tremor, excess drowsiness, hallucinations, agitation, anxiety, excitation, dizziness, decreased sexual response, and rash.

4. A PET scan takes moving pictures of the interior of the brain and monitors how much glucose is being used by its various parts. If we could use it on our teenagers we would have a surefire way of knowing if they were thinking hard or hardly thinking. Researchers have been able to visualize amyloid plaques and tangles in the laboratory and within a person's brain. It is fair to say they are on the verge of seeing the actual moment when things go wrong and disease begins. Patterns of metabolic deficits are evident during times of mental rest particularly in the prefrontal, temporal, and parietal areas. As AD gets worse, these areas deteriorate.

In normal people and those who have mild dementia or MCI, blood flow and metabolism increase during cognitive stimulation but are markedly reduced in patients with severe AD. It has been noted that people with the APOE-4 gene have to use more of their brain, a compensation factor that may prove itself a marker for eventual development of AD. Single-photon emission computed tomography (SPECT) uses radioisotope tracers to measure regional impairment of brain metabolism, essentially showing how blood is circulating in the brain. It is easier to use and more readily available than the PET scan.

5. Early changes in the medial temporal lobe are easy to track. Normal changes of aging that progress to MCI are reliably picked up in the medial temporal lobe. As MCI converts to AD, the fastest changes appear in the hippocampus. A recent study showed that MRI was a helpful tool to support a clinical diagnosis of frontotemporal dementia (FTD) and in detecting whether its cause was due more to changes in the neurons or from damage caused by small strokes.

Chapter 6 A Rose by Any Other Name

1. J. C. Morris, M. Storandt et al., "Mild Cognitive Impairment Represents Early-Stage Alzheimer's Disease," *Archives of Neurology* 58 (2001): 397–405.

2. Fast decliners generally show a worse performance at baseline. Once symptoms appear, tests of selective attention and semantic memory appear to be particularly sensitive markers. Some studies using scores from the MMSE cognitive assessment (see chapter 5) in combination with an estimate of symptom duration and a calculated pre-progression rate, have found ways to predict whether a person will progress at a slow, intermediate, or rapid rate. Other approaches have focused on age at diagnosis, other health issues like cerebrovascular disease, and MMSE scores.

Chapter 7 What We Know We Did Not Know Thirty Minutes Ago

1. Medical conditions include hypertension, hyperlipidemia, carotid artery disease, arrhythmias, diabetes, and polycythemia (high red blood cell counts).

2. M. M. Rice, A. B. Graves, S. M. McCurry et al., "Postmenopausal Estrogen and Estrogen-Progestin Use and Two Year Rate of Cognitive Change in a Cohort of Older Japanese American Women," *Archives of Internal Medicine* 160 (2000): 1641–49.

3. D. E. Alves, S. Moraes et al., "Estrogen Replacement and Cognitive Functioning," *American Journal of Epidemiology* 154 (2001): 733–39.

4. R. Mulnard, C. Cotman et al., "Estrogen Replacement Therapy for Treatment of Mild to Moderate Alzheimer's Disease," *Journal of the American Medical Association* 283 (2000): 1007–15.

5. S. A. Shumaker, C. Legault, L. Thai, et al., "Estrogen Plus Progestin and the Incidence of Dementia and Mild Cognitive Impairment in Postmenopausal Women," *Journal of the American Medical Association* 289 (2003): 2651–62.

6. K. M. Fairfield and R. Fletcher, "Vitamins for Chronic Disease Prevention in Adults," *Journal of the American Medical Association* 287 (2002): 3116–26.

7. M. F. Engelhart, M. I. Geerlings et al., "Dietary Intake of Antioxidants and Risk of Alzheimer's Disease," *Journal of the American Medical Association* 287 (2002): 3223–29.

8. G. P. Lim, T. Chu et al., "The Curry Spice Curcumin Reduces Oxidative Damage and Amyloid Pathology in an Alzheimer's Transgenic Mouse," *Journal of Neuroscience* 21, no. 21 (1 November 2001): 8370–77.

Chapter 8 The Longing for Independence

1. Oscar Wilde, *The Picture of Dorian Gray.*

2. Henry Wadsworth Longfellow, *A Psalm of Life.*

3. M. E. Nelson and S. Wenick, *Strong Women Stay Strong* (New York: Bantam Books, 1997).

4. T. Brennan, "Placement: From a Patient's Perspective," Alzheimer's Association Greater San Francisco Bay Area Newsletter (spring 2000): 1, 11.

5. R. Pear, "Nursing Homes Understaffed," *Press Democrat* (Santa Rosa, Calif.), 18 February 2002, A1.

6. P. J. Whitehouse, "Dementia: State of the Art," plenary session of the American Geriatrics Society Annual Scientific Meeting, Chicago, Illinois (2001). See also L. P. Gwyther, "Family Issues in Dementia: Finding a New Normal," *Neurology Clinician* 18 (2000): 993–1010.

7. D. Troxel and V. Bell, *The Best Friend's Approach to Alzheimer's Care* (Health Profession Press, 1997). D. Troxel, *Best Friend's Staff* (Health Profession Press, 2001). Alzheimer's Association of Santa Barbara, 2024 De la Vina Street, Santa Barbara, CA 93105, 805-583-0020, dtroxel@centralcoastalz.org.

8. See Troxel and Bell, *Best Friend's Approach,* 38.

Chapter 9 Bless the Daughters

1. Nancy L. Mace and Peter V. Rabins, *36 Hour Day,* 3d ed. (Baltimore: Johns Hopkins University Press, 1999).

2. Mary Ann Mayo and Joseph L. Mayo, *The Menopause Manager* (Grand Rapids: Revell, 1998), 261–62.

3. C. Farran and F. Keane-Hagerty, "Hope, Hopelessness and Coping," *The American Journal of Alzheimer's Care and Related Disorders and Research* 4, no. 6 (November-December 1989): 38–41. C. Farran, K. A. Herth, and J. M. Popovich, *Hope and Hopelessness: Critical Clinical Constructs* (Thousand

Oaks, Calif.: Sage Publications, 1995). Dr. Carol Farran is an Alzheimer's researcher and director of Education and Information Transfer Core at the Rush-Presbyterian-St. Luke's Alzheimer's Disease Center in Chicago.

4. L. White and B. Spencer, *Moving a Relative with Memory Loss: A Family Caregiver's Guide* (Santa Rosa, Calif.: Whisp Publications, P.O. Box 5426, Santa Rosa, CA 95402, whisppub@aol.com).

5. Robert Munsch, *Love You Forever* (Willowdale, Ontario, Canada: A Firefly Book, 1991), used with permission.

Chapter 10 Life in the Long Run

1. M. Mitka, "Suggestions for Help When the End Is Near," *Journal of the American Medical Association* 284, no. 19 (15 November 2000): 2437–38.

2. How long will you live? See Living to 100 at www.livingto100.com and Life-Expectancy Calculation at www.fastfa.com/life/life.html.

3. T. E. Finucane, "Tube Feeding in the Demented Elderly: A Review of the Evidence," The American Geriatrics Society Annual Scientific Meeting (2001, Chicago).

4. These resources may be helpful when facing the end of someone's life: Access Supportive Care of the Dying at www.careofdying.org, The Partnership for Caring at www.partnershipforcaring.org, Caregiver Survival Resources at www.caregiver911.com, AARP's Legal Services Network at www.aarp.org/lsn, National Hospice and Palliative Care Organization at www.nhpco.org.

5. Elisabeth Kübler-Ross, M.D., "The Five Stages of Dying," *Encyclopedia Science Supplement* (New York: Grolier, 1971), 92–97.

Appendix A Treatments for Dementia

1. See T. Rosenthal, "Caring for Women with Alzheimer's Disease," *Women's Health in Primary Care, Gynecology* 2, no. 5 (June 2002): 264–76.

Recommended Reading

Bell, V., and D. Troxel. *The Best Friend's Approach to Alzheimer's Care.* Alzheimer's Association of Santa Barbara: Health Profession Press, 1997. Alzheimer's Association of Santa Barbara, 2024 De la Vina Street, Santa Barbara, CA 93105, 805-583-0020.

Khalsa, Dharma Singh, with Cameron Stauth. *Brain Longevity.* New York: Warner, 1997.

Kuhn, Daniel. *Alzheimer's Early Stages: First Steps in Care and Treatment.* Alameda, Calif.: Hunter House, 2003.

Mayo, Mary Ann, with Lyra Heller. *Good for You! Smart Choices for Hormone Health.* Lake Mary, Fla.: Siloam Press, 2003.

McKhann, Guy M., and Marilyn Albert. *Keep Your Brain Young: The Complete Guide to Physical and Emotional Health.* New York: John Wiley, 2002.

Robinson, Anne, Beth Spencer, and Laurie White. *Understanding Difficult Behaviors: Some Practical Suggestions for Coping with Alzheimer's Disease and Related Illnesses.* Ypsilanti, Mich.: Geriatric Education Center of Michigan, 1988.

Sapolsky, Robert M. *Why Zebras Don't Get Ulcers: A Guide to Stress, Stress Related Diseases, and Coping.* New York: W. H. Freeman, 1994.

Small, Gary. *The Memory Bible: An Innovative Strategy for Keeping Your Brain Young.* New York: Hyperion, 2002.

Snowdon, David. *Aging with Grace*. New York: Bantam Books, 2001.

Tanzi, Rudolph E., and Ann B. Parson. *Decoding Darkness: The Search for the Genetic Causes of Alzheimer's Disease*. Cambridge, Mass.: Perseus, 2002.

White, Laurie, and Beth Spencer. *Moving a Relative with Memory Loss: A Family Caregiver's Guide*. Santa Rosa, Calif.: Whisp Publications. Whisp Publications, P.O. Box 5426, Santa Rosa, CA 95402.

Mary Ann Mayo, M.A., MFT, is a licensed marriage and family therapist and the author of twelve books on women's and children's mental and physical health. She cofounded A Woman's Place Medical Center with her husband, Joseph L. Mayo, M.D., FACOG. Until his retirement, their professional life frequently overlapped and he remains her chief editor, consultant, and sounding board. They have two children: Joseph, who is married to Mary, and Malika, who is newly married to Bert. Joseph and Mary (sounds familiar) are the parents of two delightful boys, Caden and Coleman.

The Mayos live on a farm in lovely Dry Creek Valley and find peace and a healthful lifestyle easy to maintain among the vineyards, flowers, friends, and produce of Northern California's Sonoma County.

You can reach the Mayos at P.O. Box 1039, Geyserville, CA 95441; by e-mail: joseph@sonic.net; or by visiting their web site: *www.mayo.meta-ehealth.com*